SEVENTEEN FATHOMS DEEP

THE SAGA OF THE SUBMARINE *S-4* DISASTER

JOSEPH A. WILLIAMS

CHICAGO
REVIEW
PRESS

Library of Congress Cataloging-in-Publication Data
Williams, Joseph A., 1973–
   Seventeen fathoms deep : the saga of the Submarine S-4 disaster / Joseph
A. Williams.
        pages cm
   Includes bibliographical references and index.
   ISBN 978-1-61373-138-3
   1. Submarine disasters—United States—History—20th century. 2. S-4
(Submarine) 3. United States. Navy—Search and rescue operations.
4. Cape Cod (Mass.)—History, Naval—20th century. I. Title. II. Title:
Saga of the Submarine S-4 disaster.

   VK1265.W55 2015
   359.9'3832—dc23

                              2015018522

Interior design: PerfecType, Nashville, TN

Printed in the United States of America
5 4 3 2 1

10/15

In memory of my father,
Gunner's Mate Third Class Paul J. Williams (1947–1998)

CONTENTS

PREFACE

THE YEAR 1927 WAS ICONIC. It started with a January 7 telephone call across the Atlantic—the first in history. In February, the Federal Radio Commission began to regulate radio, which was then in its golden age. On March 11, Gloria Swanson's silent film *The Love of Sunya* was the first motion picture shown at New York's legendary movie house the Roxy Theatre. But the age of the silent movie came to an end later that year with the release of *The Jazz Singer* starring Al Jolson. The Model A Ford replaced the venerable Model T, and in May Charles Lindbergh made his famous nonstop transatlantic flight. That year saw the apogee of Babe Ruth's awesome prowess at the batter's box as he delivered a sixty-home-run season. New heights were reached on Wall Street, aided by a steady conservative government headed by Calvin Coolidge.

But the year also had a dark side. It was in the era of Prohibition, when gangster Al Capone reached the apex of his powers in Chicago, and a twenty-four-year-old Elliot Ness joined the US Treasury Department to enforce the controversial dry law of the land. In May, a disgruntled school board treasurer from Bath Township, Michigan, murdered his wife, bombed his own homestead followed by the school, then killed himself and several others by detonating his own car in front of the school. Forty-five people were killed, including many children. The Mississippi River suffered massive flooding from April to August, inundating more than twenty-seven thousand square miles and affecting the lives of hundreds of thousands of people. Flooding, too, occurred that November in Coolidge's home state of Vermont, killing eighty-four people and leaving more than ten thousand people homeless.

But on the whole, 1927 was a year of optimism. World War I had long passed, and in some quarters it was thought possible to abolish war altogether. It was not only the quintessential year of the Roaring Twenties, it was ebullient.

Then, at the end of the year, there was the submarine *S-4* disaster.

As a librarian, writer, and researcher, I know firsthand the perils of getting lost in other people's lives. Forgotten letters, faded photographs, lost diaries, etc.—these are the building blocks of history. To explore them is a serendipitous passage through time and imagination. Finding lost manuscripts is even more delightful, because it is a secret that only you know and cannot wait to share.

On one of these trips through time, I was exploring the archives at the Stephen B. Luce Library, State University of New York Maritime College. The college specializes in educating students for careers in the maritime industry and related fields. The library, located within a nineteenth-century fort, is archaic and modern all at once—where history meets digital alacrity. The library has an extensive but not well known collection of manuscripts from its graduates going back to the nineteenth century. In fact, it holds a chronicle of American maritime history that is largely untapped.

I was researching the collection in preparation for my first book. One old steel-gray archival box after another was opened, dust carefully wiped away, and new discoveries made. Eventually I came upon the papers of John S. Baylis, an alumnus of the school who had died in 1971. As I pored through scrapbooks, antique tomes, and worn-out ephemera, I found a set of three dusty boxes labeled THE *S-4* INCIDENT.

I took the first of the boxes from the shelf and laid it on a credenza. I carefully cracked open the lid. It felt stiff—as if it had not been opened for decades. I peered inside. I was struck by how it was jammed with materials—and this was but one box of three!

The first item I removed was a yellow envelope. The glue on the flaps had long dried, and the envelope probably needed to be replaced. But my attention was drawn to the solid object that it was storing. Reaching in with a white-gloved hand, I removed a circular glass object, roughly the size of my fist. I held it up to the light. The pale fluorescent light gleamed opaquely through it. Then, looking at the envelope again, I saw scrawled writing in faded pencil: "Periscope Glass of Submarine *S-4*."

At that moment, I felt like Indiana Jones without the hat or bullwhip.

After I finished my first book, I was able to return to those boxes and explore them at great length. In them were the building blocks for a story—a dark tale, but one with incredible heroism, moments of poignant humor, and ultimate redemption. Looking deeper into the story of the submarine *S-4*, I found that it had only been written about in limited ways. But before me was a virtually complete record: hundreds of pages of transcripts of navy hearings, photographs of divers, telegrams, and letters—all the essentials to make a story that ultimately is a test of human nature. It was an archival secret that I had found and wanted to share.

I then conducted a multiyear quest to learn the meaning of the *S-4*. I ranged far and wide, searching other archives, talking to descendants, and contacting experts in salvage and submarines. The result is this book, which explores the themes of the *S-4* incident: ingenuity, technology, and cleverness can always be tested by powers beyond human control. The question really then becomes whether or not humanity learns from the testing.

The Rum-Chaser

ON A BRISK MID-DECEMBER DAY in 1927, the Coast Guard cutter *Paulding* patrolled off Provincetown, Cape Cod. To the east on the coast loomed a tower, the 252-foot-tall Pilgrim Monument. Commanding officer John S. Baylis's eyes were drawn to the blood-scarlet pennant over a red-and-blue flag that flew before the tower.

Lieutenant Commander Baylis's stony-handsome face held a penetrating stare accentuated by a stiff, impeccably clean uniform that gave the impression of formality. Yet from time to time this veneer would crack with the smile and bright blue eyes of a dignified patrician. Being forty-three, he was on average two decades older than his subordinates. He looked at himself as a teacher to his officers and crew.

Baylis directed the men on watch to rifle through their manuals and tell him what the pennants meant. At length, they deciphered the signs to indicate a storm—a nor'easter. But Baylis corrected his crew: The wind was from the *northwest*. The flags were in error. The captain was a stickler for detail.

Northwest or northeast, a storm was coming, but Baylis was unalarmed. The *Paulding* was close to the protection of Provincetown Harbor. There was time enough for him to carry on his mission and catch a prize. But Baylis's quarry was not a pirate ship stuffed with

Lieutenant Commander John S. Baylis (USCG), commanding officer of the *Paulding*.
Courtesy of the Stephen B. Luce Library Archives, SUNY Maritime College

holds of shimmering bullion and hard jewels. Rather, he hunted illegal booze.

In 1924, the Coast Guard had vowed to suppress the smuggling that sprouted in the face of the national prohibition on alcohol. Smugglers found a thriving and profitable trade in New England, where it was easy for mother ships in international waters to load small boats, which hustled the contraband to one of the region's many hidden coves and lonely shores. The illegal trafficking had grown so rampant that the US Navy had lent the Coast Guard twenty World War I–era destroyers to hunt the rumrunners. The *Paulding*, which had been used by the navy during the war for escort duty, was one of these so-called rum-chasers. At over 293 feet in length and 742 tons, the *Paulding* dwarfed any smuggler. The ship was capable of 30 knots, and in its mission it was sometimes forced to go at that speed.

While on the open ocean, the cutter could run down the smaller rumrunners; it was not as maneuverable in the shallows. Smugglers could find safety close to shore if they could get past the *Paulding*. If that happened, Baylis would be forced to call on the ship's four guns to force a boat to heave to.

The previous December, the *Paulding* encountered the *Marge*. It was a small but fast rumrunner with three engines capable of 1,350 horsepower. It roared across Cape Cod Bay in broad daylight to evade the *Paulding*. Baylis zealously gave chase, running after the zigzagging boat at a 30-knot clip, firing warning shots to cajole the vessel to stop. But the boat ran inshore and managed to dump all its illegal cargo before the Coast Guard could catch it. The *Marge*'s crew had vanished via a train to Boston.

Baylis was fervent in his pursuit of rumrunners, not because of a strong opinion on Prohibition but because of his fundamental dedication to service on the sea. He graduated as a cadet in 1903 from the New York Nautical Schoolship *St. Mary's*, an ancient sloop of war that trained mariners. Sometimes when he was ashore with his wife and son in Brookline, Massachusetts, he looked at old photographs of a beaming teenager grasping the oversized wheel of the square-rigged school ship. Upon graduating, he signed aboard a British square-rigger and made a voyage around Cape Horn. After his return, he joined the Revenue Cutter Service* in 1907 and remained with it ever since. He was considered one of the best commanding officers in the service. Aside from chasing rumrunners, he was involved in rescue work. In the latest incident, his vessel rescued a foundered boat on the Peaked Hill Bar during a February storm. Baylis received a commendation for the heroics. In total, Lieutenant Commander John Baylis had been on the water for twenty-six years and had even

---

*The Revenue Cutter Service merged with the US Life-Saving Service in 1915 to form the US Coast Guard.

returned to his alma mater as its superintendent before reassignment to the *Paulding* in 1924.

On this outing, on December 17, 1927, Baylis possessed a secret list of nearly three hundred vessels with which his division commanding officer, Commander Leroy Reinburg, had furnished him. These vessels, if encountered, needed to be stopped, searched, and potentially seized. The *Paulding* and its eighty-two men had been out since nine in the morning and found no smugglers, only a couple of schooners carrying fish and other legitimate cargo.

By three o'clock, the sun was descending behind a choppy sea. Since visibility was decent, and it was frigid on the bridge's outdoor wings, Baylis allowed his men to stay inside the glass-encased bridge. From here, they could clearly see the roughening seas batter the coast of Wood End.

Wood End was a narrow spit of land that curled into Cape Cod Bay, ending with a stretch of shore named Long Point. It was a lonely but beautiful place, lined with wind-driven sands, salt marshes, and grasses. The only sounds were the crash of waves and the call of seabirds. The clearest marks of civilization were two lighthouses that stood sentinel along the shore, the distant Pilgrim Monument, and the masts of ships anchored in Provincetown Harbor, which appeared on the far side of the point. The only thing that seemed strange was that the Nantucket Lightship was off its station. A note of it was made in the log.

The *Paulding* rolled by Wood End at 18 knots. Then, at three thirty, they sighted a small fishing boat that they could not immediately identify. There must have been a piratical buzz on the bridge as Baylis gave the order to pursue. The excitable helmsman, James Milazzo, spun the *Paulding*'s wheel.

All binoculars bore on the small craft as it came into view. At one hundred feet away, the quartermaster, a former navy man named Charles Reed, had stepped outside to observe the vessel. He sung out, "It's the *William Landry*." Baylis, and all hands, could now clearly see the name on the vessel's side. It was a known fishing boat, and not on Baylis's secret list.

Baylis ordered a course toward Provincetown. Milazzo turned the wheel, and the vessel changed its heading again. The *Paulding* drew closer to the shore, where there were a series of white can buoys. The navy had laid these out in 1909 for use in testing vessels along Wood End and Long Point. The length of the courses had been plotted, and they were referred to as "measured mile" courses. There were two such courses, an inner one that was closer to Provincetown Harbor, and an outer one. Baylis was nearing one end of the inner course—the buoys were useful navigation aids for vessels coming into Provincetown Harbor.

It was obvious to the crew that the day's hunt was up and that the *Paulding* was heading in for the night. But Baylis had another idea.

He turned to the officer of the deck, a fresh-faced ensign straight out of the Coast Guard Academy named George Phannemiller. Baylis ordered him to take command and follow the white buoys toward Provincetown. The young officer hurriedly stepped up with a probable air of nervous authority contained only by a starchy uniform.

Baylis left the bridge and stepped into the adjoining chart room. It was a cramped space with a smooth table that had a chart of Cape Cod Bay set on it. He laid his fingers on the chart and began to estimate distances and time. He was close enough to the bridge that he could hear if there was any trouble. But there was none expected. Phannemiller was navigating the ship along the course of the white buoys. The ensign had just given the order to alter the course 5 degrees to port.

Baylis had roughly an hour of daylight left, maybe a little less, but it was enough time to bring the *Paulding* into Cape Cod Bay in order to scrutinize the western Plymouth shore. He decided that would be the *Paulding*'s last action of the day and maybe they would find something among the small boat traffic into Plymouth. He just needed to plot the best way to bring the ship to the optimal spot.

But Baylis was interrupted by a shout from the bridge.

"Right full!"

Baylis's head jerked up. It was Phannemiller. Thoughts of Plymouth and smugglers evaporated as he rushed out of the chart room and onto the bridge.

Baylis saw through the glass windows what appeared to be two brown iron sticks just ahead under the ship's port bow. The weather-beaten spars looked like markers for nets that fishermen used at times to flag traps so that they could leave them and pick them up later. They were less than seventy yards away and quickly closing. Hitting a fishing marker might foul the *Paulding*'s propellers.

White feathery foam trailed behind the sticks, making them hard to discern in the choppy water. Strangely, the foam showed signs of motion, as if it were a wake. But real fishing markers should not move. Instantly, revelation crashed onto Baylis; it was confirmed by the quartermaster, who rushed inside the bridge.

"It's a submarine!" Charles Reed shouted.

The supposed fishing sticks were, in fact, the twin periscopes of a submarine. They were just peeping above the sea's surface and rising. They were heading at the *Paulding*'s prow at a right angle.

"Full astern!" cried Baylis. He grasped the lever to telegraph the order to the engine room and found that Reed had already gripped the lever. They pulled it together, giving the order to reverse the engines.

The siren of the general alarm peeled through the decks. Baylis felt the engines groan as the engineers below set them in reverse. Loud thumping noises boomed throughout the *Paulding* and the vessel shook. But a sizable ship going 18 knots does not just stop on command.

The *Paulding* slowed and started to veer right, but the periscopes kept rising and closing. As the *Paulding* turned, the periscopes changed from a 90-degree to a 45-degree angle in relation to the ship. The submarine was still going to strike the *Paulding*. The vessel's staying cables emerged. These were long wires that were attached forward on the submarine from the conning tower to the bow—they were used as an extended antenna for the submarine's radio systems. Then the conning tower started to appear. The *Paulding* was laden with oil and stores and drew deeply in the water. There was nothing Baylis could do. The impact was to be immense.

Baylis's gut must have churned as he gave an order that any veteran sea officer would pray never to have to give.

"All hands, prepare to abandon ship!"

2

The Pigboat

SUBMARINE STANDARDIZATION TRIALS WERE A safe assignment; no hunting destroyers, no unexpected crash dives, and no enemy depth charges along the well-known measured mile course. For the *S-4*, there was just the quiet serenity of Cape Cod—though the view of it was limited inside a submarine.

The trials meant that the boat* would spend more than a week pacing up and down the same mile of cold sea. With the expected monotony, there were outsiders present from the navy's Board of Inspection and Survey, which disturbed the submarine's isolated and intimate universe.

The *S-4*'s captain, Lieutenant Commander Roy Kehlor Jones, had endured the tedious trials before. The thirty-four-year-old son of a dry goods merchant was a boyish-looking but conscientious commanding officer who had left his native Oklahoma for the US Naval Academy, from which he graduated in 1916. He had seen a fair share of action aboard the battleship *Michigan* during World War I, escorting convoys and training personnel. U-boats were a hidden menace during the war, and Jones probably admired how much submarine technology

---

*Submarines in naval terminology are called "boats." Early submarines were so small and short-ranged that they were often carried on the decks of larger vessels. Strictly speaking, a *boat* is a vessel that can be carried on a *ship*.

had matured in the three decades of his life. In 1920, he enrolled in
the navy's submarine school and five years later earned the command
of the *S-4*. It was not unusual for a young navy officer to gain his first
command aboard a submarine. It was considered a fast track to promotion. So, the depths of the sea were now home to Jones, though it
was no Oklahoma.

The *S-4* had a complement of forty men, a small command, but
that did not matter to Jones. It was *his* "pigboat," a nickname for the
old diesel-powered submarines that reflected the crowded, sometimes
squalid, conditions found therein. But the name itself was derived from
the fact that the earliest American submarines had no periscopes. A
submarine captain had to frequently surface to see, and after a brief
check of his bearings he would take the boat down again. The legend
was that the movements of these exotic vessels amused sailors at the
surface. The movements of the early submarines reminded them of
porpoises, otherwise known as sea-pigs.*

The S-class submarines were the first built to navy specifications in
response to anecdotal reports of the capabilities of German U-boats
during World War I as well as a desire to have a submarine fleet on
par with foreign navies. Up to 1920, private manufacturers, chiefly
the Electric Boat Company of Groton, Connecticut, took responsibility for designing submarines. They patented features that, in effect,
prevented competing companies from using similar designs. The navy
was critical of this monopoly and felt the company was wielding too
much power and control through political influence.

The navy decided to design its own submarines. It set up a board
and sent specifications to different manufacturers to create a vessel to
its liking. The result was six different subgroups in the S-class made

---

*Submarine history expert David Johnston added that the nickname "became an
even more appropriate title when the conditions inside the boats were considered.
There was little or no fresh water and the sanitary facilities consisted of an open
bucket. Ventilation was poor . . . and the air was permeated with a combination
of gasoline or diesel fumes, ozone, smoke from frequent electrical shorts, human
sweat and sea spray. Combine that with stifling heat and humidity and you can
imagine what our first submariners must have looked and smelled like when they
returned from a run at sea."

by four different manufacturers. The S-class really was not a true class of vessels because it was so diverse. But since the navy took a greater stake in design, it had an interest in making sure the new submarines were effective. The *S-4* along with its sister vessel, the *S-8*, had recently completed overhauls at the Portsmouth Navy Yard. The subs had been fully repaired and tested to withstand a depth of two hundred feet, thus the inspectors and sea trials.

Two inspectors were assigned to the *S-4*, and Jones knew them both: Lieutenant Commander William Callaway and Charles Ford. The thirty-eight-year-old Callaway was *the* submarine man for the Board of Inspection and Survey. He had been involved with submarines since 1917, and he became the submarine division commander in 1923. Callaway joined the board in April, three years later.

Charles Ford was a dapper fifty-three-year-old engineering draftsman who assisted Callaway by reporting data and plotting curves. He was in effect the board's calculator. Since he started working for the navy as a civilian in 1902, he had been on ninety-three different trial voyages, of which twenty-nine were on submarines.

When Callaway and Ford came to Provincetown on December 12, 1927, they did not stay aboard the *S-4* but rather the *Wandank*, a 156-foot fleet tug that served as the station ship for the submarine. The tug's staterooms were roomier than anything aboard the *S-4*. In fact, the entire crew of the submarine came aboard at the end of each day's work to use the *Wandank*'s facilities, including the galley and showers. Every day, Jones met with Callaway and Ford aboard the *Wandank* before taking them to his submarine.

The *S-4* was composed of five cramped compartments separated by four solid steel bulkheads with watertight doors allowing for passage. Starting forward, there was the torpedo room, which contained all the launching devices to fire the submarine's weapons. The *S-4* could carry fourteen torpedoes, which were hoisted by chains into one of the compartment's four torpedo tubes. These were launched by using two large tanks of compressed air that stood next to the tubes.

Aft of the torpedo room was the battery compartment. This section of the vessel was so named because the eponymous batteries were stored here. The batteries were broken into two sections of sixty cells

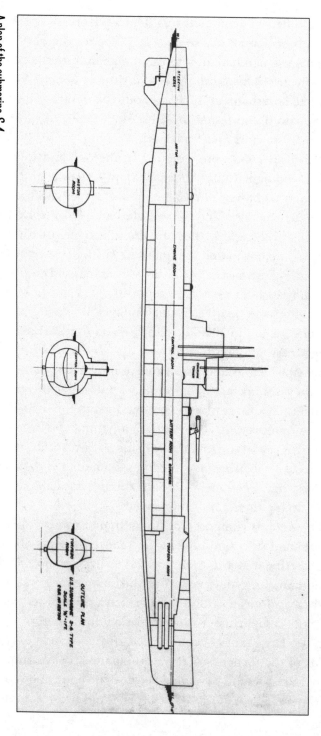

A plan of the submarine S-4.
Naval History and Heritage Command, Photo Archives, NH-41859

each and had a total capacity of 1,240 kilowatt-hours. To put this into modern perspective, the average American home in the early twenty-first century uses between 900 and 1,000 kilowatt-hours per month. The batteries were used to power the boat when it was submerged, since it was impossible to run the diesel engines underwater. The *S-4* had no means to exhaust the noxious diesel fumes while submerged nor draw in the vast quantities of oxygen necessary for combustion. If the diesel engines were turned on while submerged, every man aboard would be quickly killed.[*]

The batteries were kept out of sight beneath the deck plates so the dominating feature of the compartment was berthing for the crew. With room being limited inside the submarine, space was optimized to accommodate a crew of about forty men. Lockers were built into the bulkheads. Bunks, stacked three high, were suspended from the bulkheads and were retractable by chains that "triced" upwards so that the space was easier to pass through, to clean, and to access the batteries below the deck plates. The crew also had folding tables and chairs, which they opened at times to play games. More important, this compartment had a large coffee urn efficiently close to the vessel's only head.[†] To celebrate the holiday season, the crew had hung a paper Christmas bell over the urn.

At the rear of the battery room were the officers' two staterooms. The term "stateroom" was generous, since they were more like medium-sized closets. One was for Lieutenant Commander Jones, and the other was for his three officers: navigator and executive officer Lieutenant Joseph McGinley; Graham Fitch, the junior lieutenant in charge of the torpedo room; and the chief engineer, Lieutenant Donald Weller. The executive officer had a close working relationship with his commanding officer, but it was about to end. McGinley had been transferred to another submarine, but he had volunteered to do this one last tour to allow the incoming executive officer to spend time with his family over the Christmas holiday.

---

[*]This scenario occurred in 2003 when a Chinese *Ming*-class submarine's diesel engines failed to shut down after it submerged. All seventy crew members were killed. The boat drifted for ten days before fishermen discovered it.
[†]Navy parlance for lavatory.

To give a personal touch to his stateroom, Jones hung across the door to his quarters a thin, green *portiere*. It was a delicate curtain and seemingly out of place in a modern naval machine. But it did, like the paper Christmas bell, lend the *S-4* a human touch. Despite these efforts to decorate, there was no escaping the fact that conditions aboard were cramped, and there was absolutely no privacy. It is no wonder that Callaway and Ford needed, and probably wanted, to stay aboard the *Wandank*.

Aft of the battery room through a bulkhead door was the heart of the ship, the control room or central operating compartment, known as the COC.* It was filled with electrical panels, navigation devices, wheels, gears, valves, and levers. Each device controlled some critical component of the vessel that if operated incorrectly at the wrong time, could mean disaster. Here, the captain commanded the submarine through crewmen who used compressed air and control wheels that adjusted diving planes to maneuver the boat. The planes were moveable, wing-like fins that were affixed to the sides of the boat's hull forward and aft, controlling the depth of the vessel by changing its angle.

Also in this compartment were the periscopes that any layman associates with submarines. The *S-4* had two that could be raised above the waterline to spy for enemy targets as well as navigate the boat. The periscopes, when measured at full extension from the top of the vessel's structure, reached about twenty-four feet. A person on the surface, though, would see only a portion of the periscope, which was most distinguishable when under motion since it created a foamy wake of water, called a "feather." Originally, the *S-4* had three periscopes, but the third was removed during a redesign. Captains of S-class submarines found that two were sufficient for their work.

In many ways, submarine warfare at this time was blindman's bluff. After a submarine spotted an enemy vessel through the periscope, the crew would retract it and submerge. The captain would then set a course for a spot where they thought the enemy ship was heading

*While COC was the official navy designation, this compartment was most often referred to by submariners as the control room.

based on the observations. When they got to the spot, they would inch up blindly, deploy the periscope, and see if they were right. Without advanced sensing devices, there was always a danger of coming up in the wrong spot at the wrong time and colliding into something. To make matters even more challenging, the periscope had a limited field of vision with many blind spots. Caution was always necessary.

To the rear of the control room was the engine room. Well-lit and clean, the compartment had a narrow walkway that ran between two 700-horsepower diesel engines. The engines were exhausted through piping that ran through mufflers in the superstructure. Here too was a hatch for more ventilation and crew access. Beyond the engine room was a smaller motor room and tiller room, where there was a secondary steering system. There was also a small machine shop complete with a lathe and vises to repair equipment and fabricate new components

The control room of the submarine *S-4.*
Naval History and Heritage Command, Photo Archives, NH-41850

as needed. The *S-4* even had an early type of inverter, a device that converted DC to AC electrical current. The S-class submarines were the first to have mechanical refrigeration that used AC power. Still, the refrigeration was for food stores only. S-class submarines had no general temperature control of any kind.

The *S-4* was double hulled. That is, the submarine had first an outer casing, called the superstructure, which gave it its shape; then a space used for ballast tanks that controlled the boat's buoyancy, or its tendency to float in the water; and finally an inner pressure hull that separated outside sea pressure from the interior of the submarine. The reinforced steel framework allowed the boat to safely withstand water pressure at depths of two hundred feet.

The *S-4* was larger than prior submarine incarnations at 231 feet long, and it displaced 1,092 tons of water. This, however, is paltry when compared with later submarines. An American *Los Angeles*–class submarine is typically about 362 feet and displaces 6,927 tons. Russian *Typhoon*-class submarines reach over 574 feet in length and displace up to 48,000 tons. But for its day, the *S-4* was quite advanced. It could make 15 knots while on the surface and up to 11 while submerged.

Jones's pigboat was not a place for the claustrophobic or the faint of heart. While submarine technology was developing in the nineteenth century, accidents and deaths were commonplace. Yet even after the technology had advanced, dramatic losses continued. Between 1900 and 1927, there had been eight American submarines lost due to accident or human error. In addition, there were numerous incidents in which the crew was lost, but the boat recovered. Internationally, in the same period of time, there had been 111 losses. These statistics hung over submariners like the sword of Damocles and were a constant reminder of the perilous nature of the service.

Some of the more notable incidents among American submarines included the *F-4*, which lost all hands (twenty-one men) in 305 feet of water off Honolulu when it failed to return from testing runs in 1915. Then in 1917, the *F-1* was rammed by the *F-3* off Point Loma, California. Only five of the twenty-four crew, who happened to be on the deck of the submarine at the time of the collision, survived. In 1920, there was the *S-5*, which went down in the Atlantic off the Delaware

Capes. Remarkably, the captain managed to save the boat and all hands by blowing the air tanks to raise the stern to the surface. Then in 1921, the *S-48* sank off Bridgeport, Connecticut, in sixty-seven feet of water while on builder trials. In this instance, an internal manhole cover on the aft ballast tank was left unsecured by the builder during construction. All the trial crew escaped through one of the torpedo tubes when they managed to bring the bow to the surface. Then in 1923, the *O-5* was rammed and sunk off the entrance to the Panama Canal. Three lives were lost in that incident.

The last significant American submarine loss was in 1925. The *S-51* was running along at night on the surface with a single warning light. A merchant steamer, the *City of Rome*, could neither make out what direction the *S-51* was heading nor how fast the boat was moving. Twenty-two minutes after sighting the submarine, the steamer plowed right into it and kept going. The *S-51* went down quickly. Out of thirty-six men, three survived. At that time, it was the worst submarine disaster in American history. This sinking happened off Block Island, close to the same New England waters where Jones was conducting the standardization trials.

The submariners knew the dangers, and it might be said that the unique culture that developed in the submarine service was a direct result of intense confinement colored with the risk of sudden death. Intense profanity, practical jokes, and a blurring of the line separating men from officers was the nature of the culture aboard the pigboats.

There was a feeling among some submariners that the government was not investing enough money into the submarines. Donald F. Goering, an electrician's mate on the *S-4*, wrote to his parents, "We have a lot of jobs on the boat which are necessary, but they won't do them as they have no money. After they lose a couple of boats they might fix them up. If they don't want to keep them in good condition they ought to junk the whole navy."

On December 17, 1927, Jones couldn't have been concerned about a collision like the *S-51*. It was daylight, and they'd be in the relative safety of the navy testing area. While he did not wish for the trials to occur so close to Christmas—he wanted to go home to his family in Baltimore—everything was routine and had been so since December

12. The testing was getting to its final stages by the late morning of December 17.

Callaway and Ford had, for days, laid all the equipment out to monitor the submarine's performance. Data collection boards made up of bells and lights were set up at various parts of the boat to monitor the engines as the submarine warmed to life in the cold sea.

While Jones, Callaway, Ford, and the other men were all busy in the control and engine rooms, some of the crew were idle. This was especially the case in the torpedo room. Since the weapons were not being tested, the men headed by twenty-five-year-old Lieutenant Graham Fitch may have taken to gossiping.

Fitch had recently married a woman from Puerto Rico named Maria Christina Gerrerra who was reported to barely speak English. They had met at a ball three years earlier in Costa Rica, and despite the language barrier, it was love at first sight. The men probably teased their officer about it.

But any chattering would have been interrupted when a horn was sounded throughout the boat on electric speakers: *Diving stations— man your diving stations!*

Hatches and valves were shut. The diesel engine stopped, and the quiet electric engines stirred to life. The *S-4* slid into the sea, but not too deep, just enough so that its periscope peeped through the water.

In the control room, Jones and his executive officer, McGinley, would have peered through the twin periscopes. One swept the horizon looking for vessels, while the other concerned itself with the target buoys of the measured mile course. Callaway and Ford monitored the electric motor's performance. Jones assigned six of his crew to assist the inspectors by being armed with stopwatches to time the monitoring devices. The cables that networked the equipment were run over the watertight bulkhead doors' coaming from the motor room forward to the control room, preventing them from being quickly shut. This might prove a problem if the *S-4* took on water, but Jones made sure there were knives, hammers, and even meat cleavers available to cut the cables in case they needed to slam the doors closed. Jones was a prudent commander—so much so that his colleague, the captain of the *S-8*, thought him overly cautious.

The *S-4* carefully lined itself up for the beginning of the measured mile. Jones peered through the periscope looking for the appropriate buoys and beacons. He needed to place the submarine perfectly.

The control room hushed as the submarine fell into alignment. It was time.

Jones gave the command to begin. The submarine began its first run of the measured mile. It was 1:30 PM.

Back and forth the *S-4* went at 6 knots, surfacing at the end of a run, like a swimmer gasping for breath while turning a lap. Callaway and Ford collected their data. Jones and McGinley manned the periscopes and navigated. Everything was routine. Time clicked by, and by three thirty they were coming to the end of their testing trials.

Then as the *S-4*'s periscopes swept the sea, they would have seen in the distance a cutter with "CG-17" emblazoned white on its bow. It was the *Paulding*, one of the destroyers lent by the navy to the Coast Guard to enforce Prohibition. The ship was outside the course, and its heading showed that it was not a danger to the *S-4*. Still, Jones was cautious. It was better to just surface and let the *Paulding* see him. He gave the order.

His men turned the diving plane wheels in the control room. These changed the angle of the diving planes on the submarine's side. The *S-4* slowly crept upwards as a myopic watch was maintained through the periscope.

Then, as the periscope slowly turned to look straight in front, dead ahead was a flash of horrible white. It was the *Paulding* rapidly closing on a collision course. Something had happened. The *Paulding* had changed course, or the *S-4* had miscalculated.

Jones sounded the alarm for impending collision. He tried to lower the periscope in an attempt to mitigate the damage. However, he had neglected to fold in the handles all the way, and the periscope jammed.

Within moments, a sudden tumult ripped throughout the boat. Men and loose gear were thrown about. There was the sound of inrushing water. The air became permeated with the salty smell of the sea.

3

The Fate of the *Paulding*

VIOLENCE SHOOK THE *PAULDING*. THE ship struck the submarine just in front of the conning tower on the *S-4*'s starboard side. The *Paulding*'s bow gouged a hole into the *S-4* and then barreled over the submarine. Baylis's ship was lifted bodily out of the water, forcing the *S-4*'s prow downward and stern upward. For a moment, the submarine's stern, propellers still spinning, was pushed into the air before plunging downward at a 45-degree angle. The *Paulding* crashed forward into the sea.

Baylis and the men of the *Paulding* were thrown off their feet. Only the helmsman, James Milazzo, remained standing. Milazzo's head had smashed into the wheel but his knuckles burned white from his vise-like grip on it.

A surreal split second of stillness followed as Baylis and his men pulled themselves together. Milazzo seemed to be only bruised, but he continued to clutch at the wheel, not daring to look up. Baylis glanced at the clock. It was 3:37 PM.

Baylis gave the order to stop the engines. He then ran out onto the starboard wing of the bridge. The submarine had been converging on them at a 45-degree angle on the *Paulding*'s port side before the collision. Logically, he expected to see the submarine on the opposite side of the ship. But when he looked, all that was visible were bubbles and a trickle of oil that bled upward from the deep.

The depth of the water off Wood End was 102 feet at low tide. If the submarine was wrecked, there was little that Baylis could do to recover it. A rescue and salvage operation would require the navy, which had the divers and equipment that could raise the vessel from the bottom. The navy needed to be notified as soon as possible. In the meantime, Baylis immediately moved to assess his ship and try to render assistance to the *S-4.*

Baylis first sent Ensign George Phannemiller below to check the water in the lower compartments in the bow. He then ordered Charles Reed to get cross bearings on the Wood End and Long Point lighthouses. He needed to report the exact spot of the collision. He also had Reed hoist a distress signal for any ship in the vicinity to send a boat. If the *Paulding* sank, Baylis would need any craft nearby to pick up the survivors. Also, there was a chance that some of the submariners might be found.

The destroyer *Paulding,* launched in 1910, was lent by the US Navy to the Coast Guard to enforce Prohibition.
Courtesy of the Trustees of the Boston Public Library, Leslie Jones Collection

Phannemiller returned, dripping. The lower compartments were flooding with seawater. All the men had escaped. Some even managed to get out through the escape hatch in the wardroom. However, there was a foot of rising water in the crew's compartments. Crew members were securing the bulkhead doors to prevent further flooding.

Phannemiller, who was the officer of the deck, must have been most anxious over the collision. He was the man who first thought the periscopes were fishing markers. He was the officer who gave the order for "right full." Baylis ordered him to a launch to look for survivors. While we do not know why Baylis chose the young officer for this task, some might conclude that Baylis may have been angry with Phannemiller since it was he who was in charge when the collision occurred. Or it may have been that it was simply the young officer's duty station. Or it may have been Baylis's decision to give a surely traumatized young officer something to do and get him out of the way.

The ensign rushed off the bridge and onto the deck. Phannemiller assigned some of the crew to an open rowboat, which they referred to as a whaleboat, and ordered them aboard. Some of them had come up so quickly from below decks that they were not wearing their cold-weather gear. One was even barefoot. Despite this, Phannemiller got them aboard the boat and had it lowered over the side. The crew manned the oars and began slow circles amid the oil slicks, looking for survivors.

Meanwhile, lifeboats were swung out and made ready. Despite Phannemiller's report that the hatches were secured, Baylis felt there was an even chance that he was about to lose his ship. He issued orders to double-check the hatches, man the pumps, and form a bucket brigade. Meanwhile, Baylis was close enough to shore that he could, at worst, run the ship up on a beach.

The *Paulding* dropped a buoy to mark the spot of the collision, then proceeded forward, its gashed bow sadly sagging in the water. The ship turned toward Provincetown Harbor and steered toward a series of mudflats. That would be an ideal place to beach the *Paulding* if necessary. Baylis hoped it wouldn't come to that—he wanted to reach the harbor.

As the *Paulding* rounded Long Point, reports came to the bridge. The cook, an African American named Joseph MacMillan, suffered a third-degree burn in the galley when a steam pipe broke loose. An ensign named Davis sprained his ankle. One of the men in the crew compartments was thrown up into the bulkhead. They'd all have to be sent into Provincetown for treatment—but there were no deaths or serious injuries. Then there was an update on the ship's condition. The men fighting the flood of water were winning—they were going to make it to the harbor. But the *Paulding* was horribly wounded. A large chunk of its prow was missing and presumably embedded in the submarine's hull.

Still, the *Paulding* was neither going to sink nor be beached. Baylis should have been relieved by this—and he was. But there was also a growing sense of anxiety for the men aboard the submarine, who were either dead or trapped alive within it.

Just then, a powered lifeboat raced up to the ship. It had come from the lifesaving station at Wood End. But Baylis waved them off and requested that they assist Phannemiller in searching for survivors.

Baylis ordered a radio telegram dispatched to his superiors in the Coast Guard and the commandant of the Boston Navy Yard:

RAMMED AND SANK UNKNOWN SUBMARINE OFF WOOD END, PROVINCETOWN.

Soon enough, Baylis would learn that the boat he sank was the *S-4.*

4

Trapped

THE *S-4* LISTED TO PORT, then lurched, its bow downward. Men were thrown about as water rushed into the *S-4*'s battery room. The sea was rapidly filling the submarine, but no water had entered the control room yet because of the submarine's descendant angle. Crew in the battery compartment evacuated either fore or aft into the control or torpedo rooms. Lieutenant Commander Roy Jones needed to act fast.

He gave the command to blow the ballast tanks.

His men turned valves to release compressed air into the tanks that ran alongside the submarine. If Jones's plan worked, the air would force seawater out of the tanks and right the vessel, perhaps reversing the calamity. In an instant, air was pumped from banks one and two to all the ballast tanks.

But nothing happened. The air gurgled uselessly into the sea—the ballast tanks had been damaged. Jones ordered them to stop. He needed to reserve what air they had remaining.

Meanwhile, men leaped into action. One rushed to the watertight door to the bulkhead, waited a few moments for any survivors, then slammed it shut before water could enter the control room. Then men turned the dogs, the clamps that sealed the watertight doors. The control room was now cut off from the forward part of the ship. All hands braced themselves for the crash on the muddy bottom.

• • •

When the collision alarm was sounded, Fitch and his men in the torpedo room jumped to action. They rushed to the bulkhead door and waited a moment as two seamen on duty in the battery compartment, Joseph Stevens and George Pelnar, fled into the torpedo room. The ship, pitching down at a 45-degree angle, forced water into the submarine at a furious rate. Fitch and his men struggled against the encroaching water and gravity. With great effort they slammed the door and dogged it. The flood was halted, although there was a shallow layer of seawater pooling on the deck of the torpedo room.

Even though Fitch had gotten the door sealed, the *S-4* was still careening downward. The six men braced themselves as the submarine slammed into the soft and muddy bottom. The hull did not rupture. They were safe, but cut off from their shipmates and Captain Jones. Immediately, they prepared gas masks in case toxic chlorine fumes should enter their compartment from the batteries and waited.

There was nothing more they could do. The electric lights flickered out and coldness seeped into the compartment. Fitch and his crew took out blankets and flashlights and tried to keep themselves as warm and dry as possible.

• • •

On Jones's side of the flooded battery room, there were thirty-four officers and men including himself. Fortunately, when the *S-4* slid into the seafloor, it wedged itself into an upright position. This allowed the captain and his men to move about inside the vessel.

Jones also had the control room. Despite the failure of the ballast tanks, there were other mechanisms through the control of compressed air that he could use to save his boat. In no accident in which a submarine crashed to the bottom had a crew been able to rescue themselves if they lost the control room. Also to their advantage was the relative shallowness of the water. They had sunk in 102 feet of water, but the submarine was over 200 feet long. The *S-4* still had air left in banks three and four. If done correctly, Jones could float the stern to the surface even with the front end stuck in the mud. Then, if he couldn't open an exterior hatch himself, the navy could cut into the hull from the outside to release them. Fitch and the men in the torpedo room would be in greater danger since they would likely be trapped until the navy could raise the whole vessel. Although they had been struck less than two minutes prior, there was no time to lose. Jones needed to lay plans with the senior officer present, Lieutenant Commander Callaway, and his executive officer, Lieutenant McGinley. Not all was lost.

Then water burst into the control room, not through the bulkhead door, which was closed and partially dogged, but through a ventilation shaft meant to carry exhaust from the batteries above the door. This meant that the battery compartment had completely filled with water and was looking for new outlets.

Near the duct was a lever that operated an emergency flapper valve to seal the ventilation shaft. On the sound of the alarm, men were supposed to seal the valve. Apparently, somebody had neglected to do this minor but critical duty. Still, if they could shut the valve now, they could completely seal off the control room. But the space was confined by the bulkhead so that only one man at a time could reach the valve. So urgent was this new crisis that the man securing the dogs to the door to the battery compartment abandoned this task, leaving only three dogs turned. He yanked at the valve, and while the flow of water lessened somewhat, it continued to come in. Something was stuck in the valve.

No matter what Jones's men did, they could not stop the water. Jones would have been most concerned with the electrical control switchboards that were beneath the ventilation valves. Inevitably, seawater sprayed onto it. Then, in a sudden blue flash, the switchboard went up in sparks. One man fell back, burnt from electric flames. Then the bleach-like smell of chlorine gas started to fill the air as it seeped into the compartment through the compromised ventilation ducts.

Jones's men smothered the panels with blankets. While not a perfect solution against seawater, it could buy them time. They needed to close the valve to the ventilation shaft and stop the inflow of water.

But it would not budge despite desperate strength. Little did Jones know that the delicate green *portiere* that hung across his cabin door had flushed into the ventilation pipe and was choking the valve. There was nothing his men could do from their side of the bulkhead to remove it.

Men coughed from the chlorine fumes. The seawater continued to rise. Out of options, Jones gave the order to abandon the control room. Men, throats burnt from gas, stormed into the engineering room. With finality, Jones used a jackknife to cut the cable used during the standardization tests that blocked the bulkhead door. They slammed the door shut and turned the sixteen dogs that sealed off the rear part of the vessel from the submarine's heart and brain. All the control over the air, all the power over the ballast was gone. Jones, with thirty-three other men, jammed into the engineering and motor rooms. Water was slowly leaking in through the gasket in the watertight door, but the situation was manageable.

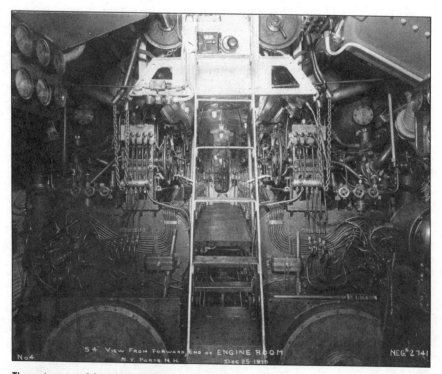

The engine room of the submarine *S-4.*
Naval History and Heritage Command, Photo Archives, NH-41854

Time ticked by. After about fifteen minutes, the control room beyond the door was completely flooded. The sea pressure against the door grew and grew until the little leak suddenly became a sheet of water.

The battle was rejoined. Men hammered the dogs down until they could go no farther. But water still came through. The men hammered again. They drove five of the dogs so hard that they sheared off their stops. But it was no use. Water still came.

Then men seized gear to deal with the emergency. They grabbed two-inch planking and with other materials jammed it against the door. The flow subsided. Imminent death had passed, though there was a good deal of cold water that flooded the deck of the engine room.

Most of the men would have been drenched in the cold seawater, gasping either in relief or panic. There was little comfort to be had in the engine or adjacent motor room. There was hardly a place to stand much less to lie down. And each breath meant a little less breathable air. With thirty-four men in two compartments, there wasn't much time, as there was no way to expel the building carbon dioxide.

Then the lights twinkled out.

5

The Boatswain

CLAD IN HIS PEACOAT, BOATSWAIN Emmanuel F. Gracie slogged over four shivering miles of soft, sandy beach inspecting the telephone poles and wire that connected his little Coast Guard outpost to the wider world.

While he had been inspecting the telephone poles along the beach that morning, Gracie saw a ship and recognized it immediately as the *Paulding*. Usually, when Coast Guard vessels passed, he had signal flags raised to greet it. It was never anything official, just an exchange of pleasantries such as one would make when passing a neighbor on the sidewalk. Although Gracie had never met the *Paulding*'s captain, he knew him by the way the ship was sailed and the natural fraternity of the Coast Guard. By the time Gracie returned to the small white house that served as the Wood End Lifesaving Station, his cheeks were reddened from the gusty December wind.

Gracie had been in charge of the station since 1925 and was responsible for reporting shipping activity off the tip of Cape Cod. This meant that after his return from inspecting the poles he needed to catch up on office duties. He was so taken up with work that, hours later, it was only the growl in his belly and the dull ache in his forty-two-year-old head that told him to look at the clock. It was 3:00 PM. He needed food, but especially coffee.

Gracie left his office, passed through the kitchen, and entered the mess room. He sat eating and drinking, looking out through windows that gave a panoramic southwest view of Cape Cod Bay. The sea-lanes about Provincetown were normally quiet, used mainly by fishing boats rather than the great ocean liners. When a unique vessel arrived, it was a cause of notice, such as during the summer of 1926 when the battleship *Texas* hailed at Provincetown. There were sightings of other navy vessels from time to time, even submarines that used the navy testing courses along Wood End. In the three years Gracie had been in charge of the station, he had seen the exotic vessels on many occasions. In fact, it had become commonplace enough that he simply noted it in the log rather than making a direct report to his district's commanding officer.

As he sat in the mess room, Gracie saw the *Paulding* again. It was heading into Provincetown. The boatswain grew curious. Perhaps it had caught a rumrunner. He wanted to have a better look.

He hurried to the nearby watchtower. On days like today, when the visibility was good, Gracie only assigned one man to the watch.

He entered the tower and climbed the stairs. At the top, he pushed open a trapdoor and popped his head through.

"What's doing, Frank?" asked Gracie.

Frank Simmonds, a Coast Guard surfman who was at the end of his watch, was peering through a telescope. He replied to his boss, "Not much, sir. I've seen a submarine operating under the beach to the southeast." Simmonds added that it was making foamy splashes as it came up and down.

For the moment, Gracie forgot about the *Paulding*. Even though both he and Simmonds had seen submarines before, there was always a thrill at looking at such unusual vessels.

Gracie took the telescope from Simmonds and looked through it. He quickly found the *Paulding*, which was now past the Wood End Station. This was about where Simmonds had last seen the submarine. The *Paulding* was close to the measured mile course.

Gracie was uneasy.

He swung the telescope about and said, "I wonder where the submarine is now. Have you seen her?"

Simmonds peered out over the water. Visibility was ten miles. "No sir, not lately."

Gracie scanned through the telescope. He saw no sign of the submarine. He paused by the *Paulding* just as it lined up to a white can buoy that marked the navy testing course.

Then there was a flash of metal and spraying water. The sea shifted as a dark metallic shadow emerged from the deep. It was the submarine *S-4*. First its twin periscopes pierced the choppy water, and then its conning tower. It was on a direct course for the *Paulding*.

"My God, Frank," said Gracie, dropping the telescope and looking with the naked eye. "There's going to be a collision."

Gracie and Simmonds watched as the *Paulding*, as if at the last moment, saw its peril and began to veer to the right. But it was too late. The *Paulding* rode roughshod over the submarine, thrusting it back down into the sea.

The boatswain immediately bolted back to the station house. He needed his two boats back in from patrol: the picketboat and the powered lifeboat. They were due back soon, but he had his men fly an emergency hoist to recall them. He also wanted to let the *Paulding* know that help was on the way.

Yet Gracie's two boats would hardly be enough help for the *Paulding* and any survivors from the submarine. He ran into his office. He needed to notify his superior, Lieutenant Howard Wilcox, the commander of the Second Coast Guard District.

He seized the station telephone and made a connection to the district office. The secretary answered. The lieutenant wasn't in. Gracie spewed out the improbable story of a Coast Guard cutter ramming and sinking a submarine. He hung up.

Gracie ran onto the beach. The powered lifeboat was coming in, the crew switching curious glances between the emergency flag and their commander, who ran along the shore gesticulating toward the scene of the collision. Gracie pulled off his peacoat and waved it frantically.

The boatswain's men turned their vessel and headed to the *Paulding*, which was hobbling around Long Point. Gracie watched from the shore as the lifeboat neared the cutter, ready to take on survivors. Yet within minutes, it headed back to Gracie.

They beached the boat and the men spoke hurriedly. The *Paulding*'s captain, Baylis, had waved them off. He told them he'd be fine even if he had to beach the ship. Instead, he wanted them to help one of his officers, Ensign George Phannemiller, who was looking for survivors in a whaleboat.

Gracie hopped aboard the motorboat and flew to the scene. The water was rough with the coming storm, and the boat skipped over the swells. There, atop the oil-slicked waves, they found Phannemiller in the fading twilight. Gracie saw that the ensign and his crew were too lightly clad for the cold. Seawater sloshed about in their boat. No survivors had been found.

The two boats circled the spot repeatedly, covering a diameter of forty yards. With dark coming, Gracie ordered cross bearings to be taken of Provincetown, the Truro shore to the south, and Wood End, so when those who could salvage the submarine arrived, they would be in the right spot. Meanwhile, Phannemiller's boat drifted languidly to the east. They were apparently exhausted from pulling at the oars and bailing water from the little boat.

Gracie felt bad for Phannemiller and his men. Not only were they suffering in the cold, but as far as he could tell there were no survivors to pick up, and at this point there weren't likely to be any. The boatswain decided that the real people in distress were Phannemiller and his crew.

Then a large vessel suddenly appeared around Long Point. It was the 795-ton *Wandank*, the fleet tug and submarine tender that had been berthed in Provincetown Harbor.

Lieutenant Thomas Fertner, the captain of the *Wandank*, asked Gracie to direct them to the exact spot of the collision. Gracie led the ship to it, and positioned his boat over the only hint of the *S-4*—bubbles and oil slicks. Fertner then dropped anchored buoys to mark the scene. Gracie motored alongside and indicated Phannemiller and his men.

"It would be a good idea if you pick them up," said Gracie.

"It will be quite all right," Fertner replied. The lieutenant was probably too concerned with minding the spot for any navy rescue force that would arrive.

Gracie turned his boat to the east and headed where Phanne-miller had been. Since the *Wandank* was at the site of collision, it could watch the disaster site. Gracie, however, could take care of his Coast Guard brethren.

But neither Gracie nor his men could see where Phannemiller had gone. His crew drew out flashlights and swept the twilit water. There was nothing but a steadily worsening sea and mounting wind. Phannemiller had vanished.

Gracie drew the lifeboat closer to the shore. Only the rumble of his boat's motor and the wail of the wind could be heard. With the weather shaping up the way it was, it would be too easy for Phanne-miller's boat to get swamped in the swells coming off the ocean.

But then the boatswain saw a twinkle on the shore.

Gracie steered toward the light and saw Phannemiller and his crew on the beach. The lights were from their flashlights. They had hauled their boat up and were doing calisthenics to keep warm.

Gracie offered them a tow to the *Paulding* in Provincetown Harbor.

Phannemiller accepted and before long, Gracie was pulling them off the beach. The men from the whaleboat were obviously dejected and depressed. The sight of the wounded *Paulding* would have offered little comfort to them, particularly Phannemiller. He had been the officer of the deck and the man in charge when the *S-4* was sent to the bottom. Now he could not even locate a single survivor.

Gracie dropped them off and returned to the Wood End station. He exchanged his powered lifeboat for picketboat number 2339. Pick-etboats were built in large numbers after World War I in order to help suppress smuggling. Where the on-loan destroyers, like the *Paulding*, were excellent at catching rumrunners on open sea, the smaller pick-etboats were more effective in the shallow waterways. It was maneuver-able and fast and had a cabin that could shelter its crew from the cold. The entire process of finding Phannemiller, towing his crew, and then exchanging the boats took several hours, so that by the time Gracie went back to the scene it was fully dark.

Gracie motored the picketboat up to the *Wandank* and brought it alongside. Lieutenant Fertner came out again to chat. He asked Gra-cie if he could help find the submarine by grappling.

Gracie agreed as long as the *Wandank* would assist by using its powerful searchlights.

"Have you got any grapnels aboard that would be of use?" Fertner asked.

"We got a ten-pound one," Gracie replied.

But Fertner thought the grapnel was too light, especially in the rough weather, and said, "We'll give you a one-hundred-pound grapnel and as much rope as you could want."

The *Wandank* passed to Gracie's men a large four-fluked grapnel and bundles of five-inch rope. The equipment lay heavily on the picketboat's deck as it took two of Gracie's men to handle the grapnel effectively. The idea was that Gracie would drop the grapnel into the sea then tow it along the bottom until it caught some part of the submarine.

Even though Gracie knew the general location of the collision, he could not pinpoint exactly where to drop the grapnel. The *S-4* in its descent might have been hundreds of feet away from where the marker buoys were. Also, submarines were designed to be hydrodynamic and stealthy. However, it was reasonable to believe that since the *S-4* was damaged, there might be some wreckage that a grapnel could cling to.

The *Wandank* turned its searchlight on a small white buoy. This was the same one Gracie noted when he saw the collision several hours earlier, the one that marked the navy's testing course.

Gracie headed slightly northwest of the buoy. At 11:45 PM, his men heaved over the grapnel. It plopped into the sea, and the rope whirled to the bottom.

Gracie turned the picketboat to begin the first drag. As the boat made way, it hit something solid. By the feel of the rope, Gracie knew they had found the *S-4* on the first try. It was miraculous.

But the line felt jerky and tenuous. Gracie and his men immediately grabbed the rope and fastened it steady to the picketboat. If the grapnel slipped, there was no guarantee that they could find the submarine again so quickly.

Deliberately, Gracie eased the picketboat back and forth. He tried to keep the line taut enough to hold, but not so taut as to yank it clean off the submarine. If he could hold on long enough for the navy to bring a proper salvage ship, the line could be used by divers as a descending line in order to find the submarine and begin a rescue effort.

Time passed, and the ocean swelled. The small picketboat was rocked back and forth and up and down. Gracie kept maneuvering the boat, still holding on.

The *Wandank* came up, and Gracie hailed them. The *Wandank* then dropped another anchored buoy, but a bit away from the boat-swain's picketboat, extrapolating by current and wind where the *S-4* would probably lie. In the meantime, Fertner informed Gracie that the specialized submarine rescue ship, the *Falcon*, was underway. Gracie had to hold on until it arrived on the scene in the morning.

Then the *Wandank* backed off. Gracie continued to grapple with the line. He constantly maneuvered the picketboat even as the swells started to turn heavier.

Meanwhile, the entire navy establishment had set itself in motion after the *Paulding* had sent word to the Boston Navy Yard* that it had struck the *S-4*. Every ship that was potentially of use was thrown to the scene by the yard's commandant, Rear Admiral Philip Andrews. In fact, word had spread so rapidly that within hours every important officer from the chief of naval operations downward was involved in getting men and equipment to Provincetown.

At midnight, lights twinkled as two vessels came into view. While not the behemoths of the US fleet by far, they dwarfed Gracie's picket-boat, each being over 180 feet in length: the *Lark* and the *Mallard*.

Both of these ships were minesweepers of the *Lapwing* class—commonly called the "bird" class—and were built during World War I to clear explosive mines. To do this, they used grapnels and hooks to catch on underwater objects.

But both ships stood back like the *Wandank*. The submarine was already hooked, so there was no need for them to use their grapnels. Instead, they used their searchlights to scan the water, in case there were any survivors. Then at 1:30 AM, another ship came into sight. But

---

*Also called the Charlestown Navy Yard due to its location in Charlestown, next to Boston proper.

it was not the *Falcon*; it was the *Bushnell*, a submarine tender. All these ships stood off, afraid that interfering with the boatswain would make him lose the *S-4*.

Nor could they have been of any real assistance anyway—not yet. Even though these ships had pumps and divers, the weather was too rough, and more important, their gear was not the proper kind for rescue diving in these conditions. The *Bushnell* was not a specialized salvage ship like the *Falcon*, and the divers aboard only conducted their business in calm water. Moreover, it did not have men who had the experience or wherewithal to dive deep in cold water under stormy conditions. What is more, the pumps that were used to deliver air to the divers could work effectively at up to seventy feet since they were hand-cranked by large wheels. The submarine lay at 102 feet. To deliver more air would require men to work the pumps so fast that they would have to be relieved every five to ten minutes. Also, the *Bushnell* conducted its diving from a launch, which would mean the pump would have to be loaded into a small boat and inexperienced divers sent over the side. Considering the weather and the prospects of success, they waited for the *Falcon*. They relied on Gracie to hold the line.

Another vessel soon arrived, but not the *Falcon*. Instead, the submarine *S-8*, the *S-4*'s sister, had come. It too stood off.

As the hours passed, Gracie felt vibrations through the rope, which told him that he was barely clawing on. At every rise in the sea it felt as if the connection would break as easily as spider's silk. He suspected that he was hooked on some spar or a piece of dangling wreckage. He thought it might have even been a piece of the *Paulding* itself. After all, the ship had lost a good chunk of its bow. Two o'clock passed, and the struggle continued as a strong gale picked up. Gracie kept maneuvering the boat, and the connection stayed. He needed to remain attached until the *Falcon* came.

Then at 3:00 AM, the wind shifted. His feet felt the sea rise in a great swell and lift the picketboat. The vibration in the rope did not speak of metal anymore, but soft mud. Gracie's boat shifted listlessly in the sea. The grapnel had broken loose from the *S-4*.

6

"Who Wants to Know?"

IT WAS QUIET IN THE offices of the *Boston American* on the afternoon of December 17. Saturday afternoons were typically slow for news reporting; however, today seemed particularly languid as some reporters got caught up in a game of penny ante.

Chatting with the reporters was twenty-seven-year-old Mark McIntyre Spaulding, who occasionally stopped by his old offices. McIntyre, who typically omitted Spaulding from his name, had been promoted recently from the *Boston American* reportorial staff to an editorial manager of another Hearst newspaper in Cambridge. Today, he was being teased, in a good-natured fashion, about the promotion. McIntyre gave as good as he got; he (as well as any reporter worth his salt) longed for a good story—a story that would trump all the other reporters.

The editor came in. In his hand was a piece of paper with scrawling on it: "4:05 P.M. Provincetown??? Short while ago. Coast Guard??"

There had been a phone call from Provincetown. Something was going on, but nobody was talking—neither the Coast Guard nor the navy.

The editor quickly selected two reporters and a photographer to go to Provincetown to find out what was happening. McIntyre, being no longer on the staff, yearned to go. So he begged the chief, saying,

"Put me down too! My Buick's outside with a tank full of gas, and I've nothing to do till Monday. . . . I do know the navy lingo."

This was true. McIntyre, despite his youth, had an interesting career. He ran away from home to join the navy in 1917. There, he served as a signalman and became so adept at semaphore* that he was transferred to submarine duty during World War I. In 1919, he was honorably discharged.

Also, McIntyre knew about submarine reporting. In 1925, he was one of the first reporters to cover the *S-51* disaster. His knowledge of signaling proved invaluable as it got his vessel to the right spot (another ship signaled the location of the sunken submarine to him) and then helped him obtain further information. In fact McIntyre, due to his naval background and knowledge, formed relationships with the men who were conducting the *S-51* rescue effort. At one point, with covert assistance from the enlisted, he masqueraded as a chief petty officer, which gave him great insight into the rescue efforts.

The editor conceded that McIntyre was the right man to go to Provincetown, but only because McIntyre could drive the other men in a carpool to save money.

McIntyre raced to the elevator and within minutes he, two reporters, and a photographer were on their way to Provincetown to investigate.

It took three uncomfortable hours in McIntyre's open roadster to make the trip from Boston to Provincetown. This was a speedy trip considering the icy roads, occasional snowdrifts, and bitter chill that was blowing from the northwest. The newsmen were huddled in the backseat. There wasn't much talking. But McIntyre had a feeling that something *big* was happening.

They pulled into Provincetown at 7:30 PM.

When the *Boston American* men entered a coffee shop, it seemed like the whole East Coast news corps had arrived. There were reporters from the *New York Times*, the *Herald*, the *Post*, and the *Boston Globe*. Yet there was nothing but rumors. All they could confirm was that the navy would issue a statement later.

---

*The sending and receiving of signals through flashing lights and flags.

His own companions were pooling their money to rent a fishing boat to try to figure out what was going on. But McIntyre, on a hunch, hung back.

He had seen off Wood End the flicker of gathering lights. It looked like a flotilla was assembling. As soon as he was unnoticed, he left the group, returned to his car, then drove his Buick into an open shed that faced out toward the harbor. He stepped out of his car, tossed a blanket over one headlight, and stood in front of the other.

McIntyre looked at the lights and knew they were ships. There was one in the harbor, a Coast Guard cutter, that piqued his interest. He then took off his hat, held it by the brim, and swung it over the uncovered headlight of the car. He jerked it back and forth rapidly, sending semaphore signals to the ship:

WHAT SHIP? WHAT SHIP?

After a moment, the ship's lights blinked back:

U.S.C.G.C. *PAULDING*. WHO INQUIRES?

McIntyre needed to think quickly. He could try to fool the ship into believing he was another vessel that was in port, or perhaps an official. To buy time he repeated his first question.

The answer blinked back: U.S.S. *PAULDING*. WHO WANTS TO KNOW?

McIntyre decided to be honest, but he prefaced his message with "PVT," meaning that it was a private message. He yanked his hat back and forth over the light as he sent:

THE PRESS. WE WOULD LIKE DETAILS OF WHAT HAPPENED. MARK MCINTYRE.

There was no response. McIntyre at first believed that the message was being taken to the commanding officer so that there could be an official response. So he waited in his car, smoked a cigarette, and worried that he was wasting his time. Surely the navy would have broken the story by now to the other newsmen.

But he decided to stay, and after a half hour realized that the *Paulding* was not going to respond to him. So he switched on his headlights again, stepped out of the car, and decided to send a more official sounding message:

TO COMMANDING OFFICER U.S.S. *PAULDING*. PLEASE GIVE BRIEF DETAILS OF WHAT HAPPENED.

The answer was immediate:

WHILE RETURNING FROM MANEUVERS OFF PROVINCETOWN 3:37 PM
TODAY WE RAMMED AND SANK SUBMARINE S-4. BELIEVE CREW OF 40
ABOARD.

McIntyre scribbled down the message without fully realizing the implications of it until after he had fully transcribed it. Amazed, shocked—he headed back to the town's center.

In the center of Provincetown, he found the three *Boston American* newsmen. Somehow, by the look on McIntyre's face, they knew something was amiss. McIntyre, for his part, was incredulous after speaking with them. Nobody knew what was going on yet!

Even as his companions peppered McIntyre with questions, he held them off. He said he needed to buy some cigarettes first. He went into a drugstore, found a phone booth, and placed a call. He quickly inquired from the city desk if they knew anything about what happened off Provincetown. They didn't.

McIntyre told them.

The *Falcon*

ON DECEMBER 17, 1927, THE *Falcon* lay quietly at its mooring at dock "I" of the Naval Submarine Base at New London, Connecticut. A sprawling facility of several hundred acres, it had in its employ hundreds of sailors and roughly a hundred civilians. However, the normal activity of the base had ceased. Officers and men were settling into a quiet holiday routine. Machinery was overhauled, stores procured, fuel obtained, and provisions loaded. This was all in preparation for the postholiday cruise, when the fleet would remove itself to the balmier climes of the Gulf of Panama. In light of the deep cold that had settled upon New England, the cruise was highly anticipated.

But the *Falcon* and its men did not even have these mundane tasks to do since all the preparations for the winter cruise had been done days ahead of schedule. This was because of Lieutenant Henry Hartley, the efficient captain of the *Falcon*. Some days prior, he had sent a message to Rear Admiral Frank Brumby, the Submarine Force commander: "Boilers clean, fueled, provisioned, stores aboard, and ready in all respects for Winter Cruise."

Hartley was one of the most capable officers in the service, and rose to his command based on merit. As a boy at school, he became enamored with naval history and on February 1, 1901, at age sixteen, he enlisted in the service as an apprentice boy aboard the *Essex*. He excelled, and he even came in second for the vaunted Bailey Medal, a solid gold award that was given to the best apprentice boys.

Hartley quickly rose through the ranks of the enlisted, went to gunnery school, and qualified as a diver. He recovered anchors and fixed equipment under the sea. He then served on a variety of ships, and during World War I he was assigned to command a force of submarine chasers.

During the war Hartley received his first command. It was a small Eagle boat, which assisted in antisubmarine warfare. The navy was so impressed by Hartley's abilities that he was commissioned as a lieutenant in 1920. This alone was a testament to his skill, since in Hartley's day the vast majority of navy officers came out of Annapolis. Hartley was what was called a "mustang," an officer who came from the enlisted ranks. Four years later, he gained command of the *Falcon*, the navy's finest and only specialized deep sea salvage vessel. He was so excited about the command that he requested from the Bureau of Navigation every book and document they had on underwater operations.

The ship's moniker, the *Falcon*, was not a true reflection of its nature. With its single smokestack and the squat way it sat in the water, the ship bespoke of a workhorse rather than a bird of prey. All the same, it was an object of love for Hartley.

The *Falcon* was a 157-foot former minesweeper of the "bird" class that was built during World War I. After the war, it was converted into a specialized salvage vessel. It was the only ship that had a complete diving facility, which was absolutely necessary in order to conduct any sort of underwater rescue and salvage work. Special booms, winches, and stages had been installed, which allowed the heavy-clad divers to be lowered directly from the ship into the water. It also had a one-of-a-kind compressed air plant that could deliver air through multiple hoses to divers or to submarine wrecks to blow water out of them, using two separate compressors. In emergencies, the ship held a reserve of air compressed to 3,000 pounds per square inch that was maintained in banks aboard. The ship also had special attachments to handle salvage pontoons (up to six). As far as Hartley knew, no other ship had

Launched in 1918, the *Falcon* was a minesweeper converted to a submarine rescue and salvage ship.
Naval History and Heritage Command, Photo Archives, NH-54139

such attachments. Yet, most remarkable of all was its decompression chamber,* which negated the effects of the bends that would afflict divers if they were brought up too quickly from the bottom. This long, cylindrical steel chamber was called by some the "iron doctor."

All of these tools enabled the *Falcon* to carry off some spectacular salvage work. The most famous example was the recovery of the *S-51* two years prior. Since that time, the navy had put another forty thousand dollars into the vessel to improve its ability to do its job.

Hartley had memorized every specification of the ship, so entranced was he by his command. But what grated on Hartley were questions by people who did not know a thing about underwater salvage. *Why was the* Falcon *so small? Wouldn't it be better to have a larger ship*

---

*The decompression chamber was properly called the "recompression chamber." The term was used interchangeably among the sources for this book and the author has also chosen to use the terms interchangeably.

to provide a more stable platform for divers? But as Hartley, or any officer who worked in deep sea salvage knew, large ships were more susceptible to pitch and yaw in greater amounts than a smaller vessel. Since a diver was connected physically to the ship above, any pull on his line could be disastrous. The maneuverability afforded by a smaller ship allowed it to respond almost instantly to changing conditions at sea.

Hartley's efficiency at preparing his ship for the winter cruise ahead of time was rewarded by receiving permission from Brumby to release the *Falcon*'s crew for the holidays with the caveat that they would be recalled in the event of an emergency. Hartley was to take leave and go home to Bladensburg, Maryland, to celebrate a honeymoon. He had gotten married on the weekend of December 11.

So on the morning of December 17, money due was paid to the crew, and by noon half of the *Falcon*'s complement of five officers and sixty-one men were released. These quickly began to disburse themselves all about the East Coast, with one going as far as Tampa, Florida. This group would not be back until December 26, when the other half of the *Falcon*'s complement would receive their liberty, which would last until after the New Year and the commencement of the Caribbean cruise.

Even the deep cold and the mounting wind did not seem to bother Hartley. "Snugly secured at the dock," he later wrote. "Let it blow."

· · ·

Then at 5:05 PM, an orderly from Captain Adolphus Andrews, the base commandant, rushed aboard. He had a message: "Captain Andrews says that he has an unconfirmed message from the Cape Cod Coast Guard Station that a submarine has been sunk or badly damaged. This is not official, but he advises you to raise steam and prepare for sea."

Hartley ordered the boiler fires lit, and the *Falcon* prepared to sail. His most pressing need was men. Half of his crew was gone and in terms of officers, he only had his executive, Edward Burnett, aboard.

He had telephone messages sent to the police department of New London as well as the movie theatres (where he assumed many of his crew could be found), to spread word that all the crew members of the *Falcon* were to return immediately. With some luck, he managed to get in touch with one of his officers who lived in New London. Still, he was terribly shorthanded and had no time to lose.

Hartley compiled a list of the men he needed and hurried over to Admiral Brumby's flagship, the *Camden*, which sat several hundred feet from the *Falcon*. The ship, at four hundred feet, dwarfed the *Falcon*. He hoped for news about what was going on—he undoubtedly harbored a hope that the whole thing was a hoax. But Hartley knew, as well as most of the other officers in the submarine service fleet, that the pigboats of the Twelfth Division were conducting trials off Provincetown after their overhauls. There were the *S-8* and the *S-4* with the *Wandank* serving as their tender.

When Hartley came aboard the *Camden*, he found the calm of the preholiday slowdown displaced with frenetic activity. Anybody whom Hartley spoke to did not know more than he did about what was going on at Cape Cod. All anybody knew was that they were to prepare the *Camden* for sea.

Hartley found the ship's executive officer and had a quick discussion about what to do. The *Camden*, while an able ship, would be difficult to get underway to Provincetown that night—wind and tide were against it. Also, to get to the tip of Cape Cod, the *Camden* would need to travel around the length of the cape, rather than going through the shortcut of the Cape Cod Canal since the *Camden* was far too large. But Brumby himself planned to go to the scene, and it was assumed that the *Camden* would go.

Then, at 5:35 PM, one of Brumby's aides told Hartley, "A message just received, the *S-4* sunk in collision by the Coast Guard destroyer *Paulding* off Wood End Light, Cape Cod in 102 feet of water."

Even as Hartley considered this, there came a change of plans. Admiral Brumby must have been told of the troubles of getting the *Camden* to Provincetown; the aide informed Hartley that Brumby would embark on the *Falcon*. The admiral would take Hartley's cabin. The gap in the complement of men aboard the *Falcon* would be filled by the *Camden*'s men, as well as by any men with diving experience.

Sailors, clad in peacoats to fight the cold breeze off the Thames River, rushed across the frozen quay to the *Falcon* as rumors circled of disaster. Within an hour, Hartley had more than his full complement.

Yet a storm was coming. Ferocious gales and frigid water would make diving conditions exceedingly difficult, if not impossible. Hartley could not simply take a diver and put him on the bottom if he had never been proven. He badly needed his own trained men and whatever veterans of the *S-51* job could be scraped together.

Of the divers of the *S-51* salvage there was only one who was still assigned to the *Falcon*—William J. Carr, who went by Bill. Carr was on liberty at his home in Jamestown. Hartley knew also of two others, Tom Eadie and Fred Michels, who were at the navy diving school at Newport. He had to get them.

Hartley consulted the rosters. He sent telegrams to his most valuable men who he knew were within traveling distance of Cape Cod: JOIN SHIP AT PROVINCETOWN, MASS. IMMEDIATELY. Then he had a cable sent to the diving school at Newport: SEND ALL DIVERS AND MEN IN THE DIVING SCHOOL TO PROVINCETOWN, FASTEST AVAILABLE METHOD, ALSO PICK UP *FALCON*'S DIVER, WILLIAM J. CARR AT JAMESTOWN. He then notified the navy office in Cape Cod that the *Falcon* was coming.

At 6:36 PM, the *Falcon*'s horn sounded. The ship cleared its moorings and turned into the night. Brumby complimented Hartley on the speediness with which he got the *Falcon* underway. But Hartley and the admiral had little hope for any survivors. The water was cold and the coming storm could well end their mission before it even started. Hartley would feel better once he had his divers aboard.

Although Hartley never stated it, he must have also had questions about Brumby. Brumby, a genteel fifty-three-year-old from Athens, Georgia, came from a traditional southern military family. His grandfather, Arnoldus Vanderhorst Brumby, was a graduate of West Point and served as a colonel for a Georgia infantry regiment during the Civil War. Likewise, Admiral Brumby's father, John Wallis Brumby, was a captain for a Georgia cavalry regiment. After the conflict, the family switched its affiliation from the army to the navy. His uncle, Thomas Brumby, had been the flag lieutenant for Admiral George Dewey during the Battle of Manila during the Spanish-American War. As for Frank Brumby, in 1895 he graduated third in his class at Annapolis, where he'd excelled at mathematics. He also served in the Spanish-American War and during the subsequent Philippine Insurrection.

Brumby eventually earned his own commands, including that of the battleship *New Mexico,* before being selected for rear admiral.

He was young for an admiral and new to the position, having been promoted only in June 1927. The navy opted to give him his first flag command not in the surface fleet, where all his primary experience had been, but as commander of the submarine control force.

Brumby did not have direct experience with submarines or diving. Knowing this, he actively sought the assistance of those who did and made himself responsible for overall command. He was a delegator who leaned heavily on others when necessary. Brumby never pretended to know more or better than his expert subordinates. Captain Ernest J. King, who had overall command of the *S-51* salvage operation, was being sent up from his command in Virginia and was to join the *Falcon* at Provincetown. King was to act as Brumby's senior aide.

Another person whom the rescue force might have wished for was Edward Ellsberg, the salvage officer of the *S-51* with whom Hartley had worked closely for more than a year. Ellsberg was a passionate, brilliant salvage expert and one of the few officers in the navy who was also a qualified deep sea diver. His assistance would be invaluable, but Hartley knew that Ellsberg had suffered a falling out with the navy over promotion and was now working for private industry.

● ● ●

The *Falcon* passed over the choppy seas near Fishers Island, then along Rhode Island off Newport near the navy's diving school. He knew the divers from there were now heading to Provincetown, or should be, at a breakneck pace. If all went well, then the divers should arrive at the scene before the *Falcon* did.

Meanwhile, Hartley conversed with Admiral Brumby about the various possibilities. He carefully explained to him the various vicissitudes of submarine salvage. Meanwhile, the executive officer prepared the ship for rescue. Mooring gear was taken out and hooked up. Diving equipment was rigged. Booms that held the diving platforms were made ready. Hawsers were threaded into their reels. To Hartley, not even the command of "battle stations" would have produced more activity. There was to be no sleep.

As the night progressed, radio messages buzzed in. The *Wandank* was on the scene and had dropped buoys to mark the approximate site of the wreck. All men and officers who were still active in the navy and who were involved in the *S-51* salvage were ordered to Provincetown immediately. Minesweepers and tugs were hauling anchors, anchor cables, hawsers, diving hoses, air hoses, and all sorts of equipment from Boston to Provincetown. Sister submarines of the *S-4* were coming out of Portsmouth, New Hampshire. Commander Harold "Savvy" Saunders, a submarine expert and constructor, was steaming in on the *Bushnell*. The Merritt-Chapman & Scott Wrecking Company also sent an offer of its services in the form of mighty derricks. Hartley also learned that the *Wright*, coming up from Norfolk, was bringing two salvage pontoons, and that the powerful tugs *Iuka* and *Sagamore* were hauling six more through Long Island Sound from the Brooklyn Navy Yard. These pontoons might prove critical, in that they were a reliable, if slow, way to raise a sunken submarine. Hartley later wrote that it seemed that the entire resources of the navy were now at the rescue team's disposal. The navy sent everything it had, including extra heavy winter clothing, extra rations of hot food, and gallons of coffee so that they could work through the night. Everything material that Hartley could have wished for was provided to him—except forbidden booze.

Hartley ordered the ship through Buzzards Bay to the Cape Cod Canal. They passed through in the dark, saving precious hours by bypassing the long way around Cape Cod. They emerged into a cold, windy dawn that rose over the long arc of the New England strand. Morning lights twinkled on the Plymouth shore. It was full steam ahead until they came in sight of Provincetown.

At roughly 7:55 AM, Hartley saw ahead of them a small flotilla waiting for them: The *Wandank, Bushnell, S-8, Lark,* and *Mallard.* There were also several small Coast Guard craft.

As the *Falcon* approached, a boat from the *Bushnell* came skipping across the waves toward them. Two men reported aboard: Commander Edmund Strother, the commanding officer of Submarine Division

Twelve, the unit that the *S-4* was attached to, and Commander Harold "Savvy" Saunders.

Saunders and Strother had come from the Portsmouth Navy Yard. They had arrived the night before with divers and equipment, but it was readily apparent that without the expertise of the *Falcon's* men and its specialized gear, the *Bushnell* could not send divers down. The *Bushnell* conducted all its diving from a separate small boat and used hand pumps to deliver air to the divers—the vessel's diving plant was too amateur for what was needed.

But Strother and Saunders had not been idle. Saunders, an expert naval architect and highly analytical,* spent the time going about with Strother and other officers to find any person who knew anything about what happened. Saunders wanted to know where and how the *S-4* was damaged so that when a diver finally got to the bottom, the team would be ready.

Saunders had gone into Provincetown Harbor, where he met with the commanding officer of the *Wandank*. Saunders assumed that since the ship was the tender of the *S-4*, it would have been an eyewitness to the collision.

But they quickly found out otherwise. The *Wandank* was inside the harbor and only arrived on the scene later, after it was alerted to what happened by the *Paulding*. Still, the captain of the *Wandank* described the small amounts of oil and bubbles that could be seen in the waning daylight. By the description, Saunders thought it too few bubbles and too small a trail of oil for a submarine that had been cut open less than an hour prior.

Saunders and Strother then prepared to visit the *Paulding* to see Lieutenant Commander John Baylis. But before they got there, a picketboat came chugging into the harbor and up to the *Bushnell*. It had the number 2339 etched on its side. This was Boatswain Gracie's boat. The boatswain had a long night since his grapnel slipped from the *S-4*. He was now helping the navy by transferring men among ships. The officers invited him aboard the *Bushnell* for food and coffee.

---

*Saunders graduated from the US Naval Academy in 1912 with the highest scholastic average since 1885.

Saunders quickly learned that Gracie and Frank Simmonds, who was also aboard the picketboat, had witnessed the collision from the shore. After they were done eating, they transported Saunders to the *Paulding*.

On the way to the *Paulding*, Saunders learned much about what happened. The *S-4* had been rising, its periscopes visible. Gracie was filled with consternation as he described how there was nothing he could do to stop the collision.

Then, aboard the *Paulding*, Saunders and Strother quizzed Lieutenant Commander Baylis and Ensign Phannemiller. From Gracie's account, and from what he learned on the *Paulding*, Saunders figured the *S-4* was struck in the battery room. Based on what he could learn about how high the periscopes were, Saunders figured the submarine's hull to have been about seven feet under the water at the time of the collision. This might have been low enough that the *Paulding* could have just damaged the outer superstructure of the submarine and not its hull. But then Baylis told them that the *Paulding* was carrying heavy stores and oil. The cutter was drawing ten feet of water. To Saunders's mind, the submarine was not scratched but lacerated.

This was the grim news that Saunders reported when he came aboard the *Falcon*. All might be fruitless. The collision may have been so horrible that the *S-4* was flooded beyond all hope for life.

Saunders joined Hartley on the bridge. He pointed out the three marker cork buoys that had been laid the previous evening. These were set up like a triangle, each about one hundred yards apart. Saunders said, "The submarine must be somewhere between those buoys." Coast Guard boats and vessels from navy ships were dragging the area with grapnels.

Finding the *S-4* was one thing, but Hartley still needed his divers.

Just then, a small surfboat came running out to the *Falcon*. Attached to its stern was a smaller boat that it was towing. Hartley could see clearly the men aboard and was undoubtedly more than happy to see the cohort of expert navy divers. These included veterans of the *S-51* job including Fred Michels, Bill Carr, and ace diver, Tom Eadie.

8

The Ace of Divers

TOM EADIE ONCE PHILOSOPHIZED ABOUT deep sea diving. "This game is a constant gamble with death. . . . For when you go down you never know what's going to happen to you before you come up. So every dive is an adventure, and there's a fascination about the work that makes one forget its risks and dangers."

Eadie always felt like a different man on the bottom of the sea: the strangeness of the underwater world, the futuristic diving suit, and the fame that diving brought to him gave him a rush. But Eadie's background lacked any hint that diving was to be his destiny. He was born in Scotland in 1887. His father was a stonemason from Partick, who became a widower shortly after Tom, the youngest of three sons, was born. There wasn't much work in Scotland, so when Eadie was still a boy, his father moved the family to the United States, first to New York City, then New Jersey.

By this time, Eadie's father had remarried—to one of his late wife's girlfriends. This never bothered Eadie, who always insisted that she was as tender to him as a real parent. His stepmother bore eight more children, bringing the total number in the Eadie household, including parents, to thirteen.

With so many mouths to feed, Eadie and his older brothers had to work whenever possible. As a boy, his father would come home with newspapers he bought downtown. He gave these to his sons and sent them on the streets to sell them. When Tom was old enough, he got a job in a factory. First, he worked at the Hartshorn Shade Roller Factory and later, the Worthington Hydraulic Pump Works. He used machines and lugged heavy materials. In the process, Eadie picked up a great deal of mechanical knowledge. He grew strong. His face transformed into that of a handsome young man, sporting a boyish smile and twinkling gray eyes. Tom Eadie would develop into a playful man who reveled in camaraderie, pranks, and simple working class pride.

Eadie did not see any value in the grueling lot of a turn-of-the-century factory worker. Like many others of his social and economic class, Eadie did not seem to have the opportunities to make a better life for himself. So in a spontaneous act, at the age of eighteen, he and his friends decided that they should join the navy. They headed to the nearest recruiting station and walked in.

While they waited for the recruiter, they began to have misgivings about the prospect of enlisting in the service. Sheepishly, they slipped out to the street.

They talked again, screwed up their courage, and went to another recruiting office. They opened the door and marched in. They were told to wait.

Cold feet set in quickly. They hurried out again.

By this point, Eadie was disgusted. "Oh, let's get somewhere," he blurted. He led the way and took his friends to the navy's recruiting office inside the post office at Newark. Five of them lined up. One by one his friends dropped out until he was the only man left standing in line. On July 6, 1905, Tom Eadie became a navy man.

He shipped as a seaman, second class, aboard the battleship *Alabama*. He worked as a helper to the blacksmith and shipfitter. But Eadie did not take well to the service, being young, somewhat stubborn, and mischievous. On this first part of his enlistment, Eadie accrued a bad record. He was put in the brig for hitting an officer with the handle of a sledgehammer. Eadie claimed to have been walking down the gangway of the ship while an officer was walking up. The officer stopped short, and Eadie ran into him. He was bawled out and put on restricted liberty.

Eadie felt it was unjust that he should be punished for an accident. In retribution, when he finally got liberty he overstayed. He was punished again by more restricted liberty. But the next time he got leave, he overstayed again. At the hearing over the matter the captain asked, "You're looking for a kick-out, aren't you?"

Eadie smiled.

"You aren't going to get it," said the captain.

Eadie began to question himself. "What's the use of acting like this? You aren't going to hurt anybody but yourself."

The moment was transformative for the young Tom Eadie. He screwed up his pride and began to follow rules and regulations. He even began to enjoy his time in the service. Eadie was aboard the *Alabama* as part of Theodore Roosevelt's "Great White Fleet" and circumnavigated the world as part of America's demonstration of its growing sea power. He voyaged with the *Alabama* to places like San Francisco, Honolulu, Guam, Manila, Egypt, Italy, and Gibraltar.

When the ship returned to America, it went to the Brooklyn Navy Yard for an overhaul. There, Eadie was detached from the *Alabama* and sent to the navy base at Newport, Rhode Island, to finish out his enlistment. It was there that he met Jake Anderson, a Danish man who was a civilian instructor; he taught the seaman gunners how to dive. Eadie watched as the navy men, under Anderson's tutelage, put on the heavy diving outfit and took shallow-water dives.

It was a magical moment for Eadie, who became spellbound at the prospect of diving. Over the course of several days, Eadie went to Anderson asking to dive. Anderson kept putting him off until somebody explained to him, "You'll never get a dive till you're a seaman gunner going through the class."

To qualify to be a seaman gunner, Eadie needed to reenlist. So he did with the provision that he could take the diving course. At Newport, he received instruction from Anderson.

Training at first was basic. He was shown all the equipment. Aside from the leaden suit, there was a hose that delivered compressed air to the diver, and a heavy lifeline to tether him to the surface. Tom had watched so many of Anderson's classes that he was already familiar with the gear.

Eadie also learned the basic signals that a diver used in case other forms of communication were unavailable.* It was done through a

---

*In the early twentieth century, a telephone wire was inserted into the diver's lifeline that allowed for direct voice communication with a telephone man topside.

series of tugs given to a diver's lifeline or air hose. One tug on the air hose meant *More air.* The same tug on the lifeline meant *I am all right.* Two tugs on the air hose meant *Less air.* On the lifeline it meant *Give me slack* or *Lower me.* It depended on the context of the dive. Two repeated pulls meant that a diver was caught on something and another diver had to be sent down to free him. Three meant, *I am coming up.* Four was the emergency signal to *Haul me up.* And five, *Send me down a line.* This last signal was used if a diver found something he was searching for and wanted a line for support. He found that divers had created a virtual language telegraphed by yanks at the lifeline.

Eadie wanted to be the first man in his class to make a dive. He found that he wasn't alone and that there were three others in the class who wanted to be first. Eadie said to them, "We'll draw straws for it; the longest straw wins."

Eadie held the straws, but he held five instead of four. The fifth was the longest, and he palmed it in his hand and out of sight. All the others picked short straws and did not notice when Eadie withdrew the longest straw, hidden in the palm of his hand. Nothing would stop Eadie from getting into the water.

Eadie's diving instruction under Jake Anderson lasted two weeks. He learned about the impact of water pressure on the human body and how to adjust the air intake on his diving helmet. He studied how it was only by the delivery of compressed air to his diving dress that a diver could work on the bottom by negating the heavy embrace of sea pressure. He mastered, through practice, all the minor but still important details, such as clearing his ears while diving.[*]

---

[*]Water pressure affects the diver's sinuses and ear canals. As a diver descends he feels pain in the ears. This is the effect of compressed air pressing against the seal of the inner ear—the eardrum. This canal is connected to the lungs by a vessel called the Eustachian tube, which allows air to equalize in the body. If a diver cannot get air to pass through the Eustachian tube to the back of the nose, the throat, and then the lungs, the pain will grow until eventually the eardrum bursts. Naturally, if one's sinuses and other canals in the body are clogged from a cold or deviated septum, one would have trouble diving to even modest depths, since there is no way to equalize the air pressure. Some traditional divers who did not use diving suits, but who suffered the same problem due to water pressure pushing against the inner ear, purposely punctured their own eardrums.

At the same time, Eadie learned all the other aspects of being a gunner's mate. There were torpedoes, air compressors, and mines. When he finished training in 1909, he volunteered for submarine duty aboard the *Tarpon*.

Eadie spent four years aboard the *Tarpon*. This was a true "pig-boat." The vessels were cramped, often untidy, and filled with diesel fumes, sweat, ozone, and sea spray. The distinction between officer and enlisted broke down since the men were living on top of each other.

On one occasion, Eadie smelled chlorine gas in the air, caused by the sea getting into the submarine's batteries. Eadie was sent below by the commander to warn the others. He ran to his locker, grabbed his clothes, and soaked them in water. He ran through the submarine, slapping men awake and handing out the wet clothes to breathe through to prevent poisoning. "Keep that over your nozzle!" he told them.

He found the executive officer and slapped him awake.

"What's the matter?" he asked.

"Chlorine," said Eadie handing him a piece of wet clothing. "Keep that over your face."

The gas worked off by the morning. When the officer saw Eadie he said, "I thank the Lord I'm here this morning."

Eadie replied, "Stick around awhile, sir; you ain't seen nothing yet."

In Eadie's time aboard the *Tarpon*, he became known as a good, reliable diver. He helped free the anchor of the *Tarpon* on occasion as well as test experimental diving equipment. He loved the thrill of danger found underwater.

Then in 1911, Eadie got married. His wife, Margaret, who had heard dozens of stories of Eadie's near misses, did not want him aboard submarines. The next year, when Eadie's enlistment ran out, she urged him not to reenlist but to take a vacation.

Eadie agreed. The couple traveled and eventually ran out of money.

Eadie went to work at a factory for $1.92 a day. The work, hauling chains, looked easy. In his memoir, he recalled seeing an old man doing the work. Eadie seized the chains and within an hour, he had quarter-sized blisters all over his hands. By noon they burst open. Eadie's hands had gotten soft during his vacation. When he got home and washed his hands for dinner he screamed.

His wife heard him and said, "Quit it and go back in the navy."

But Eadie didn't go back in the navy. Instead, he found a new job as an assistant diving instructor to his old teacher, Jake Anderson. When he told his wife that he was getting paid $3.04 a day for the work, they did a little dance. Margaret said, "We're rich. We can have anything we want now."

Eventually, Eadie became an instructor in his own right and contracted himself out to the navy and businesses to salvage lost items from the water. It paid better money than being directly in the service.* He recovered all sorts of things: torpedoes, watches, and rings. He once made $50 for finding an officer's ring in the mud. It was the quickest money Eadie ever made.

He especially liked finding lobsters, although this was just incidental to the job. He would locate them around rocks. To get them out, he teased them with a spear. The lobsters, like boxers, would spar and grab the spear. Eadie would then grab them. He claimed to have once brought up seven at a time holding them by the tail. The largest was more than three feet long. A store offered him twenty-five dollars for it.

After America's entry into World War I, Eadie enlisted in the fleet reserve while still working as a civilian diver. The next year he was activated into service and became a chief gunner's mate. After the war, he remained in the navy until his enlistment expired in 1920, then he returned to work as a civilian diver but still served in the naval reserve. It was during this time, in 1925, that Eadie took part in one of the hardest jobs he ever experienced. The *S-51* had been sunk, and he had been called upon to assist in the salvage effort aboard the *Falcon*.

Eadie was impressed by the salvage team's commanders, Captain Ernest J. King and Lieutenant Commander Edward Ellsberg. King, who was in charge of the submarine base in New London, headed the entire operation. Ellsberg was a naval constructor who handled the details of the work. To assist in the effort, Ellsberg even invented an underwater torch that could cut metal. But the sinking of the *S-51* presented new challenges to the team; the submarine had sunk in 132 feet of open ocean.

---

*Henry Hartley noted that in 1927 a civilian diver could receive $45 per dive while a US Navy diver received an extra $1.20 per hour for diving. To Hartley, the only explanation as to why a diver would work for the navy instead of for private interests was "Esprit de Corps."

It was decided that the best thing to do would be to dig tunnels under the submarine, thread chains through the holes, then use pontoons to raise the submarine. It was experimental, since neither King nor Ellsberg knew exactly what would work. Eadie was to be part of the experiment.

The interior of the *S-51* was a death trap filled with the corpses of lost submariners. At every turn, every little piece of debris, if caught on the diver's lines or heavy suit, could mean disaster. Eadie, along with the other divers, had to go through this maze to turn the valves and levers to seal tanks, lines, and doors in order to prepare the submarine for lifting. Then, when this was done, he was one of the divers charged to dig tunnels under the submarine using a high-pressure water hose.

Tom Eadie in diving gear.
Courtesy of the Library of Congress, Papers of Ernest J. King

One time, Eadie was working hard at using the hose to clear the mud from under the hull of the *S-51*. As he did so, silt was kicked up and swam around his helmet. When he was done, he headed to a diving stage to lift him to the surface. As he sat on the stage he suddenly felt himself starting to rise. Air was coming into the suit, but not going out. The silt had clogged the exhaust valve. His suit was swelling like a balloon. This was one of the most feared accidents a diver could have, what was called a "blowup."

He tried to reach for the valve to turn off the air. But his suit became so inflated that he became spread-eagled and could not reach it. He barely managed to hang on to the stage with his foot. The last thing he wanted was to fly up and smash into the hull of the *Falcon*.

The air kept coming in. His helmet rose above his head. He shouted at his telephone to the surface, "Turn off the air!" But Eadie's suit was now lifting over his head. Those on the *Falcon* could not make out what he was saying since his head was out of the helmet and away from the transmitter.

Then his suit began to fall apart. His weighted diving belt popped open and dropped to the bottom. Then, with a pop like a gun, the suit exploded. The immense pressure of the sea, which was being held back by the compressed air in the suit, bore down on him. Overhead, he saw his helmet floating with a bubble of air within it. He grabbed it and thrust it over his head.

He drew a deep breath. He now had access to the transmitter. "My suit has carried away and my weights are down around my feet."

They heard him on the *Falcon*. "All right; we'll haul you up."

The men on the stage pulled on the lifeline, which was attached to the helmet. Eadie, who was grasping the helmet and fighting the crushing water, felt his right arm go numb with the strain as he struggled to keep the helmet over his head. As men on the surface yanked his line, the helmet slammed against his nose. Blood splattered everywhere. When he got on the *Falcon*'s deck, men rushed to assist him. Eadie claimed, however, that by the next day he was fine and ready for another dive.

The *S-51* was brought to the surface on July 5, 1926, using the pontoon plan; the boat was then brought to New York. The *S-51* salvage was highly publicized, and Eadie was so commended that he was given a Navy Cross.

There was talk of giving him a navy retirement right then and there with full continuous service, including his years out of the service (since he had worked for the government anyway as a contracted diver). The secretary of the navy, Curtis Wilbur, thought this decision would set a bad precedent, since Eadie was working as a civilian. Besides, it could only be done by a special act of Congress. Instead, the navy gave Eadie a tantalizing offer. If he reenlisted in the navy they would keep all his prior service intact and allow him to retire after sixteen years at half pay. This would mean he could retire in 1932 and be guaranteed a navy pension for continuous service. What is more, they would make him a chief gunner's mate with a permanent appointment and promise him duty at his home of Newport. With his fortieth birthday coming up the next year, he reenlisted on December 15, 1926.

In August 1927, Eadie was sent to recover a buoy mooring. In this case, he went in a small diving boat with a young dive-tender and two civilians. He went to the bottom; he had failed to check the air levels in the compression tanks on the surface boat. He soon found the air getting foul. He was gasping.

He yanked his lifeline once for more air. No response. He then tried opening the control valve to the airline until it was fully open. There was no fresh air. He pulled his lifeline four times, giving the emergency signal to haul him up immediately. But the pulls were misread by the tender, who thought it meant that he was coming up and didn't need assistance. It was only because of the concerns of the civilians, both of whom knew something of diving and had been in the navy, that he was saved.

After Eadie recovered, he went down again and finished the job.

That night, his heart rattled like a drum. It didn't get better the next day or the day after. The least exertion set off his heart. He saw a doctor who told him that his heart had been under severe strain and needed to rest. He was treated by the doctor for three months.

During this interim Eadie must have harbored doubts about his continued viability as a diver. He was past his prime, and maybe it would be good if he never donned the diving suit again.

Then on December 17, 1927, Eadie had been in Fall River, a town about twenty miles outside of Newport on the Rhode Island–Massachusetts border. There, the family had been shopping for

Christmas. They just returned to their home in Newport and finished supper when the phone rang. He picked it up. It was the navy.

"Come to the station immediately. The *S-4* has been sunk."

A hurricane of activity began. Eadie was in civilian clothes and had to change. He cast off his shirt and suit. His wife stood by, growing more agitated by the moment. There was an unspoken question: *What about your heart?*

With a kiss to his nervous wife and his daughter, Marion, he was off.

He hitched a ride to the ferry about a mile away. He made the 6:25 PM boat and arrived at the base. He was the first diver to report in. There he met Lieutenant Lewis Causey, the base's executive officer. He filled him in on what was known and that the *Falcon* was underway to Provincetown out of New London. Causey then asked, "What gear do you need?"

"Hardly any," replied Eadie. "Only men will be needed. The *Falcon* will undoubtedly have all the gear that is needed."

Then the other divers started to arrive one by one. There were eleven total; three were veterans of the *S-51* salvage. There was Fred Michels, a tall man who was a good friend of Eadie's. He had become a diving instructor at Newport. Then there was Bill Carr, whose leave at his home at Jamestown, Rhode Island, was cut short. These were the elite of America's deep sea divers.

The eleven men divided themselves among three cars. As they loaded the vehicles, Causey called the Rhode Island State Police and requested an escort. The automobiles' engines roared to life. They were underway at 8:30 PM. They were met outside of Newport by a Rhode Island motorcycle policeman who cleared a path up to the Massachusetts state border. There, on Pleasant Street in Fall River, they were handed over to a policeman in the new jurisdiction who escorted them out of the town.

Eadie heard the policeman say to a Lieutenant Matthews, who was driving the car, "You've got a hundred miles straight away now. Good luck to you; I wish I could go with you."

Matthews thanked the policeman and then said to the divers, "All right. Now, boys, you can settle back for a sleep."

But sleep was far away from Tom Eadie. The job ahead was on his mind—and undoubtedly his heart. Eadie had amassed almost nineteen years of diving experience. Yet he questioned his ability to be an effective diver anymore.

As they wound their way up toward Cape Cod, the men discussed the possibility of there being any survivors aboard the submarine. Everybody in the car concurred that there was no chance. This was just going to be another salvage job, like the *S-51*.

They raced to Cape Cod. It was the wildest ride Eadie had ever been on. He wondered why they should rush if everybody aboard was dead. The submarine was struck while submerged. Everything would be open below. The boat would be filled with water. Yet, in the corner of his mind, there was a chance, a small one, that there might be people still alive on the submarine *S-4*.

They were forced to stop several times for directions. In New Bedford, they narrowly missed hitting a trolley car. Fortunately, with the start of winter just days away, the tourist traffic had thinned. They reached Provincetown at 12:30 AM on Sunday, December 18. They had beaten the *Falcon*, which was not expected to arrive until the morning. At 2:00 AM Matthews got rooms for them in a lodging house.

Eadie found that newspaper reporters had descended on the sleepy village in packs. The docks were alive as crowds gathered to watch the lights of the small flotilla that was gathering off Wood End. Newsmen had been renting fishing boats, trying to get to the scene of the accident. The price of chartering a boat had steadily risen to the point that one Portuguese man told reporters that he would rent out his boat for the absurd sum of $150.

In this case, the reporters rented the boat, but only after frantic bartering. In the meantime, the Coast Guard and the navy gave the order not to talk with reporters.

This did not stop them from peppering Eadie and the other divers with questions: *Who were they? Where were they from? How many of them were there? When were they going out to the wreck?*

They were so persistent that one man even came into their room after they turned in. The divers were so annoyed at the intrusion that they began making up wild stories. An overtired Eadie was laughing himself sick. After each story he would snort, "Tell him another."

But as Eadie drifted off to sleep he thought, "When you kid a reporter you are really kidding the public."

• • •

The next morning, Eadie and the other divers went to the harbor. There they boarded a Coast Guard surfboat. Another small boat, called a dory or wherry, was attached to the surfboat. Almost absently, Eadie wondered what the dory was needed for.

They left the harbor and turned into the mounting gales about the cape. The water was choppy, frothy, and cold. Ahead, Eadie saw a familiar sight—the *Falcon*. He'd had many an adventure on that vessel. But as they neared, Lieutenant Henry Hartley waved them off. The conditions were too rough for the surfboat to get close to the *Falcon*. There was too much of a chance that it would smash on the larger vessel's side.

The surfboat circled to the *Falcon*'s windward side, the side protected from the gales. Now the purpose of the dory became clear. Two at a time, divers got into the dory, which was eased out toward the *Falcon*. When there was a lull in the waves, Eadie threw his suitcase aboard and scrambled aboard.

Hartley greeted him and shook his hand. "Eadie," said Hartley. "You'll be the first man to go down."

Eadie replied, "All right, sir, as soon as I get into my gear."

The *Falcon* was there and ready. Eadie and the other divers were ready to go—despite the conditions. But there was a snag. During the night, a Coast Guard boatswain named Gracie had hooked the sub with grapnels, but lost it at 3:00 AM.

Now, as Eadie looked out at sea, he could see Gracie circling the spot, casting and dragging grapnels doggedly from a picketboat.

Gracie wasn't the only one, as the navy was also pitching for the *S-4*. The *Bushnell*, *Lark*, and *Mallard* had all launched their boats and were fishing with grapnels. It was so frustrating that Henry Hartley thought the marker buoys dropped by the *Wandank* were probably wrong.

Soundings were taken. Lead lines were cast. Again and again the soundings came back with a thick sticky mud. Nobody could find the *S-4*.

9

Hide and Seek

IT CERTAINLY HAD BEEN SOME time since the unflappable Boatswain Emmanuel F. Gracie had felt so frustrated. Since losing the *S-4*, he'd had no sleep, hardly any food, and no coffee.

After the grapnel had torn loose from the submarine, Gracie ordered it hauled up to the deck of his picketboat. His men seized the hawser and pulled at the line. But they discovered they could not pull the one-hundred-pound grapnel off the seafloor; the weight was too much and the rope too thick. What Gracie really needed was a capstan.

"There's one way we can get it up," said Gracie. He had the grapnel's rope securely tied to the stern of his boat. He then jammed the engine. The motor of the picketboat strained as the boat lurched toward the shore.

At length, they were right beside the beach at Wood End. Gracie urged the boat closer. As the grapnel was pulled into the shallows, he and his men took in slack from the line. Then, when there was about twenty feet of rope left, he gunned the picketboat right up on the beach. All hands hopped out. From the shore he and his men pulled the line until the grayish shape of the three-fluked hook emerged from the waves. They brought it back aboard.

It was time to check in. They got back into the boat and reported to the *Lark*. But there was nothing to be done at the moment. Gracie told an officer that he would beach his boat, and that if he was needed to signal by flashlight.

They dropped their anchor about a fifth of a mile from the collision scene. It was pre-dawn. With some time to kill, but not enough time to sleep, Gracie brewed coffee. The warm smell intermingled with the salt of the sea.

The radio crackled with a call from the Coast Guard Station. Gracie clutched the radio transmitter and reported in. The district commander wanted them to report to Railroad Wharf* at Provincetown.

The coffee had to wait; Gracie headed to the harbor. As he tied up at the dock in the town's center, a boatswain from the main district office arrived. With him were a mix of men in uniform and civilians. Gracie had no idea who these men were; no information was given to him. He was to transfer these men and others to the *Bushnell* and other navy ships that had come into the harbor.

Back and forth Gracie and his crew went between ships. Finally, at about 7:00 AM, he reached the *Bushnell* for a second time. The officers aboard offered the coastguardsmen a meal. Gracie and his men clambered onto the *Bushnell* and were served sandwiches—seconds if they wanted—and hot coffee. One of the officers asked if they might be able to find the submarine again.

Gracie agreed, supposing that they may have better luck in the daylight. He complained about the four-inch hawser and the hundred-pound grapnel they got from the *Wandank*. The *Bushnell* was more than happy to provide Gracie with as much new three-inch rope as he could want.

Gracie's next task was to transfer some of the officers to the *Paulding*. As they made way, Gracie told them what he had seen—this interested them greatly. Apparently, Gracie and Simmonds were the only eyewitnesses to the disaster from the shore. The officers questioned him, particularly Commander Harold Saunders, who wanted as much information as possible regarding where the submarine was struck to help the rescue effort. Gracie dropped them off and headed back to the disaster scene.

---

*Now MacMillan Pier.

As the boatswain left the relative safety of Provincetown Harbor and passed around Long Point, the seas turned rougher. In the gathering gray light, the rescue flotilla had grown. He took especial note of the *Falcon*, sitting squat, competent; it had arrived in the dawn. Its number, 28, stood out bright white next to the black fish, the symbol that indicated its role as a submarine salvage and rescue ship.

At about 9:00 AM, Gracie used his picketboat to start dragging the new grapnel in the area marked by the cork buoys. Other navy vessels were also dragging for the submarine. In nicer weather and under less dire circumstances, the whole affair may have been fun, with them trying to beat the navy boats in locating the wreck. But the rough weather and the danger of fouling a grapnel into one of the navy ships' anchors was a real hazard.

Unlike the last time, Gracie did not hook the *S-4* on the first try or the second. The hours passed. None of the vessels had any luck. The grapnel was, however, now much easier to handle with the thinner rope.

Gracie was bemused. They had been pulling the grapnel right over where they took the cross bearings the previous night. He had an impromptu conference with his second-in-command.

"What is your opinion? Do you think we are placed right? Have we been dragging in the right place?"

His second replied, "Sir, we have been dragging every time across the bearings."

Gracie then thought that perhaps they were too far away from the buoy.

His second-in-command agreed. The bearings were taken in the dark. In daylight, the distances would seem different.

Gracie, by a hunch, made the decision to try to drag away from where he took the bearings. It was a last resort, but since he hadn't had any luck for two hours, there was nothing to lose. He brought his boat by the stern of the *Falcon*, which was just finishing anchoring. They then dropped the grapnel, and Gracie turned the boat northeast. He throttled the engine and immediately the grapnel caught on something solid.

Gracie ordered his men to take the grapnel line and tie it to the small dory that they had been towing through the night to transfer men between ships. He turned his picketboat to the *Bushnell.* As he neared, he waved to the men on deck and asked for a buoy.

The men of the *Bushnell* were happy to assist. They handed to him a fifty-gallon oil drum rigged with wires. Gracie returned to the dory and swapped it out. The oil drum marked the spot. One might imagine the boatswain's satisfaction.

● ● ●

Meanwhile, Lieutenant Hartley, in command of the *Falcon,* had seen through hand signaling that Gracie had found something. He maneuvered the *Falcon* to windward, slowly paying out its three-thousand-pound anchor, and neared the dory. As the *Falcon* approached, he needed to steady the vessel, so Hartley released his starboard anchor. Even so, the sea was rough, and the wind fierce. To Hartley's amazement, the *Falcon* was dragging its anchor along the muddy bottom. This was the first time that this had ever happened, and he had been in command of the vessel for more than three years. What made it more remarkable was that the anchors the *Falcon* carried were far heavier than those anchors from other minesweepers in the "bird" class like the *Lark* and *Mallard.* Hartley was forced to engage the engines in order to prevent colliding with Gracie's boat. Hartley weighed anchor and steamed farther windward. The *Falcon*'s anchors paid out again, this time with 110 fathoms of chain. Slowly the ship drifted toward Gracie's boat, but the anchorage held.

With conditions as they were, it was obvious that the *Falcon* by itself could not provide a steady platform for divers to descend the line to confirm Gracie's catch as the *S-4.* So orders were sent to the *Lark* and *Mallard* to cease sweeping and to anchor off each quarter of the *Falcon.*

The two minesweepers maneuvered into position and let loose their anchors. When they seemed secure, the *Falcon* ran eight-inch hawsers to each of the ships. These were tied to the *Lark* and *Mallard* and made taut.

Hartley thought it neither a secure nor pretty mooring, but it was the quickest way to provide some stability to the *Falcon*. Then, when all looked ready, Hartley ordered more anchor chain to be released. This allowed the *Falcon* to drift closer to the grapnel line, which his crew seized and brought up on the starboard quarter. Simultaneously, the *Falcon* dropped a one-hundred-pound buoy to mark the spot—just in case the grapnel broke free.

The *Falcon* was in place, the divers were present, and all were ready to see if Gracie's line led to the *S-4*.

10

Where's Ellsberg?

WHILE LIEUTENANT HARTLEY WAS HOOKING Gracie's grapnel line to the *Falcon*, Edward Ellsberg was puttering around his house at 714 Hanford Place in Westfield, New Jersey. Since it was a Sunday morning, he was not on his job as the chief engineer of the Tidewater Oil Company of New York, but rather picking up the newspaper from his front stoop. All signs pointed to a lazy day. This change of pace was something that Ellsberg did not relish in his new civilian life. He was a man of activity.

Ellsberg graduated first in his class from the US Naval Academy in 1914. After receiving his commission, he was assigned to the battleship *Texas*, and he was also trained in a postgraduate course in naval architecture at the Massachusetts Institute of Technology. His postgraduate education took a hiatus during World War I, but he returned to receive a master's degree in 1920. After that, he made the momentous decision to give up being a line officer and to join the staff corps as a naval constructor. He went to work at the Brooklyn Navy Yard doing all sorts of jobs, but his great joy was to build big ships—battleships specifically. But construction of them was cut short after the 1922 Washington Treaty, which limited naval construction among the major national powers. Instead of building ships, he had the heartbreaking task of dismantling them for scrap. Ellsberg had become so disenchanted that he had considered transferring his talents to the navy's aviation division.

On September 25, 1925, Ellsberg, for no particular reason, woke up at 5:00 AM. Without anything else to do, he left his officer's quarters in the Brooklyn Navy Yard and ambled down to the docks to look at the two battleships he was to disassemble. At this time of the morning the docks were normally serene. Yet when he arrived, he saw a large crowd of men preparing a minesweeper, the *Falcon*, for sea.

Among the people was Ellsberg's commanding officer, Captain Wright, who was speaking with a man Ellsberg had not previously met, Lieutenant Henry Hartley. Puzzled at the assemblage, Ellsberg approached. He later wrote about the conversation that occurred:

"For heaven sakes, Captain," said Ellsberg. "What's going on?"

Captain Wright handed him a piece of paper. It was a radiogram:

COMMANDER CONTROL FORCE TO
COMMANDING OFFICER U.S.S. *FALCON*:
S-51 REPORTED IN COLLISION LATITUDE 41° 12' N., LONGITUDE 71°
15' W. *FALCON* PROCEED TO SCENE IMMEDIATELY PREPARED FOR RES-
CUE WORK.

Ellsberg gave the radiogram to Hartley and asked, "What have you got in the way of divers?"

Hartley replied, "I got two."

"Got anybody aboard who knows anything about submarines?"

"No," said Hartley. "All I've done is tow them in when their machinery is broken down, which is plenty. But I don't know anything else about subs."

Ellsberg then turned to Captain Wright and asked, "They'll need somebody who knows something about submarines. Can I go?" While Ellsberg didn't know much specifically about submarines, he was a naval architect, and the prospect of action was exciting.

Wright replied, "Yes, if you want to go, Ellsberg, you can go. But this ship is leaving in five minutes as soon as I get the rest of the stuff aboard. If you are back here in five minutes, all right."

Ellsberg spun around, ran to his quarters, grabbed his gear, and hurried back to the dock. He hopped aboard just as the *Falcon* was casting off. The ship passed up the East River, into Long Island Sound, and past New London. They received a message. A diving launch from the Newport Torpedo School had arrived at the scene off Block Island. They also learned that destroyers had found the wreck of the *S-51* by a stream of oil and air bubbles.

● ● ●

The *Falcon* arrived off Block Island that night at 10:00 PM. Ellsberg saw several ships doing work. There was a constant stream of bubbles flitting to the surface of the seawater. This showed the exact location of the *S-51*. Nearby, the *Camden* swept blue searchlights across the water. The light revealed a submarine at the surface. Its hull showed it as a sister ship of the sunken submarine, the *S-1*. It was bobbing at the waterline; air hoses were draped over its side as it desperately pumped air into the *S-51*, more than 130 feet below. However, whatever air was being pumped in was coming out at an equal rate. All those bubbles rising to the surface were wasted air.

Then Ellsberg heard a keening note that vibrated through the water and struck the *Falcon*'s hull. The submarine was using its oscillator to send signals to the *S-51*, hoping for a return signal. Ellsberg listened carefully in a pair of headphones for a reply. None came.

The *Camden* signaled to the *Falcon* to prepare for diving in the morning. Hartley moved the ship aside to wait. The anchor was set. All fell silent. Then a motorboat sputtered out of the dark. They were transporting a petty officer who had dove down to the wreck.

"Bends," said his shipmates as they brought the limp man aboard and ushered him to the *Falcon*'s decompression chamber. The *Falcon*'s iron doctor did its duty, and by midnight, the diver, a chief torpedoman named James Ingram, had recovered, and he told Ellsberg his story.

Ellsberg later wrote that Ingram was the first man to go down, submerging from a little diving launch. They were in such a hurry that there was no time to hook up a telephone transmitter to the diver's helmet. When he landed on the sub he found it hard to walk on its deck because it lay heavily on its port side. He then carefully made his way to every hatch he could find. He banged on them. There was no echo, no sound inside, and no return sound.

"They're all dead down there!" said Ingram.

Ingram was anxious to report what he had found, but since he did not have a telephone, he gave four pulls to the lifeline—the emergency signal. He was hauled up quickly. However, Ingram had been working under compressed air. His body had been absorbing excess nitrogen. As he suddenly surfaced, bubbles of nitrogen formed in his tissues and blood, threatening to block vital organs and lodge into joints, much like how a shaken bottle of soda water explodes when suddenly opened. Ingram could become paralyzed, or even killed. This condition, known as caisson's disease, the staggers, decompression sickness, or divers' disease, is most well known as "the bends," so-called because of the position its victims would assume.* Ingram had to wait until the *Falcon* arrived for treatment.

Despite Ingram's findings, the navy was desperate and hoped that maybe somebody was alive within the submarine. Another diver went down and hooked up hoses. Air was being pumped into the *S-51* in the hopes that it may somehow help. But it was no use. The *S-51* had drowned as well as any man who had been trapped inside of it. Ellsberg returned to the Brooklyn Navy Yard.

While the initial rescue efforts failed to recover any survivors, there was a great clamor in the press. The public demanded that the navy salvage the wreck. Ellsberg learned that the navy was planning on outsourcing the salvage work to the Merritt-Chapman & Scott Company in a generous contract. After Ellsberg heard about the company's plans to raise the stern of the submarine by using floating derricks, he believed the navy should do the job. Despite Ellsberg having no experience with submarine salvage, he was convinced that he had a better plan.

Ellsberg wanted to moor a ship over the wreck and lower it in the water by pumping its tanks with water. He would thread cables under the submarine and attach them to the ship above, then pump the

*The condition was called caisson's disease because it was first diagnosed among laborers who worked in caissons, underwater engineering structures that were pumped with compressed air to force water out.

water out of the ship's tanks; as it rose, so would the submarine. He knew something similar had been done to salvage the wreck of the *F-4* near Pearl Harbor in 1915. All he had to do was sell the idea.

Ellsberg met with Rear Admiral Charles Plunkett, commandant of the Brooklyn Navy Yard. Plunkett was one of those maritime figures synonymous with the word "admiral." Old and caustic, Plunkett had piercing eyes and a sweeping, bristling mustache that spoke of many years of command. To Ellsberg, Plunkett looked like an austere, lanky walrus.

But Plunkett was a walrus that could fight. During World War I, Plunkett was assigned an office job at the Bureau of Ordinance, but the old seadog really wanted to get into combat. After the Battle of Jutland, when the British Grand Fleet destroyed any German naval power to speak of, there was no action to be had except on land. The admiral then decided to bring the navy ashore in a scheme in which he took the fourteen-inch guns of a battleship under construction, sent them to France, mounted them on a railway, and fought the Germans on the Hindenburg line. It was a navy battery on wheels.

Since Plunkett knew that he would not be allowed to use regular navy personnel for his land-based guns, he recruited US Navy Reserve personnel. He got the guns and men in place and then angled the huge guns to such a degree that they fired behind the line and destroyed rail yards. The rest was history. With the help of Plunkett's unorthodox navy battery, the Hindenburg line soon disintegrated. It was this decisive figure whom Edward Ellsberg spoke with in 1925.

Plunkett had seen Ellsberg's work on ships and he had full confidence in his ability. After Ellsberg gave him the details about what was going on, Plunkett said, in a voice laden with profanity, "This is a navy job! If we can't take care of our own ships, we ought to get out and let someone run the navy who can!"

Plunkett, however, insisted that they use pontoons to raise the *S-51* instead of a ship, as Ellsberg originally wanted, since the job was to be done on the open sea. Pontoons were a more flexible method of floating the submarine, which was needed to counter the effects of heavy swells that could jerk around the *S-51* as it was raised. The pontoon method was also proven to work, as it had on the submarine *F-4*. Also, the idea of trying to raise a submarine right under another ship was alarming. If the boat came up too quickly, it might strike the surface ship's hull and sink it.

Plunkett sent Ellsberg to Washington, where he promptly convinced the navy to delay the contract with Merritt-Chapman & Scott. Plunkett then arranged his own meeting with the Washington navy representatives and the company. At the meeting, the admiral browbeat everybody into submission and took control of the entire operation, justifying it on the grounds that the collision occurred in his naval district. He ordered Captain Ernest J. King, the commander of the New London Submarine Base, to head the operation. Ellsberg was to command the technical work as the salvage officer. The *S-51* salvage would be a navy job.

When the Merritt-Chapman & Scott representative found out that they were not getting the contract he remarked to Ellsberg, "I don't know who is going to do this job, but whoever he is, he'll wish before he gets through that he had been born a girl baby!"

He left. Plunkett turned to Ellsberg and said, "Well, Ellsberg, now you've got the job."

And so began Ellsberg's education in diving and salvage. He came to the conclusion that the sea was really a person, a person that fought back all the time and was filled with devilish tricks. The conditions were such that he and the men were forced to be innovative. Nobody had ever tried to raise a submarine at such a depth (130 feet), on the open sea with pontoons before.

To raise the *S-51*, men spent months diving, first by going into the submarine and sealing off compartments, a great risk since a diver's air and lifelines were always threatened by entanglement in the wreckage. Littering the inside of the submarine were the corpses of the *S-51*'s crew, which were passed to the surface by lines. Ellsberg had been particularly struck by two crew members who had apparently suffocated to death by locking themselves into a watertight trunk to escape the flood.

As October passed into November, the water grew colder and the men wearier. Ellsberg wanted to quit the job until the spring. But he was told that public opinion would not allow for it. By November 20, only four divers remained fit for duty. Then between November 22 and 29 storms prevented diving altogether.

November 30, 1925, was a frigid day, but the storms had passed, and the seas had calmed enough for diving. Ellsberg ordered divers Tom Eadie and Fred Michels down into the wreck to remove the corpse of an officer that was jammed between the engines. Eadie was to do the work and Michels to attend him.

Both men were suited and lowered to the deep. Within moments the radio cracked, "On the bottom." Both divers had arrived safely, and Eadie entered into the submarine. Michels waited outside, monitoring Eadie's lifeline and air hose.

Meanwhile, on the *Falcon*, Ellsberg stayed by the radio and waited. After a minute, Michels's voice called through the telephone, "On deck! There's something the matter with my air. I'm coming up."

Ellsberg had Michels hauled up. They inspected his air valve. Everything looked normal, but Michels said that he was getting air sporadically.

As Ellsberg pondered this, Eadie telephoned up. He had found the body. "I've got him by the legs, Mr. Ellsberg, but I can't pull him free! If I tie a line on him you could pull on him with the winch up there, but I think you'd pull him in half! He's stuck tight!"

"Never mind, Tom!" Ellsberg yelled through the radio. "Let him stay. Come on up!"

Eadie was back on the deck in twenty minutes. As he was undressing he said, "The water is awful cold down there, commander. It makes it hard to see, because the faceplate on the helmet all fogs up from your breath."

Ellsberg decided that no more real work could be done on the submarine until it was warmer. But he wanted to secure the *S-51* for the winter first. He sent Henry Bailey, their smallest diver, to check the hatches and seal up everything he could.

Bailey went into the water. He landed on the submarine and headed over the deck. Ellsberg watched Bailey's air bubbles trickle across the surface as he moved. Bailey's tender let out more line. The bubbles started to grow smaller then suddenly vanish.

Without warning, there were four jerks on his lifeline.

"Emergency signal from Bailey! Take him up!"

Eight men seized the line and reeled in Bailey. After he surfaced, the diver was hauled on deck. Men ripped off the diving suit to see a distorted blue face. Bailey gasped for breath before he finally murmured, "No air, no air!"

They rushed him into the decompression chamber as Ellsberg inspected the air hose. Air would not pump through it. He increased the air pressure and then cylindrical blocks of ice suddenly popped out of the hose and onto the deck. The cold of the water was condensing the compressed air and freezing it inside the hose. Under the advice of the ship's doctor, Camille Flotte, Captain King stopped work and disbanded the mission until the spring. Ellsberg returned to New York.

Ellsberg spent the winter of 1925 to 1926 preparing for renewed efforts to salvage the *S-51*. He collaborated with other divers and created an improved underwater cutting torch. But Ellsberg's chief concern was to find enough adequate deep sea divers. He brought a number of shallow-water divers to New York and had them trained to qualify as deep sea divers. He signed up for the training himself and was taught to dive by some of the men he commanded aboard the *Falcon*. He, with twelve others, passed the course and became qualified for deep sea diving, which at that time was considered below ninety feet. In doing so, Ellsberg became the first commissioned officer to train and qualify as a deep sea diver. When the *Falcon* returned to the site of the wreck on April 25, 1926, Ellsberg had twenty-four divers ready to go to the bottom, double what he had in the autumn.

The second go at the *S-51* was an onerous process of continuing to seal up the submarine with the addition of digging tunnels beneath the wreck to pass chains through so that the pontoons could be latched on to the vessel. Ellsberg himself made dives. On his first, he felt like he was going to pass out but absolutely refused to jerk the lifeline with the emergency signal. He wanted to set an example to the others. Eventually, he acclimated and even enjoyed his descents.

By making dives himself and by being so hands-on with the entire operation, he won the loyalty of the divers, officers, and crew of the

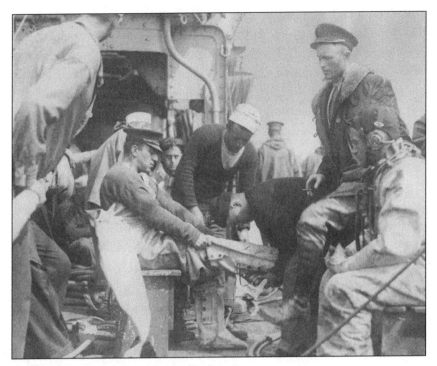

Edward Ellsberg, seated left, preparing to dive to the *S-51*.
Courtesy of the Edward Ellsberg Historical Archives

Falcon. In Ellsberg's opinion, facing death was simple compared to what deep sea divers experienced.

To dig the tunnels under the *S-51*, the divers used a high-pressure hose. Ellsberg wrote about the first diver he sent down to make the attempt—Henry Bailey, the small, but determined, diver. Bailey went down with a hose until he touched the gravelly bottom. Attached at his wrist was the gleaming brass nozzle of the hose. Ellsberg, who was on the *Falcon*'s deck, heard Bailey call up through the telephone, "On deck! Turn on the water!"

The valve that held back a torrent of pressurized water was released. The hose swelled as it was pumped below. In moments, the telephone crackled again.

"On deck! Turn off the water! I'm about fifty feet from the sub and I don't know where the hose is!"

A modern fire hose usually takes several men to control since the water pressure is so great. In this case, the hose was too much for Bailey alone to handle; and with the added buoyancy of the water, even while wearing an almost two-hundred-pound diving dress, the water pressure blew him away. After some adjustments to the pressure, the job went easier. Eventually, the salvage team developed a balanced nozzle that reduced the kickback on the diver. However, to dig, or "wash," the tunnels was a thoroughly meticulous process.

On July 5, 1926, everything was ready to raise the *S-51*. Twenty hoses were attached to the submarine and the pontoons. Water was blown out of them, the sea bubbled, and the *S-51* was recovered. Ellsberg, with many of his shipmates, gallantly threw their caps into the sea at the moment of their long-fought victory. After months of dangerous toil, Ellsberg said, "Now we can go home again!" On July 8, the submarine was put into dry dock at the Brooklyn Navy Yard, and the bodies of the final eighteen remaining crew were recovered.

• • •

Ellsberg gained national celebrity for his role in the salvage of the *S-51*. Captain King gave commendations to the divers but reserved his highest praise and recommended promotion to the rank of commander for Ellsberg. The navy, for its part, gave Distinguished Service Medals to King, Hartley, and Ellsberg—the first time ever for a peacetime mission. Navy Crosses were given to nine of the divers.

Then came an exchange that Ellsberg later recorded in a book about his experiences on the *S-51*. At the very end of the job, just as Ellsberg was in his cabin and rolling up the blueprints of the *S-51*, there came a loud knock at the door.

Ellsberg, startled, turned and saw the door had swung open. In the frame stood one of the divers—Boatswain's Mate Bill Carr. Ellsberg recalled a red face with angry blue eyes. In his hard fist was a piece of paper. Ellsberg momentarily pondered why an enlisted man would barge suddenly into an officer's cabin before Carr thrust the paper at him.

"Say, Mr. Ellsberg, look at that!"

Ellsberg took the paper. It was an order that contained the list of honors given to the divers. Bill Carr's name was on it for a letter of commendation.

"This order's all wet, Mr. Ellsberg," said Carr. He then pointed out the names of his fellows who were to get Navy Crosses. He wasn't to get one—instead, he was recommended for promotion.

"To hell with that promotion," said Carr. "What's it amount to in my case? I'd've made a chief's rate before this cruise's over even if I'd never seen a diving rig! But when'll I ever get another chance at a Navy Cross?"

Carr had made more dives on the *S-51* job than any other man. Ellsberg considered him a workhorse—and his physique was that of a bull. Yet even though Carr had been down more than the others, it happened that he never had to do anything particularly heroic. Ellsberg told him so, then added, "I'm not saying you couldn't have, Bill, any less than those who did, but it was your hard luck that things broke down on the bottom so they got a chance to be heroes and you didn't. I can't help it. So you better take your promotion and that letter of commendation and be happy. It's a lot more than some of your shipmates are getting. Come on, Carr; say you're satisfied."

Carr calmed down, but he was still not satisfied. He smiled. Ellsberg wrote that Carr said, "Gimme that Navy Cross anyhow. Sure an' you know I've earned it! An' what good's a letter o' commendation to me anyway? I reads it once an' stows it away in my diddy box an' nobody ever knows I got it. But a Navy Cross is different. There's Jim an' Tom an' Tug an' Joe an' those other lads that's gittin' 'em can pin their Navy Crosses on their coats every time they makes a liberty, an' the girls ashore all knows they're heroes! How about me? Can I pin that letter o' commendation on my chest when I goes ashore so the girls'll know I'm a hero too? Like hell I can! Come on now! Be a sport, commander, an' gimme that Navy Cross! It'll look grand on that new chief's uniform you're promotin' me to!"

Ellsberg, however, was unmoved, and Carr had to go without a Navy Cross.

As for Ellsberg, he too was disappointed. Despite Captain King's recommendation, there was no mention of promotion for him—something he greatly wanted.

The problem was a so-called equalization bill that was signed into law by President Calvin Coolidge on June 7, 1926. The legislation was meant to equalize promotion of staff officers with those of the line. The thought was that line officers were promoted faster, and it would allow staff officers, who had given equal service, time to catch up to their peers. As a naval constructor Ellsberg was a staff officer, but his problem was that he had already received quick promotions. The law had a catch, which said that staff officers who were promoted too quickly had to wait until the corresponding line officers had caught up. Ellsberg's advancement to the rank of commander was to occur when the next vacancy happened. By his estimation, the new law would make him wait for promotion for eight years.

In the meantime, Ellsberg began speaking publicly about his experiences on the *S-51*. In July 1926, he gave an after-dinner oration at the Engineers Club. These unauthorized talks began to irk even some of his closest allies. At one point, Admiral Plunkett gave him a public bawling about paying more attention to the newspapers than his job.

Ellsberg also wrote up a series of recommendations to the navy dated October 5, 1926. The navy needed more divers—cutbacks after World War I had cut down the total number of navy deep sea divers to twenty. These men needed to be experienced. He also recommended that S-class submarines be equipped with lifting eyes,* and that pontoons for rescue and salvage work be available at ports on the Atlantic and Pacific Coasts. In addition, the navy should have its own separate salvage section.

But the navy did not implement these suggestions. Rather, they were submitted to and subsequently ignored by the Bureau of

---

*The idea of installing lifting eyes on submarines was heavily debated at this time. However, the navy had concluded that to install lifting eyes would require a massive amount of reconstruction into the hull of the submarine and would consequently add too much weight to the boat, detracting from its main purpose—to sink ships.

Construction and Repair. To Ellsberg's mind, this decision made another disaster like the *S-51* inevitable. He estimated that it would be two years until the next one. Between this and the equalization law it was easy for him to tender his resignation and leave the navy in December 1926 to join Tidewater. In the meantime, he started writing a book on his experiences with the *S-51* salvage titled *On the Bottom*.

Still, Ellsberg was stunned when he opened his front door and picked up the newspaper on Sunday, December 18, 1927. The headline screamed, SUBMARINE *S-4* SUNK! FORTY MEN TRAPPED! The next disaster had arrived.

The story of the *S-4* had gone national. Newspapers ran headlines about the collision and how, if the crew could not be rescued, it would be the worst submarine disaster in American history—worse than the *S-51*. The newspapers were not sanguine about the fate of the men aboard the submarine, citing naval authorities who feared they may all be dead. Still, there was a faint ray of hope from the likes of Captain Adolphus Andrews, the commander of the New London submarine base, who said it was possible that some, if not all of the crew, were alive. Andrews said, "Provided the *S-4* was not crushed in such a manner as to be entirely flooded. The members of the crew probably would have an air supply to sustain life for seventy-two hours. If the *S-4* was rammed amidships the chances of any of its crew escaping alive would appear very remote, but if it were struck on the bow or stern, the immediate closing of the bulkheads might easily save them from drowning."

The information provided by the press was scanty. Ellsberg was in a peculiar position of being one of the few persons in the world who really knew about deep sea diving and salvage. He knew of nobody else, even Captain King, who was more qualified to help if there was the possibility of life aboard the submarine *S-4*.

He went to the telephone and called Axtell J. Byles, the president of Tidewater. He quickly explained to him the situation and what he wanted to do. It was a quick conversation. He was to take a leave of absence.

Ellsberg then called the Navy Department in Washington and offered his assistance as a civilian volunteer. They accepted. He then contacted the Brooklyn Navy Yard. He hoped that Admiral Plunkett was still in charge. He was in luck: the admiral had not yet retired. Plunkett was happy to hear from him and told him that of course he could volunteer to help. He just needed to get down to the Navy Yard.

Ellsberg took his old uniform cap and navy overcoat out of the attic. He tossed all the heavy socks he had into a bag. He said goodbye to his wife, Lucy, and daughter, Mary, and then headed to Brooklyn. Despite his misgivings, despite his frustration with the navy, the *S-4* needed his help.

● ● ●

In Wallabout Bay, a little recess in the East River before it empties into New York Harbor, is the Brooklyn Navy Yard. In later days, the yard would abut the trendy Brooklyn neighborhoods of DUMBO and Williamsburg. In 1927, however, the area was populated with navy men, naval contractors, and ships. It was the premier shipbuilding and repair facility in the country. Even in the cold week before Christmas, the Navy Yard was bursting with activity. The ring of hammers, the clash of tools, and the smells of diesel mixed with seawater created a palpable industriousness that would have brought a longing to Ellsberg's heart to build ships again.

But Ellsberg was on other business. He needed to see Admiral Plunkett. He had to get to Provincetown.

He found Plunkett. Ellsberg gave a salute and asked that he be sent to the disaster scene as quickly as possible.

"We'll send you right up to Provincetown," said Plunkett. The Admiral made some calls and arranged for a destroyer to meet Ellsberg in Boston. It would shuttle him to the *Falcon*. Ellsberg was also filled in on the details of the disaster and what was being done.

Plunkett then explained that he couldn't fly to Provincetown since Captain King was taking the only available plane to the site. "The fastest way to go is by train," said Plunkett, looking at the clock. "There should be one leaving from Grand Central Station in twenty or thirty minutes."

Ellsberg suddenly became distressed. He didn't know how he could possibly get from Brooklyn to the station that was in the middle of Manhattan in that short of a time.

"Don't worry," said Plunkett. "You'll make it all right. I've a navy ambulance below waiting to take you through; if I know that driver, he won't need twenty minutes."

Ellsberg said, "That's fine. I am ready to go."

Plunkett smiled and said, "Oh no, not yet. There is one more thing you've got to do."

"What's that?"

"I've got to swear you into the Naval Reserve first."

"Oh no," said Ellsberg. He now realized why Plunkett summoned him to Brooklyn instead of sending him straightaway to Cape Cod. "When I resigned from the navy I was through, and I have no desire to come back in the Reserve or any other way. I'm a civilian, but I'll do everything I can to help."

"That's all right with you," Plunkett replied, his blue eyes flashing, "but I know your wife and I can't allow that. If you get killed on the *S-4* as a civilian that's just too bad. But if you're in the Naval Reserve, there is something we can do for your widow."

"All right," said Ellsberg.

Ellsberg raised his right hand and repeated after Plunkett, "I, Edward Ellsberg, do solemnly swear that I will bear true faith and allegiance to the United States of America; that I will serve them honestly and faithfully against all their enemies whomsoever; and that I will obey the orders of the President of the United States and the orders of the officers appointed over me, according to the Rules and Articles of War."

Moments later, Ellsberg found himself in a navy ambulance rushing to Grand Central Station, its sirens screaming in the city streets. As Ellsberg clasped on to a stretcher in the back of the vehicle, he concluded that the driver must have learned to drive among the shell holes of the Western Front. Police officers held traffic as the ambulance burned through red lights.

With Ellsberg was a reporter from the *New York Times* who asked questions concerning the operation. Even as the ambulance jostled them about, Ellsberg said to the reporter:

The *S-4* is in 102 feet of water. The *S-51* was in 135 feet when we finally raised her and she weighed 200 tons more than the *S-4*. We have six pontoons on the way. Our pontoons will have a combined lift of 480 tons, and there must be some buoyancy in the boat. With that lift and her own help we may be able to raise her.

The *New York Times* further reported, "Mr. Ellsberg told how he had designed lifting hooks after the *S-51* disaster to be attached to all submarines, with which, his figures indicated, a helpless submersible might be raised in four or five hours. The pontoon method, naval men said, might take two weeks or longer. They declared the pontoons were good for salvage work, but worthless when it came to saving life."

Ellsberg arrived at Grand Central with time to spare. He boarded his train and was on the way to Provincetown to help those men he worked so closely with, including his old superior officer, Captain Ernest J. King.

"An Olympian Zeus"

CAPTAIN ERNEST JOSEPH KING, BEING off duty, had been Christmas shopping for most of the day in Norfolk, Virginia. A tall and lean forty-nine-year-old man, King was the newly appointed commanding officer of the seaplane tender *Wright,* which was moored at Hampton Roads. Upon his return to the ship at 5:00 PM, shopping bags in hand, his executive officer, Victor D. Herbster, met him. The Navy Department had been calling every thirty minutes. The chief of naval operations, Admiral Charles Hughes, was looking for him.

King got to the telephone and while he could not get in touch directly with Hughes, the message was clear. The *S-4* had been sunk. There may be people still alive inside the submarine. He was to go to Provincetown immediately.

Ernest King to this point had experienced a highly varied, successful career despite or maybe because of the fact that he was a tactless hard-ass.

The son of Scottish and English immigrants, King had grown up in Lorain, Ohio, chiefly influenced by his outspoken father—a workingman who built bridges. He enjoyed being taken by his father to the shops, where he would learn the intricacies of machinery and mingle with the engineers. He came to admire such blue collar men and picked up on their traits of bluntness, profaneness, and stubbornness.

As a child when visiting a family acquaintance named Rawley, King was given a pumpkin pie that had too much pepper on it.

In front of the hostess King said, "I don't like Mrs. Rawley's pie."

To this his mother replied, "Ernest! You shouldn't say that."

"It's true," said King. "I don't like it."*

This trait, which was more of a compulsion by the time he reached adulthood, to say exactly what was on his mind may have drowned another man's career—but King was also brilliant. He was a natural leader. By the time he was in high school he felt that he had been "born to manage things." He was attracted to the navy after reading an article in the magazine *Youth's Companion* at the age of ten. He graduated from his high school as valedictorian and entered the Naval Academy after placing first in competitive exams.

As a cadet at Annapolis, a drunken upperclassman accused King of boasting that he'd graduate first in his class. King denied this, but a classmate who was present asserted that he instead would be the one who graduated first. The upperclassman then turned his attention on the classmate and berated him. King came to the realization that he did not wish to graduate as number one from the academy since it would draw too much scrutiny. It would be far better to graduate third or fourth—which still gave respect, but not as much attention. King's ambition was to become no less than the chief of naval operations, the highest-ranking officer in the navy. He put himself to task and became battalion commander of his class, and the senior midshipman officer. He graduated fourth in his class in 1901.

The officer that came out of Annapolis proved to be thoughtful, disciplined, gregarious, and willing to accept advice from those more experienced than he. He was an active team player. King also adhered to a philosophy of giving unusual initiative to his subordinates to allow them to do their jobs, as long as they were competent. He did not discriminate between those officers who came through the old boys' network of Annapolis and those who "came up through the hawsepipe," working their way up the ranks like Lieutenant

---

*The author cannot help but agree with King that pepper and pumpkin pie do not mix.

Henry Hartley. King's measure of a man was based on his ability, not parentage. This is perhaps why Hartley had such respect for Captain King—something that is clear in all the correspondence between the two men.

But there was another side to it. King was prone to outbursts of temper if a subordinate failed to be responsible in his duties. King's acidic tongue would lash the offender into submission even in front of the victim's comrades. Biographer Thomas B. Buell later wrote of King:

> He was an egoist, intellectually arrogant and supremely confident in his ability to distinguish truth and righteousness and to reduce the complex to the simplest terms. Subconsciously he sought to be omnipotent and infallible. There were few men whom he regarded as his equal as to brains; he would acknowledge no mind as superior to his own. Yet he also realized that there were things he did not know and things he could not do, and in such matters he would have to depend upon others. But once convinced he had the right answer, he was unyielding toward any suggestion that he might possibly be wrong. Unyielding may be too mild an adjective. Stubborn. Adamant. Tenacious. And fortified with a violent temper—in the words of Walter Muir Whitehill, like an Olympian Zeus returned with lightning flashes and roaring thunder.

It was no surprise that this "Olympian Zeus" would often come into conflict with his superior officers. He picked fights indiscriminately. King had an intimidating air that his biographer noted made older officers feel uncomfortable. In his early career, he was also a hard drinker who became known for erratic performance. All of this had a negative effect on his career, but he had enough backing from supporters in the officer corps to give him more chances.

At length, King contemplated himself and his goals—while he would not give up partying he swore never to be late. His punctuality became legend. He further developed himself by writing for the *Naval Institute Proceedings*. King then made a choice to select only those assignments that would give him a broad experience in order to bring about promotion and eventual flag rank.

In 1914, he earned his first command on the USS *Terry*. Then two months later, he took another command on the *Cassin*. By the end of World War I, he had risen to the rank of captain. However, he was so junior in the seniority system that governed the navy's doling out of assignments that he found that there were no suitable commands in the surface fleet for him. So he decided to transfer to the submarine service in 1922. He immediately took command of a division, but soon found that new tactics he introduced did not produce the results he wanted. It did not help that he became seasick inside submarines.

In 1923, King took his fifth command ashore as the commanding officer of the submarine base in New London. The navy provided a mansion, a car manufactured by the Marmon Company complete with chauffeur, and four enlisted men who served his family. It was luxurious. King felt a personal loyalty to his retinue. An aide once put his driver on report for a minor infraction. When the case came before King for official action, he glared at the aide, dismissed the case, and the aide was given a tongue-lashing. It is perhaps for these reasons that King did not have many friends in the navy—but nevertheless his talent was considerable. Critically, King decided that he would become an admiral purely by merit.

The future chief of naval operations, Admiral Charles F. Hughes, was one of King's supporters. He warned King that he was being looked upon negatively by the selection board. King was spending too much time ashore and needed to put in his time at sea. Hughes wrote, "I do not know what to advise but it should be at sea and in no fancy job—a tanker, beef ship, or repair ship and not a division commander."

King then began to make career moves to take him out of submarines. But there were no surface ships available for him that he found desirable. The service wanted to see King do duty on lesser ships. But King needed major commands to become an admiral. So he started making plans to switch to Naval Aviation.

After two years of command and his career stagnating, King and his wife decided to take a vacation in September 1925. The Kings cut themselves off from newspapers and the radio while touring through rural New England up the Connecticut Valley, through the White and

Green Mountains and on to Lakes Champlain and George in New York. They then headed to Ticonderoga, Crown Point, and then home again through the Berkshires.

Upon their return their children rushed up to him. Something was wrong. Then his daughter, Elizabeth, said, "Daddy, wasn't it just awful about the *S-51*?"

The *S-51* made a huge splash in the newspapers. But King was only indirectly involved—he prepared a speech concerning the dangers of the seagoing profession for a memorial service. But he found that a Rear Admiral Christy, who had been directing the rescue operations, had just arrived. The admiral, not having the time to prepare his own speech, used King's.

Then a couple of weeks later, he returned home after playing golf on a Sunday. There was a message to call Rear Admiral Charles Plunkett, commandant of the Brooklyn Navy Yard. King thought it strange that Plunkett would be contacting him on a Sunday. After many attempts, King finally got him on the telephone.

Plunkett informed King that he was to be in charge of the raising of the *S-51*. There was no negotiation, no deliberation. King, always the planner, knew nothing about naval salvage and wanted to think about how this would affect his career. But Plunkett was Plunkett. "Since you don't seem interested in the job, I'll try to find someone else to do it."

"Why, admiral," replied King, taking the hint, "of course I'd like to have the job. I just didn't believe my ears. Of course I'll take the job and welcome it."

Apparently, Plunkett, who had been convinced by Edward Ellsberg that the navy should conduct the salvage, felt that a senior officer was needed to manage the operation as a whole. It would mean coordinating the ships, logistics, working with senior officers, and dealing with the press. Ellsberg with his own aides would work directly on the salvage.

It was King's experiences with the *S-51* that led him to meet Hartley, Ellsberg, and the divers. This last group, King later wrote, were the bravest men he had ever met. How else could he explain men who dove into the dark interior of submarine wreckage more than one hundred feet below? For his performance as commanding officer of the *S-51* salvage, he received a distinguished service medal. He was well on his way to the flag rank he coveted.

King, shortly after raising the *S-51* in July 1926, left submarines entirely. He moved from the underwater world to the skies. While he had been hoping for command of the light cruiser *Raleigh*, he learned that no commands of those types of vessels were going to officers below the classes of 1898 and 1899.

However, Rear Admiral William A. Moffett, chief of the Bureau of Aeronautics, was looking for senior officers to command the burgeoning wing of naval aviation ships. Moffett approached King, who was mulling over what to do since the *Raleigh* was out of reach. King took up the offer and entered naval aviation.

King was to be given command of the *Wright*. He trained for his wings as a pilot. King's course was abbreviated since Moffett wanted

Edward Ellsberg, Ernest J. King, and Henry Hartley on the job during the *S-51* salvage.
Courtesy of the Edward Ellsberg Historical Archives

him to return to the *Wright*. So after a five-month course, rather than the usual ten, King was graduated from flight school and earned his wings as aviator 3368 on May 26, 1927. He conducted aerial bombing tests and learned about the effectiveness of dive bombing—although he could never fly solo due to his age. By December 1927, he was fully comfortable with his new command. King had become one of the few officers in the navy to serve in its three divisions: surface, submarine, and air. Now he was plotting to gain command of one of the new carriers in the service, the *Lexington* or *Saratoga*. Either of these commands would give him the step he needed to make admiral.

But his plans were interrupted when news of the *S-4* reached him.

Normally, King would have flown to Provincetown in such an emergency. But the storm that was creeping toward New England had already reached Virginia. Planes were grounded. He took the night train instead. When he arrived at Pennsylvania Station in New York at 8:00 AM the next day, the weather had cleared somewhat. Officers (with accompanying police and blaring sirens) escorted him to the Brooklyn Navy Yard. King put on his flight suit and approached a seaplane that lay next to the battleship *New York*. News photographers were present and snapped photos of one of the heroes of the *S-51* salvage going to save the *S-4*. It made the papers.

King drank some strong coffee, then crammed himself onto the seaplane. The pilot maneuvered the aircraft out of the Navy Yard and into the East River. King noted the coldness of the air, and the strong gusts coming from the north.

They took off, and flew at one thousand feet over Long Island Sound, Buzzards Bay, and the Cape Cod Canal. In three hours, they landed in Provincetown, where a boat from the *Bushnell* escorted King to the *Falcon* just as the first diver was going into the water.

12

One Man Down

THE *FALCON* RODE ON ITS anchors but was also tied by its hawsers to the bows of the *Lark* and *Mallard*. The two minesweepers anchored themselves off the *Falcon*'s starboard and port quarters, trying to stabilize the rescue ship. On the *Falcon*, two large steam-driven reels paid out or hauled in line from the minesweepers as the rescue force rolled, yawed, and pitched in the sea. Lieutenant Henry Hartley considered it the best mooring he could do, considering the circumstances. He did not have the luxury of establishing mooring buoys all about the *Falcon* as they did in the case of the *S-51*. It was doubtful that anything could fully stabilize the rescue ship. Then there was the cold gale. Ice was forming on the rails and deck.

Hartley believed that there was nobody alive on the *S-4*, just like the *S-51*. But, despite the sea, despite the cold, and despite his misgivings, an attempt had to be made by a diver to go to the bottom. But these were conditions that no diver had ever gone down in before. There was no question as to who the first diver would be.

Hartley told Tom Eadie, "If the grapnel catch proves to be the *S-4*, hammer on the hatch covers as you come to them. Note if any air is escaping from the hatches. Listen for signs of life. Do not hurry, but allow a reasonable amount of time for anyone alive in the *S-4* to answer you. Telephone where you are from time to time. Note how she lays, get as much general information as possible, especially as to location and extent of damage."

• • •

Eadie began the laborious process of getting ready to dive. Since this dive was going to be in cold water—the sea temperature was 33 degrees Fahrenheit—it meant additional protection. He put on as many layers of woolen underwear as he could find; Hartley wrote that up to six pairs were typical for water that was 32 to 37 degrees. Then there were multiple pairs of wool socks, usually up to three, which were covered by wool-lined moccasins.

After dressing, Eadie came out onto the pitching deck and sat on a small stool, which had below it an assortment of nuts and wrenches used to fasten the diving gear. Two men then took charge of Eadie. In diver parlance these men were called "bears." (The origin of the term is unclear.) Their especial duty was to dress the divers and care for the diving equipment. One of the bears headed to the engine room, where all the diving gear was kept warm and dry on a rack.

The suit was a one-piece design of two layers of duck canvas or cotton; between the fabric layers was a layer of vulcanized rubber. Patches to prevent wear were attached at the knees and elbows. Eadie, who was familiar with wear done to the suit, always put on extra patches where a diver's tools, belts, and various lines were likely to rub against the outfit. To actually get into the diving dress, Eadie slipped his legs through the wide opening at the neck before working himself into the entire outfit. To keep water out of the sleeves, the rubber cuffs were sealed with "snappers" made from sections of rubber tubing. These held a talon-like grip on Eadie's wrists that, if he stayed out of the water, would cause his hands to turn blue. Yet underwater, the pressure of the air pumped into the suit eased their hold. The bears also slid on waterproof gloves over Eadie's woolen gloves and cemented them to the suit. The gloves were cumbersome things, having only two fingers and thumb molded in the form of a half-closed fist. Eadie wrote that these gloves were a big improvement that was made during the *S-51* salvage. Previous diving glove designs were essentially clumsy mittens. The suit portion of the diving dress weighed between twenty-five and twenty-seven pounds.

Next came lead-soled shoes that weighed about fourteen pounds each. Once the shoes were put on, a tinned copper breastplate followed. On the suit's rubber collar there were twelve holes that lined up to holes on the breastplate. Studs from the breastplate poked through. Over the studs and collar, the bears fixed a curved metal strap that was divided into four sections. The bears used screws to anchor the strap, making it watertight. To further prevent leakage, an inner collar called a "bib," made of the same material as the suit, was pulled up Eadie's neck.

Then there was the diving belt. It was hung on Eadie like a pair of suspenders. Up to one hundred pounds of lead weight were inserted into the belt to provide more stability. The actual weight was selected based on the depth of the dive. The deeper a diver was to go, the more weight.

Then the bears put a skullcap on Eadie, which held in place the receiver for his telephone. Then at last came the Mark V deep sea diving helmet. This helmet and the associated diving dress, which was adopted as a standard by the navy in 1916, was the iconic headpiece that the general public associated with traditional deep sea diving.* This was screwed to the breastplate. The helmet had four ports of thick glass reinforced by gratings that allowed Eadie to look ahead, up, right, and left. The one in the front, called the faceplate, was on a hinge that opened in order for a diver to speak with his tender when out of the water. It also had a non-return valve, which allowed air to enter the diving dress but not escape up through the same air hose. It is important to remember that the helmet was a bubble over the head of the diver and did not turn as he swiveled his neck. This is why the diver needed to have separate ports. The helmet and breastplate added fifty-nine more pounds.

Inside the helmet was the transmitter for Eadie's telephone and an emergency button, which Eadie could use to open his exhaust valve all

---

*The durability of the diving dress's design is revealed by the fact that the navy used the Mark V as late as 1980.

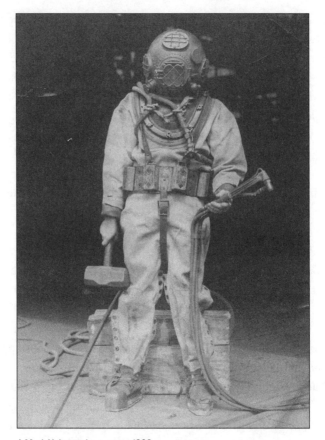

A Mark V diving dress, circa 1926.
Courtesy of the Edward Ellsberg Historical Archives

the way by pressing it with his chin or seal it by pulling it with his lips. In the rear of the helmet were two valves; the one on the left was for the one-inch-thick air hose through which compressed air was driven into the suit through a non-return valve that ensured that air would not escape if the hose became damaged. Air that entered the helmet was spread out in a three-branch tube that distributed the air to limit fogging. The valve on the right was an outlet to allow air to escape the suit, and it was situated so that the bubbles did not interfere with the diver's line of sight. The outlet was set with an adjustable spring that would release air only after it built to a certain pressure. A supplementary release for excess air was the spit cock, which was located on the front of the helmet to the left of the faceplate. This was typically used to blow out any water that may have gotten between the bib and the breastplate. On the helmet was also the connection to Eadie's one-inch-thick lifeline, which not only tethered him to the *Falcon* but also carried the wire of his telephone in its center. This line ran through a watertight connection into the helmet. Both the air hose and the lifeline were looped about his shoulders and seized together in the back, forming one line that was easier to handle than two separate lines.

The tools added even more weight to Eadie. All divers carried at the belt a metal sheath that held a knife with a cutting blade on one side and saw teeth on the other. Eadie thought it a perfect tool for cutting wire. For this job, Hartley gave Eadie a hammer so that he could tap on the submarine for signs of life and flooding. An expert diver like Eadie could usually tell by the vibrations on the hammer if the compartment was flooded. Sometimes, divers would also take submersible lamps with them. Eadie chose not to. It was day and he supposed that there would be enough ambient light at seventeen fathoms deep for him to see.

A half hour after the bears began dressing Eadie, they finished the job. The diver was now two hundred pounds heavier. Medieval armor was significantly lighter. But all this weight was necessary to keep Eadie stable and to prevent him from upending.

After last-minute checks, Eadie was turned over to the diving tenders. In the enclosed helmet, Eadie could not hear anything except the hiss of incoming air. The only mode of communication was the telephone or signaling. The telephone was checked and rechecked. Eadie spoke into the transmitter, then heard a cracking response: "OK on Eadie."

The diving helmet was then sealed using a bayonet-style lock and a quarter turn to fasten it onto its gasket. The men turned a locknut on the helmet's rear to secure it in place.

Eadie was helped off the bench and over to the side of the ship. There, suspended by booms, was the diving stage. It was made of a flat grating hung by iron straps. He clambered onto it. A tender tapped him on the helmet, signaling that everything was ready.

The stage was lowered into the icy waters that Eadie felt despite all the layers of clothing he wore. He adjusted the air hose and fiddled with the valves to test his air intake.

Eadie's telephone tender then called, "Everything OK?"

"Everything is OK," said Eadie. "Carry me to the descending line." There was a pause, as if to do last-minute checks on the surface. Then the men of the *Falcon* swung the platform outward and over to Gracie's line.

"Go to the descending line."

Eadie stepped off the stage and turned the valve of his air hose. Compressed air pumped into the suit, granting him buoyancy and easing the grip of the sea about him. The diving dress, which was stiff and incredibly heavy on the deck of the *Falcon*, had become supple and light—almost as if he were wearing regular clothes. It was air, and air alone, that countered the effect of the sixty pounds per square inch of sea pressure Eadie would feel when he reached the bottom, seventeen fathoms below. His tenders guided his line toward the grapnel catch.

Eadie wrapped his leg about the line. He opened his exhaust valve a little, to let air out of the suit. He slipped down toward the bottom, disappearing from sight. It was 1:23 PM, almost twenty-two hours since the *S-4* and *Paulding* had collided.

● ● ●

Meanwhile, Henry Hartley fretted about the deck. He worried if it was really the *S-4*. He worried about the weather. He worried if men were trapped alive on the submarine. But most of all, Hartley worried for Tom Eadie. Nobody in his experience had ever dived in conditions like this before.

Hartley, being a qualified diver himself, could imagine what it was like to make the dive. The water was silt-filled; a cold current that ran along the bottom stirred up mud, which was sure to have been even further disturbed when the *S-4* slammed into the bottom. Divers were sure not to see more than a few feet. It was far different on the *S-51* job, during which Hartley's divers could see up to twenty feet. Eadie would rue not bringing a lamp with him.

But what made matters worse was the sea itself. To a diver, as the waves above swell and then fall, the water pressure varies wildly. Even little swells can amount to hundreds of pounds of additional pressure. He also faced the real danger of fouling his lines in the wreckage. Only an expert diver, who knew instinctively how to handle the suit's intake and outtake valves, could make the attempt.

The tension that had built up over a day mounted further, when after just two minutes since disappearing from sight, Tom Eadie's voice hissed through the telephone.

"On the submarine."

Hartley could not stand it. He seized the transmitter from Eadie's telephone man.

"Where are you, Tom?" he asked.

"On deck. Near the conning tower."

Hartley asked, "Any sound?"

But Eadie did not immediately answer Hartley. It was almost as if he were teasing him. Finally, Eadie's voice came through loud and clear.

"Yes, there is life in the boat forward."

13

Six Taps

LIEUTENANT HENRY HARTLEY FACED A problem he had long studied and thought about since he took command of the *Falcon*. He later wrote that he could not describe his feelings at the instant he learned that there were men trapped alive inside the *S-4*. However, he was conscious that the entire navy, and indeed the country, would soon know that there was life inside the submarine. Even though he was not the most senior officer aboard (Admiral Brumby was present and Captain King had just arrived by boat from the *Bushnell*), Hartley felt that the burden of rescue was entirely his.

Now that life was confirmed, it was more important than ever to get as much information as they could about the damage done to the submarine since it meant that they would have to raise it as quickly as possible.

Eadie called up on the telephone. Bubbles were escaping from the conning tower hatch.

"Large amounts?" Hartley asked.

"No, just a few. I am going forward now."

That was where Eadie had heard signs of life. Then two tugs came from Eadie's line. He wanted more slack so he could walk across the deck of the boat.

The tenders paid out the lines. Hartley, with his trained eyes, could see Eadie's bubbles as they broke the surface. They slowly moved, which gave an idea to Hartley as to how the submarine lay on the seafloor. Meanwhile, Eadie's heavy leaden boots clanked over the *S-4*, telling anybody inside that the navy had come.

Eadie called up. "Hole in battery room, starboard side opposite gun mount. Gun slewed, muzzle to port, about ten feet of deck and superstructure missing."

"What does it look like?" Hartley asked.

"Torn up pretty bad," said Eadie. "Lot of wreckage."

Hartley had seen the *S-51* after it had been raised and the great gash in it caused by the *City of Rome*. He then asked Eadie, "Bad as the *S-51*?"

"Worse."

There was a long silence. It had been Hartley's practice not to bother the divers with too many questions so they could do their work. The diver, in order to speak to his telephone man on the surface, would need to close his intake so that the hiss of compressed air did not drown out the diver's voice. In addition, compressed air also affected a diver's speech so that at times his words became mushy—it was difficult for him to whisper or whistle. Even so, the telephone was a far superior way of communication than hand pull signals.

The diving tenders manned Eadie's lines, and hands waited anxiously by the telephone. His bubbles were on the move again.

Hartley broke the silence. "Still hear the sounds?"

"Yes, every time I walk."

"Where?"

"Up forward. I hear them banging every time I walk."

Eadie was then asked if he could go farther forward. He replied, "I will try, but hold me tight. No slack. This stuff looks bad."

The tenders pulled in the lines. Eadie's request for no slack would help him avoid fouling among the surrounding wreckage, which was presumably sharp and could potentially rupture his suit.

Eadie's bubbles and lines went forward, then came to a halt.

Over the transmitter, Hartley and the other tenders could hear the banging as Eadie laid his hammer against a hatch.

BANG!

There was cold thrill as all those within earshot of the telephone receiver heard the reply:

TAP TAP TAP TAP TAP TAP

Six taps. Over and over again.

Eadie's voice came hissing through the telephone. "I am up forward, the sound comes from the torpedo room. Every time I strike with the hammer, they answer back. I can show you where when I come up."

Then Eadie's bubbles moved farther forward. He then reported, "I am on the bow. Her bow is covered in mud. Going aft now. Hold me tight. No slack. Will tell you when over the bad place."

Eadie's bubbles then traveled aft.

Again, it was a lengthy process, as Eadie had to negotiate walking through wreckage. Then his bubbles stopped moving. But Eadie wasn't as far aft as he should have been, considering the length of the S-4.

Hartley decided to call down. "Are you in trouble? What happened?"

"I'm foul in the antenna," replied Eadie, "but I'm all right and will clear myself shortly."

Eadie soon reported again. He had tried to get aft to see if there were any signs of life in the engine room, but he couldn't get much farther than the control room—the submarine's gun was slewed over and blocked his progress. Eadie managed to lie down, stretch himself as far aft as he could, and try tapping. But there was no reply from any other place in the S-4 except the torpedo room.

Eadie's bubbles moved forward again until they were near the descending line. There they stopped.

Hartley asked, "Are you in trouble? What's happened?"

"I finished the inspection," Eadie reported.

"Are you satisfied with your inspection?"

"I am. What do you want me to do?"

"You've been down long enough," said Hartley. "Stand by to come up; we have another man ready to go over."

● ● ●

Eadie had been on the job for over an hour. Typically, divers were expected to be on the bottom for no more than forty-five minutes. But this was a special set of circumstances.

Eadie's tenders pulled him up to forty feet beneath the surface. He dangled there for five minutes before being drawn up another ten feet. He then hung for another fifteen minutes before he grabbed the "monkey line" that brought him onto the diving platform. He was brought aboard at 2:53 PM. This was a fast decompression time that would require him to sit in the decompression chamber for twenty-seven minutes. There he gave a more detailed report of what he found to the officers.

Eadie empathized with the poor men trapped in the submarine. It would be cold, wet, and dark inside the *S-4*. He later wrote of that moment, "If you never do anything more in your whole life, inspire those men in there with the confidence that we on the topside are onto our job, and doing every last thing we can."

14

Blowing the Ballast Tanks

THE ICY NORTHWEST WINDS MOUNTED in strength, blowing at force 9 on the Beaufort Scale.* It was clear that there should be no more diving. Rear Admiral Frank H. Brumby had to decide what to do.

The admiral must have been overjoyed to see his friend, Captain Ernest King, arrive via boat from the *Bushnell* at 1:23 PM. King was to be Brumby's senior aide and chief advisor in what became an ad hoc kitchen cabinet of senior officers.

The officers who were present all had extensive experience working on submarines, designing submarines, diving, or salvage operations. Aside from King, there was Lieutenant Henry Hartley and submarine builder Commander Harold Saunders. But there was also Lieutenant Carleton Shugg. He was a naval constructor with considerable submarine experience. He arrived with Saunders from the Portsmouth Naval Yard, and acted as Saunders's assistant. The last man to round out Brumby's advisors was Ralph F. Skylstead, a former submarine commander, who served as Brumby's flag lieutenant.

The first thing to do was to assess the situation based on Eadie's intelligence, both his direct reports while he was on the submarine and the more detailed accounts obtained via voice tube after the diver had

---

*47–54 miles per hour.

been thrust into the recompression chamber. Of paramount importance to the officers was to understand the extent of the damage.

The officers inventoried the S-4's compartments. The torpedo
room was obviously not flooded since there were men alive within it,
and the battery compartment obviously flooded; but the condition
of the other compartments was questionable. Eadie reported that
he knocked his hammer on the control room's hatch. Based on the
reverberation of the hammer and the bubbles coming from the hatch,
Eadie thought it probably flooded. But this was illogical since the damage seemed to be isolated at the battery room. Typically, if a compartment was filling with water, a diver expected to see a great amount of
bubbles streaming up from the compartments' hatches—even after
a day had passed. The hatches sealed effectively when water pressure
from the *outside* was pushing against them. But when the inside of a
compartment flooded, the hatch was not as well-designed to hold air.
Thus, if a diver saw evidence of bubbles coming out of the hatches, it
showed that water was getting in, compressing the air upward in the
compartment, and forcing its way into the sea.

There had been no evidence of damage to the rear of the control
room, and there was no reason to believe that the engineering and
motor rooms were flooded. Both of these compartments were well
away of the point of impact, and since the S-4 had crashed at a downward angle, the water would have initially rushed toward the torpedo
room at the front of the submarine. It was incredible that the men in
the torpedo room had been able to seal their compartment since they
would have had to fight the onslaught of water rushing downhill at
them. If the men in the torpedo room were able to shut and dog their
door, the men in the other compartments would have had a much
easier time of sealing themselves in.

It was rational to believe that the compartments aft of the battery room were not flooded—perhaps even the control room, despite
Eadie's assessment. So the officers worked on the assumption that
only one of the five major compartments was flooded and that the
rest of boat was dry.

The officers of the rescue force could only speculate as to what
happened to the men to the rear of the torpedo room. Chlorine gas

may have killed them when seawater got into the *S-4*'s batteries. It was possible that gas might have permeated the engine room since there were vents that connected the batteries to that compartment. However, there were ways to seal those vents, which would have been done when the submariners realized that the battery room was flooded. A far more likely scenario was that the men had been incapacitated for lack of breathable air. The rescue force knew that the vast majority of the *S-4*'s crew were aft of the battery room for the standardization trials. The submarine had already been submerged for the better part of a day when the collision occurred. With the majority of men crowded in two or three compartments, the oxygen would have run out quicker than in the torpedo room, which would have had far fewer men.

The rescue force decided that it was still highly possible that the men aft of the battery room were alive, but too weak to respond to Eadie. If fresh air could be delivered, then they could be revived and saved. But it had to be done immediately.

The only way to quickly deliver air to the inside of the submarine was through a valve located on the starboard side of the *S-4* near the conning tower that led to the compartment salvage line. This line ran across the entire submarine with outlets at each of the five compartments. These outlets had a check valve, which would allow air to enter the compartment but prevent water from backing up into the line. In addition, each compartment had an additional manual control, called a gag valve, which was to be left open at all times except when another compartment flooded. In that scenario, the men in the nonflooded compartments were to close their valves. Then, if compressed air were put into this line, it would run indiscriminately to all compartments where the gag valve was open. The idea was that if one room had flooded, a salvage force could use the compartment salvage line to force air into the damaged compartment and drive out water to the point of damage. It was not a line intended to deliver breathable air, but one used in salvage to grant additional buoyancy to the submarine.

The likelihood was that, due to operating procedures, all the gag valves for this line would be closed with the exception of the battery room. Since the men in the engineering room were unresponsive, there was no way to communicate to them to open their valve. And even in the event that they did not close the gag valve, any air pumped into the line would pressurize their compartments since, incapacitated, they would be unable to open outlet valves to vent out the bad air. Of course, this might have a salutary effect of diluting the carbon dioxide in the compartment, but that remained to be seen.

It was true that by hooking up this line that it might help the men in the torpedo room, since they were cognizant. They could open the gag valve and open venting valves to the sea. However, the men in the torpedo room appeared vigorous. Their tapping could be heard through the telephone receiver on the surface. They had at their disposal canisters of compressed air that were used to launch the torpedoes. While foul smelling, it would allow them to dilute the carbon dioxide and hold out. The conditions were miserable, but the men inside the torpedo room could linger for at least a day longer.

In the end, all of Brumby's advisors agreed that using the compartment salvage air line would not render assistance to any man incapacitated in the rear of the boat. The only possible way to save them was to raise the *S-4* immediately.

To those not familiar with submarine salvage, raising the *S-4* might seem easy—or at least there might be multiple ways of doing it. Perhaps the *Falcon* could tow the *S-4* to shallower water or maybe they could use lifting cranes to haul the submarine to the surface.

Both of these suggestions would have been summarily dismissed by King and Hartley, who had ample experience with the *S-51* salvage. Trying to tow the submarine out of the mud was unthinkable; it would have torn the *S-4* apart. The hookups for towing apparatus were meant to be used on the surface only. As for lifting it with derricks, this too was impossible, as shown during the *S-51* disaster. Any means of fastening lifting eyes to the submarine would have ripped plates off the *S-4*'s hull—it was simply too heavy. Besides, even if this attempt was possible, the proper equipment was not present. The last the rescue force had heard was that the Merritt-Chapman & Scott Company was sending lifting derricks, but they had no idea when they would arrive.

There were only two reliable ways to raise the *S-4*. The first means was to use the methods employed on the *S-51* job, which meant passing chains under the hull and using salvage pontoons to bring it to the surface. However, this meant that divers would have to dig tunnels under the submarine. For the *S-51*, this process took months. The rescue force did not have that kind of time if they wanted to rescue every man in the boat. To a man, each one of Brumby's officers advised him to raise the *S-4* by blowing the submarine's main ballast tanks.

The *S-4*'s main ballast tanks ran along its sides, in the void spaces between the inner and outer hulls. When empty, these tanks provided the necessary buoyancy to keep the boat on the surface. When full, they made the boat heavy enough to submerge. There were potentially two hundred tons of seawater to blow from the ballast tanks and there was a real possibility that emptying these tanks would provide enough buoyancy to raise the submarine to the surface. This kind of technique had been used before.

In 1921, due to human error, the *S-5*'s (a sister vessel of the *S-4*) torpedo room filled with water during a crash dive. In this case, the boat became lodged at the bottom in 194 feet of water. The captain, using the resources available to him, blew the ballast tanks in the ship dry. This tilted the stern of the submarine out of the water. Not being able to tell if their submarine had actually broken the surface, the crew carefully drilled through the hull and, to their relief, found air coming in and not water. After they enlarged the opening using hacksaws, the captain managed to hoist a makeshift flag out of the hole using a pipe and an undershirt. Soon enough, an American steamer came by. Seeing the unidentifiable stern of a submarine sticking out of the water, the captain of the steamer went in a boat to investigate. The following exchange took place with the steamer captain peering into the *S-5*'s hole:

"What ship?"

"USS *S-5*."

"What nationality?"

"American."

"Where bound?"

"To Hell by compass!"

The navy was soon contacted and liberated the men of the *S-5*.

Brumby, King, Saunders, and the other officers all had the similar hope that the S-4 could be raised like the S-5. The S-4 was over 225 feet long. It was in 102 feet of water. If the rescue force blew the ballast tanks the stern would rise to the surface, where they could cut through to the motor and engine rooms, revive those men, and then work their way to the torpedo room. Even better, if the entire S-4 came up, they could tow it toward the shore and rescue all the survivors. The S-class submarines had been designed so that if only one of the main compartments were flooded, the vessel would still float. To their best knowledge, only one main compartment had been flooded, the battery room, and the team worked on that assumption. It would be a spectacular rescue. What made the proposition chancy was if a second compartment had flooded or if the ballast tanks had been damaged in the collision.

To do the job, a diver needed to hook up an air hose to a valve located near the port side of the conning tower, opposite where the compartment salvage air line was. This valve opened to the ballast tank salvage line.

The rescue force did not consider hooking up both the compartment air and ballast salvage lines simultaneously. The job of blowing the ballast tanks alone would require a diver to descend with tools, an air hose to connect to the submarine, and his own air hose and lifeline. To go down with another air hose would endanger the diver by threatening to foul all the lines. Under ideal conditions this task would best be handled by two divers going down together.

It was to be the ballast tanks. But Brumby had another decision to make regarding the newspapers.

* * *

All through this period, the navy had kept a tight rein on information. The story, which broke through the semaphore skills of Mark MacIntyre, had created a firestorm of interest in the plight of the S-4's crew.

By the morning of December 18, aside from the broad outline that the S-4 had been sunk in a collision with the *Paulding*, no details had been given out from the navy. What is more, the newspaper men were barred from going aboard any of the rescue ships.

During the afternoon, at around the time Eadie had found the lost submarine, a fishing boat came up to the scene. The boat, a traditional fishing smack, had been rented by a number of reporters who wanted to find out what was going on.

According to Henry Hartley, Brumby spoke to them using a megaphone, answering their questions. The reporters then requested to board the *Falcon* and be present during the entire operation.

Brumby refused. There were 146 men aboard, and the *Falcon*'s complement was five officers and sixty-one crew; adding any more would jeopardize the mission. The *Falcon* was so crammed that a score of enlisted men were forced to berth in the mess deck and in the corridors.

According to Hartley: "This angered some of them and their language became sharp and nasty. A Mr. Goldberg in particular [kept] hurling insulting remarks [such] as 'Your damn navy secrets.' "

Attention turned away from the fishing smack and to the matter at hand—raising the submarine *S-4*.

• • •

Chief Boatswain's Mate Bill Carr was the acknowledged second-best diver on the *Falcon* with about ten years of experience. A tough man with an earthy sense of humor, he had lived in the shadow of Tom Eadie since the *S-51* salvage—when, as discussed, Edward Ellsberg could not, or would not, get him the Navy Cross he desired. However, Carr managed to take it all in stride (he was good friends with Eadie) and after the *S-51* job he remained assigned as a diver aboard the *Falcon*.

Divers typically had little knowledge of the intricacies of naval architecture and only learned through experience. Since each salvage job had its own set of particular vicissitudes, in practice this meant that each job was idiosyncratic. On the *S-51* assignment, the divers constantly rehearsed what they were to do on the surface before diving.

Saunders, Hartley, and King gave explicit instructions to Carr that he was to go down to the *S-4* and secure a descending line in lieu of the grapnel, being sure to clear out any debris from the area. Then he was to go to where the salvage line for the ballast tanks was, open the door to the valve, attach an air hose to it, then open the valve. The *Falcon* would then pump compressed air into the line to blow water out of the ballast tanks and raise the submarine.

It is important to remember that any work done by deep sea divers was necessarily slow. Typically, divers went down to do one job only, and their time was, under normal circumstances, limited to forty-five minutes to an hour on the bottom. It took time to get to the bottom. It took time for a diver to adjust all his valves. Then there was the job itself. As Tom Eadie later wrote, "You can't work as fast as on the surface; fumbling for tools in gloves, and the extra care you must take not to drop and lose them, slows you. So sometimes it is a wonder the diver accomplishes as much as he does." Then, after the job was done, there was time necessarily eaten up by the long decompression process.

Carr was given an air hose and a four-inch manila line—this was to be used as the permanent descending line for the divers. In Carr's case, he was not rigged with a telephone.* Carr also chose not to wear gloves despite the icy water. In his reckoning, he needed his bare hands due to the intricacy of the work. He was lowered into the sea at 3:09 PM.

Carr's tenders drew in and slacked his line as the ship pitched and rolled. Ice built on the deck and rails. Without the telephone, the only communication that came from Carr were tugs on his lifeline that indicated to give or take in slack of the lifeline, or to increase or decrease the rate of compressed air being delivered to him.

Then, a little over an hour later, Carr gave a different signal. He was ready to come up. The tenders began to pull him up and, through a rapid fifteen-minute decompression process, brought Carr to the surface at 4:27 PM. He was immediately put into the decompression tank.

---

*It is unclear why Carr did not have an operating telephone. It seems unlikely that Hartley would have let any of his divers down without an operating phone. The most likely case was that the telephone he had been given was inoperable. Since it took a great deal of time to change telephones, they may have decided to risk sending him down without one.

At the surface, Carr told his tale. He landed on the submarine without an issue, cleared the debris, and secured a permanent descending line. The real difficulty he had was getting access to the ballast tank valves. They were behind a trap door that was stuck. This may have been due to warping of the *S-4*'s superstructure or, as Carr supposed, water pressure holding the door tight against a pocket of air. He wedged his diving knife into the door edge and slammed onto it with his wrench. The knife worked itself in, and at length Carr pried it open. The rest of the job was straightforward.

It was time to blow the ballast tanks, but before they could do that, Henry Hartley insisted on moving the *Falcon*. During the *S-51* salvage they had a similar situation when the *S-51* came up prematurely and nearly struck the ship.

Hartley ordered the *Falcon* to haul on the line running from its port quarter to the *Mallard* and slacked the line they had on the starboard quarter of the *Lark*. They slowly swiveled the *Falcon* clear of the descending line. Hartley placed them approximately over the torpedo room. The *S-4*'s stern was to theoretically come up near the *Falcon*'s stern. Propitiously, the gale lulled.

They turned on the air full blast and waited.

15

"How Long Will You Be?"

IN THE SHADOW OF THE *Falcon* the submarine *S-8* slunk like a ghost. It had been lurking among the rescue fleet since midnight of December 18 at the request of Commander Harold Saunders. "Savvy" Saunders knew that having a sister ship of the *S-4* would provide an excellent technical model to refer to during the mission.

But having the *S-8* present also provided another advantage. It was equipped with a device that would allow the rescue force to communicate directly with the men trapped inside the *S-4*.

Fifteen years prior, in 1912, was the infamous *Titanic* disaster. The ship, which had been traveling from England to New York, had struck an iceberg and sank. More than fifteen hundred people perished in the North Atlantic. The incident was shocking since the ship was a cutting-edge liner. The word "Titanic" entered into the modern lexicon as a byword for disaster.

Yet 705 people survived the sinking. Their rescue was credited a great deal to the invention of radio, which allowed the doomed ship to call for help. It also gave inspiration to inventors to create devices that used sound waves to warn ships of approaching danger.

By chance, an executive of the Submarine Signal Company, which had been working on underwater communication devices, met the Canadian inventor and polymath Reginald Fessenden in the South Station at Boston. Fessenden, an early pioneer in radio, was responsible for the first voice radio broadcast. It was during this work that he had been in touch with the Submarine Signal Company to look for better transmitters. The executive invited him to come to their lab to see what they were doing. Fessenden showed up the next morning.

Fessenden saw that the company had been working on devices for underwater detection and transmission. The most advanced devices at that time worked short range. Fessenden proposed creating a device that could signal over longer ranges. After a bit of static from the company, since Fessenden was not as experienced as their own engineers, they allowed him to work on an underwater receiving apparatus. Within three months, he had developed an oscillator—a telegraphic signaling and receiving device that had a range of up to fifty miles.

Fessenden's oscillator was bell-shaped, spanning roughly two feet. To use it, the device was lowered directly into the water and charged with electricity. This generated a high-pitched sound that could be translated into the dashes and dots of Morse code. It was also discovered that by employing echolocation, it also served as a primitive form of sonar. Fessenden demonstrated this by showing at sea how icebergs could be detected using the oscillator at a distance of two miles.

By 1927, virtually every submarine was equipped with these oscillators, which were typically just called "Fessendens." The *Falcon*, being an underwater salvage ship, had one as well.

Now that it was verified that there were men trapped alive inside the *S-4*, everybody was anxious to communicate with them. Indeed, prior to Eadie's descent the *S-8* had used its Fessenden, calling to the bottom, and thought they might have heard a response. But while Eadie and Carr were on the wreck, they turned the device off to stave injury to the divers' ears, due to the high-pitched signals the Fessenden emanated.

The gale, while still fierce, had abated somewhat. The ballast tanks were being blown, and there was no more diving to do. Now there was time to attempt communication. Since the *Falcon* was too busy maneuvering itself into a better position, the *S-8* activated its oscillator. Officers on the *Falcon*, King and Saunders in particular, directed what messages were to be composed.[*]

The rescue force did not know who was in the torpedo room or how many men there were—but they had educated guesses based on the *S-4*'s roster. It would be natural to assume that Lieutenant Graham N. Fitch, the torpedo room officer, was there as well as the enlisted crew under him. If Fitch was there that would be fortunate. All submarine officers received instruction in international Morse code.

The *S-8* started simply. They sent down a series of dashes and dots that explained all they needed to do was tap on the submarine and those sounds would be detected by the oscillator. Three taps meant *yes*, five taps *no*, and seven *I don't know*. The *S-8* then sent a message asking if they understood. In a few moments they heard three taps.

Now the rescue force had to pick its first message. At 5:00 PM the *S-8* asked:

Is the control room flooded?

TAP-TAP-TAP-TAP-TAP-TAP-TAP—they did not know.

Within minutes, a second question was composed and signaled down:

Is water in the torpedo room?

TAP-TAP-TAP—yes.

Are you in the torpedo room?

TAP-TAP-TAP

The torpedo room must have been damp, cold, and dark. The air was probably fetid. Any flashlights were used sparingly in order to save the charge. The only noise would be the odd creaking of the sea against the wreck and the alien signal of the Fessenden that flitted in and out.

Since the responses came so quickly, the rescue force assumed that it must have been Lieutenant Graham Fitch who was responding. It was time to have more nuanced communication.

---

[*]The communication record is unclear as to who composed the messages to the *S-4*. Ellsberg in his own memoirs recalls King dictating some of the messages. It seems most likely that it would be King and Saunders composing the messages since Brumby would have been unfamiliar with the specific questions to ask.

The *S-4*s torpedo room in happier times.
Naval History and Heritage Command, Photo Archives, NH-41842

The *Falcon* had finished its maneuvering. It sent word to the *S-8* that it would take over communications directly. The rescue ship took its own oscillator and hung it over the side. They sent a signal to Fitch to answer directly in code. Two knocks would stand for a dash, and one knock for a dot. After this was acknowledged by Fitch, the *Falcon* signaled:

Is there any gas?

No, but the air is bad. How long will you be now?

The *Falcon* did not respond to this query, but instead asked:

How many are there?

There are six. Please hurry.

• • •

Even while all ears were engrossed in the shadowy conversation with the *S-4*, the first bubbles began boiling at the surface. At first, there might have been a brief anticipation of a rising submarine. All the officers rushed to the stern to watch.

But there was no sign of the *S-4*.

It had been an hour since they first started blowing the ballast tanks.* The bubbles indicated that whatever air they were pumping into the *S-4* was escaping into the water. Saunders tested this by adjusting the *Falcon*'s air compressors, pushing in more air, then less. Brumby, King, Saunders, and Hartley could clearly see that whenever they adjusted the air pressure, it would change the amount of bubbles coming to the surface.

All the air they had been pumping into the submarine was now leaking out and water they had pushed out of the ballast tanks was not enough to raise the submarine. It was evident that the ballast tanks had been compromised, or more than one compartment had been flooded.

They needed another plan.

---

*Several later sources have indicated that they blasted the ballast tanks for a half hour. However, primary source evidence from naval hearings all corroborate that they blew the tanks for one hour.

16

"Tonight or Never"

THE FAILURE TO BLOW THE ballast tanks coincided with a renewal of wild weather. The thermometer dipped into the midtwenties and the uninhibited wind raced along the Atlantic shore. These conditions created unpredictable and deep swells that added to the misery of the rescue force. It was now after 6:00 PM and a cold wind was blowing across Cape Cod.

Admiral Brumby met with Saunders and King. They had to do something, and they had to do it now. Pessimistically, they supposed that some of the rearward compartments on the *S-4* had flooded. And even if they weren't flooded, there was no way to get to the men there in time to revive them. There was now absolutely no hope for any man who may have been in the control, engine, or motor rooms. But there were the men still trapped in the torpedo room. Brumby's officers advised that the only thing left to do was to get fresh air to the men in the torpedo room and hope the storm blew over.

The most expedient way to do this was to use the compartment air salvage line that they had eschewed hooking up before. For this to work, the line needed to be undamaged, the gag valve to the torpedo room open, and the gag valves in the flooded compartments shut. Brumby agreed to the plan. The question was which diver was going to do it.

Eadie and Carr were both used up and in recovery from their dives. The best practices of diving allowed for a forty-five-minute dive and a rest day before the next one. In Eadie's and Carr's cases, both men were below for well more than an hour, working in cold water conditions, and each had been brought up so quickly that he needed to be placed into the decompression chamber. The rescue mission could not expect more from them.

Fred Michels, like Eadie and Carr, was a veteran diver. Originally from St. George, Utah, his first major dive had been to the submarine *F-4*, which sank off Hawaii to a depth of more than three hundred feet.* He later received formal training and qualified as a deep sea diver in 1916. He was also on the *S-5* job and was one of the regular divers of the *S-51* salvage. Since then, Hartley had appointed Michels a diving instructor at Newport, and he often had charge of the divers when Hartley was absent. Michels was a competent and quiet man with a handsome face and lanky muscles who did his work in a diligent way. He was nicknamed "Whitey," apparently for his dirty blond hair, but was usually called "Mike."

Michels was not of the same caliber as Eadie, but he was equal in efficiency to Carr. What the rescue force really needed was another Eadie. However, a quick look at the roster of divers showed that there was no one else. At that moment, there were nine qualified divers aboard the *Falcon*. But being qualified simply meant passing the tests—which were under controlled conditions. It was only when a diver actually went to the bottom, did work, and safely returned that he was considered "proved."

Meanwhile, the *Falcon*'s skipper, Henry Hartley, had been on the stern, watching the bubbles from the useless ballast salvage hose gurgle on the surface. Hartley half expected the line to rip loose due to the precarious mooring he had established vis-à-vis the *Mallard*

---

*Divers on the *F-4* salvage often suffered nitrogen narcosis, or "rapture of the deep," in which the men, working at an unparalleled depth, imbibed a greater density of air. Most gases when breathed at greater densities result in a narcotic effect in which the victim seems drunk. In the case of overexposure to oxygen, or hyperoxia, called by divers "oxygen jag," men would be afflicted with acute euphoria, but it was also potentially deadly. Because of this risk and the long amounts of time needed to decompress divers from three hundred feet, men were only allowed to work on the *F-4* for ten minutes at a time.

Clockwise from top left: Fred Michels, Henry Hartley, Bill Carr, and Tom Eadie.
Courtesy of the Library of Congress, Papers of Ernest J. King

and *Lark*. The exercise was pointless, but the *Falcon* continued to blow the ballast tanks even after it was shown that it would not raise the *S-4*. To Hartley's mind, there was no chance that the *S-4* was going to surface. It was useless to send down more divers. It was too dangerous.

Then the towering figure of Captain Ernest King loomed. He said to Hartley, "I have just been in consultation with the admiral and Commander Saunders and have come back to see you."

Hartley did not immediately respond. So King continued.

"We have arrived at the conclusion that we must try to get air on the salvage lines to the compartments of the submarine," said King.

"It would be suicidal to send another diver down," replied Hartley.

"It is life or death," replied King.

Captain King then drew close, towering over the shorter lieutenant. "Hartley, we have got to get air on that boat."

"It can't be done," replied Hartley.

Then King asked questions about the available divers. Divers on the *Falcon* were divided into first, second, and third strings. Third-string divers could work alone on the bottom at simple jobs or they could act as a third man in a three-man team, standing by a hatch and tending a line while others, more experienced, entered the submarine. Second-string divers were more experienced and could be sent inside a submarine to do mechanical jobs, but no farther than the foot of a ladder. It was the first-stringers who could be sent deep inside a flooded submarine. For the work tonight—cold water diving in the dark while a storm was underway—they needed a first-string man. Michels was the only one left.

But Hartley was hesitant. King said, "If a diver is willing, we must try. This weather may last several days and shows all signs of growing worse. It's tonight or never in my opinion. See what you can do."

Hartley, almost seemingly against his will, was forced to agree with King. Hartley later noted in his recollections that there was only one thought in his head at that moment: "Keep the trapped men in the Torpedo Room alive until the weather moderated."

In the meantime, King went to the *Falcon's* wardroom, where Brumby was speaking with some of the other officers. King then explained what should be done and that Michels was the only proved man available. King added that Michels had a wife and children.

The admiral agreed but added, "Do not order him to go over."

This was a compassionate, yet ill-informed statement by the admiral. It was custom that any diver could refuse to go over. The occupation was much too hazardous. However, to men like Henry Hartley who knew navy divers, he was sure that if any of those men were asked, even the least experienced would have gone. Hartley recalled, "There is no class of people in the world who are more proud of their profession than navy divers. I have never known one to demur or offer an excuse; all he asks for is confidence in the men on the top side."

Meanwhile, at 6:43 PM, Captain King had a message sent on the Fessenden to the *S-4* to make sure that the men in the torpedo room opened the gag valve to the compartment salvage air line:

Compartment salvage air is being hooked up now.

The reply was eager.

Will you raise us soon?

There was no straightforward answer to this question. No, the *Falcon* could not raise the *S-4* any time soon. There was no physical way to do it without the pontoons (still en route). But telling the exact truth to the *S-4* would not do, so King replied:

We are doing everything possible.

• • •

Hartley maneuvered the *Falcon* back over the wreck and prepared for diving. It took about an hour for the ship to get positioned. By this time, the weather had deteriorated even further. No matter how hard Hartley tried to moor the ship to the *Mallard* and *Lark* there was no stability. All three vessels were yawing considerably. The *Mallard* and *Lark* swung their bows back and forth at right angles to their anchor chains. This in turn swung the stern of the *Falcon* back and forth. At one moment, the *Falcon* would be over the *S-4* and the divers' descending line slack, then in another moment the stern of the ship would pull away and the line would become taut. The men on deck were forced to slack out the descending line, just to maintain the connection.

As this was going on, King and Hartley summoned Fred Michels. It was Hartley, who knew Michels better than King, who opened the discussion. "Mike, we want to try to get air on the *S-4* compartment salvage line. Who would you recommend?"

Michels did not like the idea of sending anybody down much less having to choose somebody. But on the *S-51* job he had hooked up the same type of salvage line—it was just that now the conditions were frightfully different.

But somebody had to go, so Michels said, "Guess I better go myself; none of these other men have been down on a wreck to my knowledge. I don't say I could do it myself, but I will take a chance."

Captain King said to Michels, "It is a thousand-to-one shot. But if you are successful in hooking up the air hose it would do you and the men in the sub a lot of good."

Michels got ready.

Due to the wind and current, it was impossible for the *Falcon* to steady itself for diving so that Michels could go over on a leeward side—the side shielded against the wind. Instead, wind blew directly at the diving platform and encased Michels's diving suit and equipment with ice.

Michels needed to bring quite a lot of equipment with him. He had to work with multiple lines: the descending line that attached the *Falcon* to the submarine, his lifeline and air hose, a power cord that attached a 1,000-watt underwater lamp to the surface, and the air hose that he was to attach to the *S-4*'s compartment salvage valve. There must have been a grim determination on the part of all those present on deck. Gone were the smiles and laughter that often accompanied divers. Instead, the atmosphere would have been palpably humorless, with many thinking that this might be the last time they would see Mike.

Michels was lowered into the water at 7:49 PM, almost two hours after the failure of the ballast tanks had been discovered.

* * *

Michels grasped the descending line and slid down into the inky dark. His lamp emitted a faint radiance that only allowed for a few feet of visibility.

He slid down the line as the seconds spun by. Then, instead of the steel deck of the *S-4*, the heavy-clad diver's leaden boots plopped into mud. In seconds, Michels was up to his knees, then his waist in viscous ooze. There was seemingly no bottom. His lamp was engulfed in mud as well, extinguishing all light. Michels for his part guessed that he was buried in the sea floor, out of sight.

Michels's situation was caused indirectly by the weather. As the storm swung the stern of the *Falcon*, it yanked the diver's descending line. The line tenders on the *Falcon* paid out the line, giving it slack. As the ship swung back, the tenders would haul in the line—but it was impossible because of the storm to tell if they hauled in all they needed to. Even when the *Falcon* was in a normal position, the sea tugged at the line, and the up and down motion of the *Falcon* made it necessary to give more line lest the line rip clean off the *S-4*. As a result, a loop of slack had formed on the descending line. When Michels had gone over, he fell into the inadvertent loop, which hung over the *S-4*'s side, and into a trench of mud that was rent from the seafloor when the submarine crashed there.

Michels was stuck in that mud like it was quicksand. There was seemingly nothing he could do to extricate himself. Any step he took made him sink deeper. He called to the top with the telephone, but the tender could not understand him.

In a minute or two, Lieutenant Henry Hartley's voice came over Michels's receiver.

"What is it? What is the matter?"

"I am in the mud," said Michels. "Pick me up."

Hartley knew immediately what was wrong. They needed to pull out the slack from the descending line to land him on the submarine. He commanded men to seize the line. Up to thirteen pairs of hands grabbed hold and with a massive pull hauled the line. The line strained, and then loosened. Michels, holding the line and opening the intake valve to his suit to allow in more compressed air, flew through the cold water, and landed on the ruined deck of the *S-4*.

He played his light about him. He was near the breach of the submarine's gun, perhaps about twenty feet from where he needed to be, which was by the conning tower where the descending line had been made fast. He began to take up slack from his lines and move toward the conning tower.

Yet when the diving tenders pulled Michels free of the mud, the air hose he was to connect to the salvage valve had fouled in the wreckage. Michels turned to free it, but before he could do anything, a great tug came at his lifeline and air hose. He was pulled off his feet and fell, and his light flew in the other direction.

In a moment he slammed into something hard. His fallen lamp cast its beam at him. He was still on the deck, but all about him was torn metal. This was the superstructure of the *S-4*, swept off the hull. Michels saw a lost piece of the *Paulding*'s bow, with white painted pieces of its shrapnel embedded in the stricken submarine. He was in the cut made by the *Paulding*.

He only was able to observe this for a moment, since on the surface, the *Falcon* swung its stern again, which once more pulled Michels off his feet. Hartley at the top realized this and ordered that the *Falcon* pay out more slack on Michels's lines to rectify the situation.

After the last pull, Michels managed to get back his lamp. He just needed to free the air hose then get over to the valve attachment.

Then, on the surface the *Falcon* swung again, this time more directly over Michels. The tenders pulled in Michels's lines, but they did not pull in enough. A great loop of his lifeline and air hose fouled on either side of the submarine. There they became caught in projections of the wreckage.

Michels reported the situation and that he would attempt to clear himself. He set to work, crawling toward where his lines were trapped. In the meantime, the *Falcon* hauled in his line to try to help so there was no more slack that could foul.

Then, suddenly, Michels called for them to stop.

When the tenders pulled in the lines, it resulted in them tightening in the wreckage. Michels, knowing how sharp the jagged metal was, rightfully feared that if they pulled in any more the lifeline and air hose would sever. The *Falcon* stopped and gave more slack. In the meantime, Michels went to work on clearing the lines. He labored until he was exhausted. Then he stopped, rested, and began again.

• • •

Meanwhile, on the *Falcon*, Hartley paced the deck. Every so often, the telephone tender would check on the diver.

"Hello, Mike?"

"Mike OK!"

This happened on several occasions—the only thing that Michels would ask from the top was for more slack. Because of the weather conditions and his fouled lines, it was impossible to use traditional pull signals.

Hartley, for his part, would ask the tender, "Hear his air?"

"Yes. Good and strong."

This satisfied Hartley. He knew that Michels was getting air and that the telephone was working. The diver could contact them if needed. It was the *Falcon*'s practice to leave the diver alone, since to use the phone a diver necessarily had to adjust the air valves to reduce background noise—this interfered with his work.

Meanwhile, Michels's lamp line had become hopelessly fouled in the descending line. He abandoned it and worked in the dark. He then decided that despite the fouling, he was going to try to make the connection anyway. By this time, he had managed to somehow get himself close to the air connection. He even got the door to the valve open. But he could not quite reach the connection inside. To get to it, he needed to turn around and back into the space—no easy task when you were fighting fouling in a diving suit. He got in place, and was at last able to work on the valve gear.

Then his air hose became taut.

"Give me more slack."

But the slack never came.

"Give me more slack."

But the slack did not come.

Hartley had been giving him slack. Much more slack than he needed. In the dark water neither the diver nor the tenders could see that they were forming more loops about the wreckage. So every time Michels asked for more slack, he was adding more line to get tangled. Hartley suspected that too much slack was being given, and he ordered the tenders to haul back in as much as they dared—the last thing he wanted was to cut the lines on the wreckage, so they never pulled in the optimal amount.

Michels now realized that he was trapped. The intermediate sections of Michels's air and lifelines were being made into a noose. They were winding about his back. The salvage air hose would not reach or connect. He needed to abandon it and save himself.

It had been 45 minutes since he had first gone over the side of the *Falcon*.

Then the air coming into his diving helmet started to gust in and out in gasps. Something was wrong. Michels's air was being cut off. He crawled his way toward the side of the *S-4*, near the conning tower where the wreckage was less. There was nothing he could do alone in the cold, watery dark. The murderous web about him was caught in various bits of the wreck. He figured that he needed cutters so as to cut away some of the metal that his lines were trapped on.

It could not possibly get worse.

Then metal from the wreckage pierced Michels's suit. He began to shiver uncontrollably as ice water crept up to his neck. Dizziness fell upon him. In a fleeting thought, Michels realized that his mission was a failure. He needed to stand up. He needed to get up. He needed air. He needed warmth. He needed to escape. He thought that if Eadie were there he would see his circumstances and cut him out of it.

But Fred Michels could not even stand. All about him his own lines had created a web that grew tighter. At last, he was pinned, face forward, to the deck. He felt like he was pulled down, but the reality of it was that his lines were pushing him down. By some miracle, he kept his head upright enough to prevent water from coming into his helmet. After he was down, the weaving caused by the yawing *Falcon* continued.

In the meantime, on the *Falcon*, Hartley's anxiety grew apace. On deck, a rescue diver had been dressed, ready to go down. Hartley then ordered Michels's telephone man to contact him. The tender had some difficulty in doing this, but at last said to Hartley, "Mike says he is foul."

Hartley took the telephone himself.

"Mike," said Hartley. "This is the captain. How are you making out?"

"Not so good," said Michels.

Hartley knew that "not so good" from a veteran diver can be quite bad.

Hartley ordered him to go to the descending line so that he could be hauled up.

But Michels said he could not.

"What is the matter?" asked Hartley.

"I'm foul . . ." Michels's voice hissed out, barely comprehensible.

"Can you clear the line?"

"I can't."

"Where is it fouled? The starboard or port side?"

"Cut it . . ."

Hartley could not understand what he said—Michels had to run the air in his helmet continuously to keep the water down—the hiss was drowning out his voice. Hartley asked him to spell what he wanted—this was a common practice so that divers might be better understood. But all that came through was "U-T."

Again, repeated questions. Michels talked fast, but Hartley did not understand him. Michels seemed to have difficulty speaking.

"Did you say C-U-T-T?" asked Hartley.

"Yes."

"Are you cut?"

There was a stream of unintelligible words.

"Your suit is cut?"

"Yes."

"Can you clear yourself?" asked Hartley.

"No," said Michels. "Keep plenty of slack in my air hose, it's foul in the cut."

Finally—something Hartley could work with. Michels was foul—his line caught in the cut on the *S-4* made by the *Paulding*—his suit also was cut, and perhaps he also needed cutters to help get him out of the mess. He did spell out two *T*s.

"Keep still and conserve your strength," said Hartley. He wanted to encourage Michels, not panic him.

But Hartley was panicked himself. Not only did he have a diver in mortal jeopardy, but the storm even threatened to drag the *Falcon* off the site. The diver who had been dressed to relieve Michels would not do. Hartley needed a proven diver. He had to send his ace.

"I am going to send Eadie down to clear you," said Hartley.

"Send Eadie," said Michels. "Cutters. Eadie. Cutters."

17

Two Men Down

TOM EADIE WAS LYING ON his bunk in his underwear. He had been released from the decompression chamber and was now recovering from his dive. It was a little over five hours since he had been on the *S-4*, and he could not expect to dive again for another day at minimum. He soon fell asleep.

He was surprised to find Lieutenant Henry Hartley shaking him awake.

"Eadie," said Hartley. "Michels is fouled and badly fouled. Do you think you can go down again?"

Eadie, without a word, jumped down from his bunk, grabbed his diving woolens, and started dressing.

Hartley hurried topside.

On the deck, the bears were ready for Eadie when he emerged into the icy gale. The men started to dress him in his diving gear as the storm wildly tossed the *Falcon* up and down and side to side. Water sprayed the deck. The men quickly rigged a wide piece of canvas to shield Eadie so that he could stay dry.

Eadie specified that they dress him without the diving gloves. He knew that if Michels was fouled then he would need the full use of his hands to free him. To mitigate the cold somewhat, he rubbed grease on his hands and slid a pair of woolen mittens over them. At length, he was dressed in his diving outfit. The suit's bolts were tested and tightened. All was in working order. Eadie proceeded toward the diving stage. There the tenders performed last-minute second checks. But now the telephone would not work. Apparently, water had slopped into the helmet, knocking out the telephone.

As quickly as possible a new battery box, skullcap, earphones, and telephone cable were rigged. But it did not work. It seemed that the trouble was in the helmet itself. Since each helmet was individually fitted for each breastplate, Eadie would have to get almost completely undressed again.

"Put my bonnet* on," said Eadie. "I don't need a telephone. We can use hand pull signal."

Henry Hartley was tempted to agree. But one look over the *Falcon*'s railing was answer enough. "Not with this sea running."

After thirty minutes lost, Eadie was ready.

Hartley said to Eadie, "We are still talking with Mike, but we can't hear him very well. I can't make it out, but it seems to be cutters, wire cutters, so I am giving you a heavy pair of wire cutters."

The cutters were too large to fit in Eadie's tool bag so they strapped it on him. He was also given a hammer, an eight-inch cold chisel, and pincers. Hartley could not think of anything else to give Eadie except a 1,000-watt submersible lamp.

Eadie was helped to the diving stage. They lowered him in at 9:25 PM. Michels had been struggling on the bottom for one hour and thirty-six minutes. To descend, Hartley had Eadie clap on to Michels's lifeline and air hose instead of the descending line. This made sense, since Michels was the object of Eadie's mission, not the submarine.

This method of descent was against diving regulations. A diver, when descending, had a tendency to spiral down the line, thus risking fouling. If a diver fouled on another diver's line, and especially the air hose, it could jeopardize life. Hartley threw out the manual in this case since he needed to get Eadie directly to Michels as quickly as possible. To help prevent spiraling, Hartley had Eadie's

---

*Another word for the diver's helmet.

lines set 15 feet away from where Michels's lines were set on the deck of the *Falcon*.

As Eadie descended he felt the cold 34-degree sea squeeze him like a vise. He ruefully wished he had put on more than one pair of underwear—but he had been in such a rush that he had forgotten. To him, his hands felt submerged in pickled brine.

He turned his suit's intake valve to release air. He sank quickly from the *Falcon* and down into the dark.

The descent did not take long, and Eadie found himself once again on the broken deck of the *S-4*. He traced Michels's air hose and lifeline. It wove in and out on either side of the wreck like a tangled skein. There were about 175 feet of it on the deck alone. The wreck was only 106 feet from the surface.

Then he saw Michels.

He was lying prone just before the conning tower. Michels's face-plate was pressed against the submarine's deck. About him, his own lines wove a net that lashed repeatedly about his body. He was so tightly bound that Michels could not even reach the control valve for his air intake. To Eadie, this explained why Michels's messages were garbled since he was unable to reduce the background noise caused by the compressed air entering his helmet. It was just as well that the valve was open, otherwise Michels would already be dead.

Tom Eadie faced a Gordian knot that he dared not cut, since these were the threads that kept his friend alive.

"On the bottom," Eadie reported through his telephone. "Mike is here sitting down."

Eadie moved his lamp about. Michels, who was just a dim outline in the muddy water, indicated the wreckage. Eadie followed Michels's motion to the point of impact of the *Paulding* and *S-4*—the cut.

There was a piece of angle iron that was forged into a U-shape from the violence of the collision. One bight of Michels's lifeline was caught in it, and Eadie thought that this might be the point that if he could pull it out, would release the entire line. The point was located on the starboard side, down in the wreckage, but no more than within six feet of Michels. That, however, was not the only work to do since Michels's lines were fouled in the other direction among the wreckage.

Carefully, Eadie got over to the wreckage, following the lines. As he neared, he lost sight of the line, even with his lamp, due to the obscuring silt. So he reached forward and groped below the iron. There he found it.

Eadie grasped it, set a leaden foot on the iron, and he pulled with all his strength to slide it off the metal.

It would not move.

He then tried to pry apart the metal, but this too was impossible.

The topside telephoned down. They wanted an update.

"It's quite a mess here," said Eadie. "Don't bother me."

This was the foulest fouling Eadie had ever seen. Lengths of line were caught under other lengths of line. He needed to pick a place to cut into the wreckage to free it all. The only place he could see was the bight of the U-shaped iron. If he managed to cut through it, then Michels would be able to stand up. But he needed to cut iron, not wire. The requested wire cutters were useless.

"Send me a large hacksaw," said Eadie into his transmitter. It was just as well that he had come down with a functioning telephone. A diver can't ask for a hacksaw with pull signals.

* * *

On the *Falcon*, Hartley had been monitoring the telephone. When he had heard Eadie's request for a hacksaw, he was dismayed. Hartley could not imagine what it was that Eadie had to cut through that he did not have the appropriate tools for already. Hartley did not see much chance of getting Mike off the bottom.

Hartley went himself to the tool locker and took the largest hacksaw they had aboard. But he puzzled over how to send it down.

The safest way to send it was by the descending line. But Eadie was not near that line. Also, Hartley suspected that with all the fouling and slacking, it may prove impossible to send it that way. He phoned Eadie.

"Hold on tight and say when ready, we will haul taut your air hose and send down the saw on a screw shackle."

"All right," said Eadie.

This again was against regulations, since there should never be any possible obstruction attached to a diver's lifeline and air hose. But Hartley felt that they were taking chances as it were.

Hartley slid the hacksaw into the sea and waited.

"All right," said Eadie after a few minutes. He had gotten the tool.

Eadie passed his lamp over to Michels and put it in his hand. Eadie motioned for Michels to hold the light while he worked through the iron. Eadie then began the laborious process of sawing. This was difficult work in that the iron he had to saw was loosely wedged into the *S-4*. He needed both hands: one to steady the metal and the other to wield the hacksaw.

But in less than a minute, a bright flash of light flared directly into Eadie's eyes, blinding him. Michels had dropped the lamp, and its beam shot right into Eadie's face instead of the spot where he was sawing. Eadie grew angry.

He shook Michels and shouted, "Hold it there!" He indicated where Michels should point the lamp.

Eadie turned to work.

Michels dropped the lamp.

It was then that Eadie realized that Michels was delirious, probably due to exposure from water leaking into his suit.

Eadie took the lamp and put it by the *S-4*'s gun mount. He angled the light and got to work.

Eadie needed to go slow since he did not want to break the brittle blade of the saw. It would take too much time to send down a replacement. He alternated between sawing and hammering pieces of the iron, breaking them off. It was a miserable job.

Meanwhile, on the *Falcon*, Hartley listened to the sawing and hammering through the phone. At every pause of the sawing, Hartley worried that Eadie had broken the blade. At the same time, the mounting gale threatened to pull the *Falcon* off the submarine. Hartley later wrote that at this moment he thought, "Can we hang on with the *Falcon* until Michels is cleared?"

He telephoned Eadie.

"Are you all right?" Hartley asked.

"Yes," Eadie replied.

"Are you making progress?"

"Yes."

Hartley turned the telephone back over to Eadie's tender and grabbed the connection to Michels.

"Hello," said Hartley.

"Hello," replied Michels.

This went on, with Hartley adding encouraging words to a barely coherent Michels.

After forty-five minutes of work, Eadie got through the iron. Then he began to work at unraveling the lines, telephoning to the surface to take in all the excess line slowly. Soon enough, with Eadie's help, Michels staggered to his feet. He swayed, nearly unconscious.

There was a bit of line left to free on the port side of the *S-4*. Eadie gave his lifeline to Michels and said, "Hold my lifeline. I will go over the side and clear that."

Eadie went over the side, Michels holding the line and shining the lamp light for Eadie to see.

Then Michels suddenly dropped the line.

Eadie's feet slammed into the wreckage. But he was unhurt. There, he found Michels's air hose caught under a jagged piece of iron that would sever it before long. He got it loose in less than a minute. Then, he opened his air intake valve. Compressed air poured into his suit helping him pull himself upward. He climbed back up thinking about Michels's erratic behavior. "Something is wrong with Mike."

Then, Eadie felt ice water creep against his skin. Looking downward, he saw bubbles coming from a tear in the leg of his suit.

By the time Eadie got back to Michels, the water was up to his neck. But because of the compressed air coming into his helmet, the water, while soaking his underwear and socks, did not drown him. Eadie turned up his air to keep the water contained.

Eadie telephoned to the *Falcon*. "Take up slack on Mike's hose."

And the *Falcon*, fathom by fathom, hauled in Michels's line with Eadie interjecting instructions. Michels was at last free of the fouling.

Eadie then telephoned to the top, "Mike is clear. Take him first." He then asked the top to telephone Michels and have him follow Eadie to the descending line.

On the *Falcon*, Hartley ran over to Michels's phone and took it from the tender.

"Hello, Mike."

"Hello."

"We are taking you up."

"All right."

Meanwhile, Eadie approached the descending line. Then suddenly, he felt his feet leave the deck. The *Falcon* was hauling him up.

But Eadie would have none of it. Michels was to go first.

"Stop pulling me up," said Eadie in the telephone. "Haul in Mike."

"We aren't pulling you" was the answer.

Something was wrong. Eadie spun around, and right in front of his faceplate were Michels's leaden boots.

Michels's and Eadie's lines had fouled. As the *Falcon* hauled on Michels's line, they were also hauling up Eadie.

Eadie called for the top to give more slack on Michels's lines. Then Eadie seized Michels's shoes, pulled him down and tripped the helmet's spit cock to allow excess air to leave the suit and bring him down. Apparently, when Michels heard word that he was going to be hauled up, he turned up his air intake so that he could float upward.

Luckily, it was not a great fouling. They were only caught by one turn of the lines.

"Slack on Mike," Eadie telephoned.

Eadie then brought him under the lines and freed him. He then closed Michels's spit cock so that more air could enter his suit.

Eadie motioned to Michels to head toward the descending line. Eadie went ahead, then turned around. Michels had vanished.

A voice came through the receiver, "Are you ready to come up?"

Eadie took his lamp and spun it about.

"Where is Mike?" said Eadie. He feared his friend may have fallen off the submarine.

"Stand by to come up."

"Where is Mike?"

"He's all right. Are you ready to come up?"

"Yes, please haul me up," said Eadie.

Even if Eadie had told them he wanted to stay down, they wouldn't have let him anyway. The water was so cold.

* * *

After Hartley had heard Eadie ask, "Where is Mike?" there was nothing else to feel but dread. Then, Michels's tender shouted, "Mike is coming very light and fast."

"Take Mike in faster," said Hartley.

Michels's lines came up with no resistance. Normally it took at least two men to haul in a diver, sometimes four. Hartley noticed that one of the two men hauling on Michels's line said "move," meaning that he could handle it better alone. This was bad—it was a sign of a blowup. Michels, in his delirium, had opened his air intake valve too much.

"Run away with Mike's hose," cried Hartley.

Three or four men seized the line by the railing and ran down to the opposite side of the deck, hauling the slack line in as quickly as possible. Then, when they reached the opposite railing and could go no farther, another group of men grabbed the line from where the first group started and ran to the opposite side. The teams would relay back and forth as the hundreds of feet of line came up. There was no sign of Michels.

Then Tom Eadie broke the surface. His submersible lamp, still ignited, flashed across the roiling black sea. There, beside him, floated Fred Michels, spread eagle. The rescue force did not even see Michels until Eadie's light fell on him.

A diving stage slid over. Eadie climbed on and was hauled aboard the *Falcon*. Meanwhile, other men dragged Michels close to the ship's side and lifted his head out of the water to prevent drowning. Then a seaman named Burton leapt onto the stage, and immersed himself in water up to the neck. He pulled Michels onto the stage.

Michels's suit had stayed intact and not blown apart. If it had blown apart at the breastplate, as typically happened during a blowup,

Michels would have sunk to the bottom and drowned. Instead, his diving glove had burst off, which relieved much of the excess air pressure.

When they hauled him on deck, Michels's arms and legs were rigid. The weight of his helmet and belt caused him to fall over, incoherent. They got these off. Then they cut Michels's shoes loose. He had a severe case of the bends. There was only one thing that could save Michels now.

Men ran with him to the decompression chamber.

Eadie was already in the chamber, being attended to by the other divers, including Bill Carr. They had stripped Eadie's suit, and before they were done with him, Fred Michels was passed into the chamber.

Michels's eyes were rolled back, and he frothed at the mouth. The only sounds he made were gurgles. He was frozen stiff. His fists were clenched tight about his gloves. The men cut off Michels's clothes to his skin until he was naked. Michels's hands would not bend. Two men had to force them open to remove his gloves. Eadie later likened Michels to a "cold storage bird."

Eadie was worried, and he called through the voice tube to turn up the pressure to sixty pounds per square inch. The air had to be pressurized to force the nitrogen bubbles that had formed in Michels's blood back into solution before they could kill or paralyze him. Hartley, who was standing outside, gave the order to run up the pressure.

Michels had been on the bottom for approximately three hours and twenty minutes. Eadie was down for one hour and forty-five minutes rescuing Michels, in addition to his first dive of more than an hour. Admiral Brumby, who witnessed the whole affair, later wrote, "I have never known so fine an example of cold-blooded, deliberate heroism as that shown by Eadie."

The *Boston Daily Globe* reported, "The annals of the navy record no braver act, and when Eadie, his diving suit cut open from contact with the jagged edges of the *S-4* and filled with freezing water up to his helmet, finally rose through the sea, he had written his name in letters which blazed out brightly alongside a string of fighting men going back to John Paul Jones."

But there was no time for Eadie to reflect on what he did. He and the other three divers in the decompression chamber set to work on Michels. They massaged his muscles, wrapped him in blankets soaked with warm water; they beat the devil out of him in the hope that they could bring life back to their friend.

There were two medical officers in the rescue force, one on the *Bushnell* and another on the *Mallard*. The *Falcon* sent signals to the two ships in turn to send medical assistance. But the *Bushnell* couldn't get its motorboat started, and the *Mallard*'s boat swamped next to it in the gale.

In the meantime, the storm continued. Hartley lingered by the decompression chamber. But by midnight a message was sent to him by his executive officer, Edward Burnett. The *Mallard* was dragging its anchor and pulling the *Falcon* off the *S-4*.

"I recommend we cast off the lines to the *Lark* and *Mallard*. Order them to move clear," advised Burnett. "This will allow the *Falcon* to come head to wind and sea; otherwise all three ships will wind up in a huddle with foul anchors."

Hartley agreed. The *Falcon* cast loose. He then ordered the ship to detach itself from the *S-4*. They fixed buoys to the descending line and the air hose that had been attached to the ballast tanks to mark the spot.

There could be no more diving that night.

All hands were utterly exhausted. Admiral Brumby went to sleep in the cabin that he commandeered from Hartley. Captain King reclined in a large wicker chair with a footrest. Hartley found a transom seat in the mess deck.

Even as Hartley faded off to sleep, the officer of the deck found him. He reported that a Coast Guard boat was trying to come alongside. The weather could not permit the boat to get close enough to transfer personnel, but whoever was aboard insisted that he was to get on the *Falcon*, even if that meant jumping from ship to ship.

18

Inside the Iron Doctor

EDWARD ELLSBERG HURRIED DOWN TO the dock of the Boston Navy Yard. The stiff northwest wind sapped away the heat from his body despite his old overcoat. After getting his orders from Admiral Plunkett in New York, Ellsberg had headed by locomotive to Providence, from which he was going to be hustled by an automobile to Provincetown. However, word was soon passed to the navy that Lieutenant Commander Ellsberg was on his way—even those on the *Falcon* had heard he was coming. So Admiral Philip Andrews, commandant of the Boston Navy Yard, sent an itinerary change. Ellsberg was to stay on the train and go straight to Boston. The admiral apparently had a quicker way of getting him to the *Falcon*. For Ellsberg, it had been an exhausting journey—and it wasn't over yet.

Waiting for Ellsberg was the *Burrows*, a Coast Guard cutter of the same class as the *Paulding*. The ship, much like its sister, was a rumchaser destroyer that had been borrowed from the navy to enforce Prohibition. However, this night the ship was tasked to transport personnel, stores, and equipment to the *S-4* rescue force.

At the foot of the gangplank, Ellsberg encountered Captain Clayton Simmers, who managed the Boston Navy Yard. Simmers had been overseeing the loading of stores aboard the *Burrows*. After some perfunctory chat, he showed the list to Ellsberg and asked him if he had any suggestions.

Ellsberg scanned the list: woolen underwear, air hoses, weights, diving gear, and supplies of all kinds. It had almost everything one could wish for in an undersea rescue and salvage mission—except one.

Ellsberg wrote in a rather dramatized account that he said to Simmers, "This is December captain, and you're nearly frozen through just standing here. It'll be hell on a man diving in ice water out there in this weather. He'll need some medicine to thaw out when he comes up. Got any whiskey in the yard?"

But Simmers replied, "Not since Prohibition. Not even for medicine anymore."

Ellsberg then suggested grain alcohol. "We'll mix 'submarine cocktails' with it the way we used to on the *S-51*, after a cold dive—half a pint hot coffee, half a pint grain alcohol—marvelous how a pint of that mixture will unfreeze a cold diver, captain."

Simmers agreed to try to get a couple of cases out on the next shipment.

Ellsberg saluted and boarded the *Burrows*.

• • •

The *Burrows* left the shelter of Boston and headed southeast toward Cape Cod. As the ship slipped out of the harbor, the seas grew heavy. The cold northwest gale screamed across the vessel's deck. In Ellsberg's estimation, the *Burrows* made a speedy passage considering the conditions.

They arrived at Provincetown at about 2:00 AM on the morning of December 19. To Ellsberg's disappointment, the *Burrows* would not take him straight to the *Falcon*. It was too hazardous to attempt to transfer personnel. Instead, the *Burrows* would anchor inside Provincetown Harbor.

According to Ellsberg, the captain apologized. Ellsberg was no dissembler, and it was probably easy to see his frustration. But he would have to wait.

Edward Ellsberg was a brilliant naval architect, engineer, and accomplished salvage master, but being patient or understanding, especially in matters of life and death, was a different matter. He had traveled hundreds of miles to come to Provincetown, only to be stymied at the last moment by the weather. It would not do. These were Coast Guard men. In Ellsberg's estimation, they were supposed to go out under all conditions to rescue ships. He demanded to see the officer in charge of the force that the *Burrows* was attached to.

Ellsberg took a cutter to the *Tampa*. There he met a Coast Guard captain named Harry G. Hamlet, a lean man with white hair, a cleft chin, and a soulful glance. He was, in fact, the officer who was in charge of reconditioning the twenty navy destroyers that became Coast Guard rum-chasers. Now he was the force's commanding officer.

According to Ellsberg, he was polite but firm to Hamlet. "I have to get aboard the *Falcon*, and I have to get aboard now."

Hamlet was not about to let any of his boats or men destroy themselves in that wild sea. Hamlet apologized, but just like the captain of the *Burrows*, told Ellsberg that they couldn't take him to the *Falcon* due to the weather.

Ellsberg later wrote that he thought it was bitterly ironic that the Coast Guard, whose ship rammed the *S-4*, was not doing everything in its power to set things right. He persisted and requested a motor lifeboat to take him to the *Falcon*.

Before Hamlet could refuse the indefatigable Ellsberg again, a radio message came in from the *Falcon*. They had a man who was in a bad way. They needed a doctor.

It seems that this final bit of news moved Hamlet to agree. Also, by this time Ellsberg was accompanied by an expert in decompression work named Carrig who had worked with him on the *S-51*. His presence may have been a deciding factor in Hamlet's decision.[*]

---

[*]Ellsberg had written about his experiences concerning the *S-4* several times, and the only mention of "Carrig" (possibly misspelled) is in his testimony before a Naval Court of Inquiry. Because the Court of Inquiry happened within a month of the *S-4* collision, it is certain that this is the best source. In Ellsberg's other accounts, it is implied that he traveled alone.

Hamlet gave the order to find a coxswain who could transport Ellsberg to the *Falcon* by a motor lifeboat.* In the meantime, Ellsberg had some coffee with the captain. Ellsberg then mentioned his conversation with Simmers at the Boston Navy Yard. According to Ellsberg, this exchange occurred:

"I tried to get some whiskey as I came through the Boston Yard for the divers out here," said Ellsberg, "but whiskey's not on their books any more, and the best they could do for me is some grain alcohol they're sending out today."

Hamlet replied, "Well, you've come to the right place for that. There's something at least I can help you fellows on and no argument. My district base is loaded down with Scotch we've taken from captured rum-runners, and I can honestly assure you it's the genuine stuff, right off the boat."

The promised whiskey took the edge off Ellsberg's anger as he mused over the situation. He later wrote, "Queer things happened under Prohibition. The *Paulding*, a Coast Guard rum-chaser, had sunk the *S-4* (though apparently through no fault of hers); now the Coast Guard was going to supply some captured rum for the divers working on the ship they sank."

The coxswain who was to transport Ellsberg entered the cabin. A small man in an oversized pea coat, he had no idea why he was called. Once he found out, he protested that it would be impossible to land Ellsberg and his companion on the *Falcon* because the sea would smash the motorboat to bits as he tried to lay it next to the larger ship.

But Ellsberg would not take no for an answer. He convinced the coxswain by telling him that they didn't need to get right alongside of the *Falcon* but near enough to size up the situation.

---

*In Ellsberg's account, he wrote that Captain Hamlet asked for Boatswain Gracie, who was unavailable due to overwork. Also in that account, Ellsberg wrote that they took Gracie's own motorboat. It is unlikely that Hamlet would specifically ask for Gracie in this kind of situation, and it is likely that it was added for dramatic effect—something that Ellsberg, as an author, excelled at.

Shortly thereafter, Ellsberg found himself in the cold again, this time on a motorboat. Conditions had not improved. A fine, glistening sheath of ice encased the surfboat and its riders.

Soon enough, the lights of the *Falcon* twinkled off Wood End. Ellsberg saw the great roll of the sea as waves smashed against the *Falcon*'s steel hull. The salvage and rescue ship strained at its anchor chains. To Ellsberg's mind, the *Falcon* was doing far worse than if it were free of the anchors.

Ellsberg's boat cleared the *Falcon* well away of the bow, the coxswain not daring to come closer. Then they passed the starboard side. Ellsberg watched the *Falcon* carefully to see if there was any break in the weather that would allow the boat to draw close enough to the ship to let him board. He was looking for the leeward side, where the wind broke over the *Falcon*.

But he saw no lee. Nor did he see a way to get close on the port side.

Ellsberg knew that the coxswain was correct. There was no way to bring the small motorboat close to the ship without it being smashed.

But he was still determined to get aboard.

Ellsberg wrote that this exchange occurred:

"No use!" cried the coxswain over the storm. "It's like I told you. Can't make it. I'm going back!"

"Not yet!" yelled Ellsberg. "Circle her again! We may get a lull in the gale!"

And the coxswain, despite his misgivings, rounded the *Falcon* again slowly. But there was no improvement.

Ellsberg noticed that the deck was empty, and no other ship was near the *Falcon*. Ellsberg knew that there could be no diving in these conditions, but he had an odd feeling, perhaps compounded by the news that the *Falcon* needed a medical man. This lit his already incessant desire to get aboard the *Falcon* and see his old shipmates.

They rounded the *Falcon* again and came as close as they could. Ellsberg wrote that he gave an order to the coxswain.

"Pass her as close aboard as you dare without staving in your boat, and I'll jump for it on the fly!"

The boatswain was incredulous, but he came around the port side again—perhaps he just wanted to get rid of his mad passenger. Then,

Ellsberg climbed to the gunwale. The wind blew in his face as the boat piloted in to about eight feet. Ellsberg looked ahead. The *Falcon*'s side loomed over him like a moving cliff. Up and down, at times higher than the motorboat, at times lower than it, and for an instant, even with it. The ice on the railing gleamed. There was no grip there. He would need to clear it. As the *Falcon* dipped into a trough the lifeboat came level.

Ellsberg jumped. His arms were stretched out as he landed on his stomach in a sprawl. He slid on the icy deck, skidding across before coming to a stop. Carrig followed.

Then a moment later, bags followed with a thud, heaved across by the lifeboat's engineer.

The boat sped off, heading back to Provincetown Harbor.

Ellsberg clambered to his feet and gave a shout of thanks to the distant coxswain.

• • •

It was the quartermaster, hastening down from the *Falcon*'s chart house, who first greeted Ellsberg. They knew each other from the *S-51*. Ellsberg wrote that this exchange occurred:

"Where's Hartley?" asked Ellsberg.

"Turned in, sir," replied the quartermaster.

Ellsberg then inquired about other officers he knew from the *Falcon*.

At last the quartermaster said, "I tell you, Commander, we're all dead on this ship from what we've been through all day long in this storm, and now that we can't dive, everybody has turned in. We're at anchor, and I am simply the anchor watch."

"All right," said Ellsberg. "What's going on?"

"Well, the only thing that's going on is we've got some divers that were tangled down below in the recompression tank."

The quartermaster then told Ellsberg the story of Michels and how, after being pulled up to the surface, was thrust in the tank. "It looks bad for Mike," said the quartermaster.

Ellsberg headed to the decompression chamber and opened the first round door that took him into the iron doctor's antechamber. He was shut in, then he turned on a valve that released compressed air. Because of the mechanics of compression, the air was warm— Ellsberg thought it hot enough that he removed his overcoat, hat, and mittens. The design of the chamber was such that the door to the interior compartment would only open when the pressure of the antechamber was nearly equal with it. This was to prevent compressed air from escaping the inside. Occasionally, Ellsberg would impatiently test the inner door, which would not budge until the pressure equalized.

Finally the door opened and Ellsberg peered within. Ellsberg later wrote:

> My heart sank at what I saw. On the deck, naked, stiff, unconscious, lay Fred Michels whom last I had parted from long months before at the Navy Yard in New York. Working over him, one on each side, chafing his muscles, rubbing him with hot towels, were Tom Eadie and Bill Carr, striving desperately to bring him to.

Ellsberg knelt beside the divers, who offered no verbal recognition that their old commander had returned. In dribs and drabs Ellsberg learned what had happened. Michels's fouling, Eadie's incredible rescue, and how, with a foaming mouth and eyes rolled back, Michels had to be cut from his suit. The divers had found him as stiff as a board and had been working on him for more than two hours. They had tried to give him something to drink, but his teeth were clenched. It was only a few minutes before Ellsberg arrived, at 3:30 AM, that they had managed to get a hot drink down his throat.

Ellsberg studied Michels, looking at his pale, still face.

Then, suddenly, Fred Michels's eyes fluttered open.

"Why, hello, Mr. Ellsberg!" Michels said. "What are you doing here?"

19

The Six

EVEN AFTER THE IRON DOCTOR had been fully decompressed, Henry Hartley would not allow Fred Michels to leave the chamber. While the great danger of Michels being killed by the bends had passed, it was feared that due to his prolonged exposure to the cold seawater, he would contract pneumonia or double pneumonia. The recompression chamber was warm, moist, and offered the safest haven aboard the *Falcon* for Michels. As for Tom Eadie, he showed no adverse effects from his double dive. He was released and resumed his normal activities. In fact, his heart problem had seemed to disappear. He later wrote, "There was no fluttering, no getting all haired up when I started to do anything, and I was inwardly very much tickled by my ability to go on working."

After Michels and Eadie were brought to the surface, communication resumed with the *S-4* vis-à-vis the Fessenden. At 11:31 PM on December 18, the *Falcon* messaged:

Is water still coming in?

Their response: *Slow. Hurry.*

Thirty-one minutes later the *Falcon* sent another message:

We are working as fast as possible. Have you light?

We have no light. The air is very bad.

By then, the *Falcon* had broken from its moorings to the *Lark* and *Mallard*. Diving could not continue.

But now with the *Falcon* wildly riding its own anchors, all the rescue force could do was get as much information from the *S-4* as possible. Otherwise, the *Falcon* was helpless and hapless.

At 12:50 AM on the morning of December 19, the *Falcon* asked:

Can you tell us the names of those with you?

Names are Fitch, Short, Crabb, Pelnar, Snizek, Stevens.

This information confirmed the earlier suspicion that it was the twenty-five-year-old Lieutenant Graham Fitch who had been tapping out the messages. The other five were enlisted men.

Robert Leslie Short, torpedoman first class, was originally from Boonville, Missouri. He was an eight-year submarine veteran. Aside from serving on numerous other submarines, the thirty-four-year-old had been on the *S-4* since 1923.

Russell Archibald Crabb, quartermaster first class, was also a veteran with nearly six years of submarine experience. He had been aboard the *S-4* since 1925. Like Fitch, Crabb had recently wed. His wife lived in Fall River, Massachusetts. They had no children.

George Pelnar was a new recruit, having enlisted on February 10, 1927, as an apprentice seaman. The twenty-one-year-old was from Omaha, Nebraska. After going through the necessary training of submarine service, he joined the *S-4* as his first assignment on December 1.

In keeping with the pattern of newlyweds aboard the *S-4*, Frank Snizek, torpedoman second class, had just married in September. He met his wife, Eleanor, in June when the *S-4* had stopped at her hometown of Bridgeport, Connecticut. He had just returned from his honeymoon and had taken up the habit of writing to his wife twice a day. Snizek made sure to get to Bridgeport at least once every two weeks even though he himself was from Ridgefield Park, New Jersey. After enlisting in the navy in 1919 Snizek qualified for submarine service in 1922. Even though he was new to the *S-4*—he had joined the boat in June 1927—he had accumulated a record of over nine years serving on various submarines.

Seaman Joseph Leighton Stevens was from Providence, Rhode Island. He had enlisted in the navy in 1923 but had only been aboard the *S-4* since 1926, when he had qualified for service. The *S-4* was the only submarine he had ever served on.

Admiral Brumby's most immediate concern was trying to figure out how to get air into the torpedo room once the weather eased. It was clear that raising the *S-4* immediately was impossible. With the storm blowing as hard as it was, there was some time to lay plans. The immediate thought was to hook up the compartment salvage air line again, the one that Michels had failed to connect.

Since the air compartment salvage line sends air to all the compartments of the submarine, the men inside a compartment just needed to open a gag valve to allow the air to come in. The real danger to the plan was if the line itself was compromised. The men alive in the *S-4* could solve this riddle for the rescue force by opening the gag valve in the torpedo room. At 1:30 AM on Monday the 19th, the *Falcon* sent a message to Fitch.

Have you tried removing gag from compartment salvage air line?

The response: *Salvage air line is flooded.*

This meant that, according to Fitch, even had Michels been successful, the plan wouldn't have succeeded.

There was no more conversation between the *Falcon* and the *S-4* for the rest of the night. But this did not mean that the rescue force was idle. Knowing that the compartment salvage line had been compromised, Ellsberg, Saunders, and the other officers studied the plans of the *S-4* to formulate some sort of way to renew the air in the torpedo room.

On the morning of December 19, the ferocious and ceaseless gale only showed signs of strengthening. At 6:09 AM, a new message was sent down to the *S-4*: *How deep is water in compartment?*

The answer: *Water is eighteen inches deep. Air is very bad.*

Eighteen inches of freezing seawater in the compartment would have made conditions in the torpedo room almost intolerable. But as for the air—the *Falcon* knew that the six men were running out of breathable air, but it also meant that Fitch had broken into some of the compressed air that launched the *S-4*'s torpedoes. While breathable, it was an oily, fetid air.

Meanwhile, on the *Falcon*, Lieutenant Henry Hartley went to Brumby and reported on Michels's condition. He asserted that he should be taken to a hospital as soon as possible.

This immediately started a discussion between the officers of the rescue force as to how to get Michels to a hospital. They could not transfer him to another vessel—it was too dangerous—the way

Ellsberg boarded the *Falcon* proved that. Also, the *Falcon* was the only ship present with a decompression chamber. The *Falcon* could take Michels directly to the navy hospital in Boston, but this would necessarily remove the ship from the scene.

Brumby was reluctant to leave, but Hartley argued that the barometer was still falling, the gale from the northwest strong, and the sea heavy. Diving was not possible. Hartley said, "We could get to Boston and back long before we could possibly do any work." They could have an ambulance waiting for them at the dock.

Brumby made his decision, keenly aware that whatever choice he made would be amplified by the newspapers. At 6:29 AM, he dictated a message for the Navy Department:

> BLOWING COMPARTMENT SALVAGE AIR LINE OF NO USE AS TEST OPEN-
> ING OF GAG VALVE IN TORPEDO ROOM LET WATER ENTER COMPART-
> MENT AND SHOWS LINE OPEN ELSEWHERE IN BOAT. CONTINUOUS
> BLOWING TANKS SALVAGE AIR LINE HAS BROUGHT LARGE QUANTI-
> TIES AIR BUBBLES TO SURFACE SHOWING AT LEAST ONE MAIN BAL-
> LAST TANK UNWATERED AND BLOWING OF NO VALUE. SEA ENTIRELY
> TOO ROUGH FOR DIVING AND GETTING WORSE. [ON] ACCOUNT [OF]
> VERY SERIOUS CONDITION [OF] DIVER MICHELS *FALCON* PROCEED-
> ING TO BOSTON TO LAND HIM [AT THE] NAVAL HOSPITAL AS IT IS
> IMPRACTICAL TO TRANSFER HIM TO ANOTHER VESSEL. *FALCON* WILL
> RETURN TO PROVINCETOWN IMMEDIATELY. COMMANDER STROTHER
> CMD TWELVE IN *BUSHNELL* WITH *LARK* AND *MALLARD* REMAIN.

Then the *Falcon* sailed for Boston, leaving behind the other ships of the rescue force with only the buoys of the descending line, and the air hose to the ballast salvage line showing where the *S-4* lay. The *Falcon* arrived in Boston at 12:10 PM. Michels was taken on a stretcher to a waiting ambulance then rushed to the Chelsea Naval Hospital. Photographers snapped pictures, and reporters asked questions. Meanwhile, Tom Eadie left the *Falcon* to send a telegram to Michels's wife telling her that he would be all right and not to worry.

And she shouldn't have—Fred Michels recovered rapidly—by the evening of December 20, Michels had eaten three good meals and told reporters, "I am feeling perfectly fine tonight."

20

"It's Terrible, It's Terrible"

ON MONDAY, DECEMBER 19, THE US Senate came into session with a prayer led by the chaplain Z. E. Barney T. Philips:

> Save, we beseech Thee, the valiant sons of this nation imperiled in the great deep for Thy paths are in the great waters and even there shall Thy hand lead them. Enfold in thine arms of love and mercy their loved ones and by the sacrament of our sorrowing sympathy bring us all to a deeper knowledge and understanding of the mystery of Thine infinite love.

Across the country, newspapers screamed headlines of the harrowing story of the six men trapped alive within the *S-4*.

6 MEN ALIVE IN SUNKEN SUBMARINE *S-4*; TAPS ASK RESCUE CREWS TO HURRY—*Washington Post*

SIX MEN FOUND ALIVE IN TORPEDO ROOM OF SUNKEN *S-4*; TAP PATHETIC PLEA 'HOW LONG WILL YOU BE?' TO DIVER; NAVY BATTLES AGAINST TIME TO LIFT SHATTERED CRAFT—*New York Times*

HURRY, PLEAD SIX ALIVE IN SUNKEN SUBMARINE *S-4*—*Chicago Tribune*

"PLEASE HURRY!" BEG SIX MEN ALIVE IN *S-4* BUT WRECK CANNOT BE RAISED FOR 48 HOURS—*Boston Daily Globe*

Six Men Found Alive in Sub *S-4* By Divers; Trapped Sailors
Urge Rescuers to Hurry—*Hartford Courant*

Provincetown had been in its off-season. Now the sleepy village
found itself besieged by reporters and other outsiders. Many of the
local residents gathered by the cold seaside watching the rescue force
just outside the harbor around Long Point. The Coast Guard boats
zoomed to and fro, carrying men and messages. The streets themselves were beset with out-of-town cars ranging from beat-up Fords carrying the curious to more high-end automobiles taxiing officers who
sat in the rear seat. As a December 19 *New York Times* article reported,
"The townsfolk, those who did not have rooms to let or boats to hire,
lounged on the sidewalks and watched the undue activity as though it
were some kind of show staged for their especial benefit."

The two lunchrooms and one restaurant that were open over-
flowed with patrons. Shops that sold woolen caps, shirts, and wind-
breakers were soon out of stock, forcing the proprietors to send for
more from Plymouth and Boston. The only hotel in town that was
open for business had only floor space left for reporters to sleep
on. Private homes opened their doors, but prices rose steeply as the
demand for a room, or even a floor, grew. To solve the space problem,
John Edwards, chairman of the Provincetown Board of Selectmen,
opened the town's large caucus room in Town Hall for reporters to
use. It soon became inundated with the staccato rhythm of typewrit-
ers, the sight of piles of discarded copy paper, and the heady smell of
tobacco smoke. Bunks were set up so the newsmen could sleep there.

The Coast Guard station in Provincetown became a gathering
point for reporters. But instead of finding Coast Guard personnel,
reporters only found a single watcher and a cook who worked overtime to provide meals for the reporters—all the others were involved
with rescue operations.

Provincetown resident Mary Heaton Vorse later wrote:

The news ran like fire through the town. The sinking of the *S-4*
blotted out all other interests. There was no one who could think
of anything else. It was as if we ourselves were imprisoned below
decks with those men. There was no consciousness of anything

else in the town except those men under the water. We had never seen them. We did not know them, but they were there with us, in the room with us. Our own living and dying stopped. We lived, all of us, with the imprisoned men. The town had formed itself into a formidable mass that was like a prayer for help.

As for the reporters, what they wanted most was to get aboard the *Falcon*. After the tense encounter on the afternoon of December 18, the navy brokered a deal with the press to allow a committee of reporters aboard the *Falcon*. Ernest King in his memoirs recalled two: one from the Associated Press and the other, a George C. McGuiggan from the *Boston Post*. McGuiggan ended up hitting it off with King, who later wrote, "McGuiggan told King something of his life as a reporter, including the experience of being ordered by his editor over the telephone during a Connecticut River flood to cross the river, when there was no means of doing so, if he wanted to keep his job. Thus King began to understand that reporters had their troubles too."

There were, however, more than these two newsmen since both of these reporters came with photographers. Also, newspaper articles show that reporter Joseph S. Ward Jr. from the *Boston Daily Globe* was aboard the ship.

It was hard for the crew aboard the *Falcon* to treat the reporters with civility. By this time, misinformation was getting into the newspapers. Tom Eadie later recalled:

> We read those newspaper articles out on the job, and we couldn't even recognize from them the job we were on. Carr said, "Gee, Tom, from now on I won't even believe the baseball scores!" Even after the committee was assigned, it was hard to treat them right. But those who were assigned proved themselves to be real men, and there was nothing that they wanted to see or know about that officer or man wouldn't explain to them. They ate and slept with us, had the freedom of the ship, and saw everything that was going on. We did feel badly, though, to see those stories, knowing what we ourselves were putting into it and realizing as nobody else could the conditions we were fighting against.

The fact that only a limited number of representatives from the press were allowed aboard had the unintended consequence of outraging the newspapers that were barred from the *Falcon*. On December 19 at 5:05 AM, Curtis Wilbur, the secretary of the navy, received this telegram:

RESPECTFULLY PROTEST METHOD BEING PURSUED BY OFFICERS IN CHARGE AT PROVINCETOWN IN DEALING WITH THE PRESS. ONE NEWS ASSOCIATION AND ONE NEWSPAPER HAVE MEN ON BOARD ADMIRAL BRUMBY'S OPERATING SHIP. OUR REPRESENTATIVE OR OTHER PRESS REPRESENTATIVES ARE NOT EVEN ALLOWED TO BOARD VESSEL. JUNIOR NAVAL OFFICER ASSIGNED TO CONTACT WITH PRESS CONSTANTLY CLAIMING ALL DAY HE HAD NO NEWS TO GIVE OUT. THIS SITUATION CAUSING DUPLICATION OF EFFORT AND LONG DELAY IN GETTING NEWS TO PAPERS. I KNOW YOU WILL WANT TO CORRECT A SITUATION WHICH PREVENTS FACILITATION OF NEWS AT SUCH A TIME.

RESPECTFULLY,

LEE ETTELSON

MANAGING EDITOR, *NEW YORK AMERICAN*

The submarine *S-4* was one of the year's biggest stories, right up there with Charles Lindbergh's transatlantic flight and Babe Ruth's sixty-home-run season. International newspapers were covering the story. The secretary of the navy was kept busy replying to messages of sympathy from Japan, the United Kingdom, Italy, and other countries.

Indeed, the reporters on the ground at Provincetown had been enduring enormous pressure from editors in their home offices to get as many details about the story as possible. One small plane with two men in it crashed into a marsh at the west end of Provincetown on December 23 while attempting to snap aerial photographs of the scene. The newsmen survived, but as to their photographs, that is unknown.

The radio station WEEI provided extensive coverage of the incident. "There were broadcasts at 7:20, 9, 10:30, 11, and 11:30. . . . To provide for the late broadcasts, Station WEEI operated one hour overtime." National radio covered the event as well. Thirty radio stations of the National Broadcasting Company's red and blue networks suspended broadcasting for one minute at 10:30 PM on the night of December 19 for a silent minute of prayer. It was through WEEI that the wife of the engineering officer, Donald Weller, found out about the collision. After hearing the news, Marion Weller felt there was no hope for the men of the *S-4*.

Soon a large segment of the press developed the attitude that if the navy was going to be cheap with the information it gave out, then reporters were going to go their own way. Newsmen sought to hire fishing boats. Many local fishermen would not charter their boats, fearing the storm. Those who did charged high prices. One group of reporters noted that fishermen charged between fifteen dollars and thirty-five dollars per man to get to the scene.[*] Those reporters who did get out on a boat soon learned about the weather conditions as they left Provincetown Harbor. "A photographer who went out in one of the smaller craft poised his camera just as a wave slapped the side of the boat. His picture, if he snapped the shutter, was of a pair of feet rising in an arc toward the sky."

One photograph, found in the papers of Ernest J. King, has an image of two fishing boats full of reporters approaching the *Falcon*. The image, which had been sent to King by a friend, had written on it: "Dear Capt. King, I suppose you will recall these 2 'pest' press boats readily enough." Brumby, King, and the other men of the *Falcon* viewed the press more as a hindrance than a help.

It is likely, based on King's character, that it was he who was the primary officer pushing to limit reporters on the scene. Reporter Joseph S. Ward Jr. summarized the feeling. "The newspapermen, who were paying many hundreds of dollars a day for boat hire, in an attempt to pick up scraps of information for the millions of American people whom they represented, were made to feel as though they were interlopers in a private affair, taking a peculiar glee in hampering the work wherever possible."

Even so, the navy should be given credit for providing the information it did, specifically to the relatives of the *S-4*'s officers and crew.

---

[*]This equates to roughly two hundred to five hundred dollars in 2015 dollars.

Reporters hired fishing boats to attempt to cover the story of the *S-4*, much to the annoyance of the navy. *Courtesy of the Library of Congress, Papers of Ernest J. King*

The department had sent telegrams to the nearest kin of each man at around 7:00 PM on the night of December 17, only a few hours after the submarine went down. The messages sent were form letters, such as the one to Lieutenant Commander Roy Jones's wife, Evelyn:

SUBMARINE S FOUR SUNK OFF PROVINCETOWN MASSACHUSETTS AT THREE THIRTY PM DECEMBER SEVENTEENTH. NO RECOVERIES HAVE BEEN REPORTED. LAST REPORT TO NAVY DEPARTMENT INDICATES YOUR HUSBAND LIEUT COMDR ROY K JONES WAS ON BOARD. YOU WILL BE FURTHER ADVISED.

Jones's family became a center of media attention. Reporters tried to visit Evelyn, who was so overcome with shock that one newspaper reported that a doctor administered "restoratives" to her. Newsmen found also Jones's father, John, who said, "It is hard to hope. The chances seem slight. Roy might have resigned after the war, but he thought he owed the government more service for his training at the Naval Academy. He thought his duty was to stay in the service rather than take an outside position."

News of Frank Snizek, one of the six in the torpedo room, only reached his recent bride, Eleanor, when a friend, who had seen Frank's name on a list, found her leaving mass at a church in Bridgeport, Connecticut. Eleanor was so overcome with grief that she ran through the streets hysterical. After she composed herself she revealed that in her husband's last letter he told her "to give up her job and he would meet her Dec 23 to take her to the home of his parents [in Ridgefield, New Jersey] where they were to visit over Christmas."

"It's terrible, it's terrible," Eleanor Snizek sobbed.

Brooklyn Eagle reporters found Joseph Galvin, the brother of Daniel Galvin, an apprentice seaman on the *S-4*. Joseph had been calling the Brooklyn Navy Yard repeatedly and running out for newspapers any chance he could. The brothers were close, both being orphans. Joseph told reporters that Daniel had gotten a position at a banking house on Wall Street, but found it dull. He enlisted in the service, writing to his brother, "I wouldn't give up the thrill of the navy for the best job in New York." Joseph's landlady said, "Joe's heart's broken over it."

Reporters also found Roger L. Braley, a former member of the *S-4*. He said to reporters, "I don't think there is a chance unless they can reach the trapped men very soon. It must be terribly cold down there and then, too, it is safe to say that the prisoners have nothing to eat."

The *Brooklyn Eagle* opined on December 19:

Judging from past experience, the chance of raising the vessel before life on board has been snuffed out is remote. The navy seems to be somewhat lacking in resourcefulness when it comes to such work. The operation of submarines is always extrahazardous, but when a vessel is making tests, as the *S-4* was doing at the time she was sent down, it would seem that some measure of preparedness for such an emergency as has so frequently developed might have been taken.

Others were more sanguine about the trapped men of the *S-4*. The *Chicago Tribune* interviewed Rupert Calcott, the brother of second-class fireman Charles B. Calcott, nicknamed "Lucky Kelly." His brother, who was confident that the crew would be saved, said, "Once he was with the submarine *S-7* when the crew was imprisoned underwater after the craft sank off Goat Island in the Pacific Ocean. He was rescued after several hours. Another time he had the same experience and I'm sure by this time he has become accustomed to the ordeal and is not worrying much."

Some blamed Prohibition for causing the accident. Lieutenant Walter J. MacGregor, the commanding officer of the Nineteenth Division of the Fifth Naval Militia in Hartford, said that the ships turned over to the Coast Guard as rum-chasers cruised indiscriminately along the New England shore. MacGregor said, "It is customary when a submarine is sent out on a trial trip, as was the case with the *S-4*, that the craft steer a course which will not conflict with any of the routes of ships of the merchant marine which are known and recorded. But these prohibition patrol boats go when and where and how they please, and the navy never knows when to expect one of them."

As critical as some were of the Coast Guard, there was more reproach for the navy—and this attitude was growing. Some reporters seeded the impression that the navy simply did not know what to do. When it became known that the compartment air salvage line was evidently broken, there was no lack of such opinions. Reginald Norman, a member of the Navy League and from Newport, Rhode Island, sent a telegram to the Navy Department:

AFTER THE *S-51* DEBACLE AN ORDINARY CITIZEN WOULD EXPECT HIS GOVERNMENT TO MAKE THE NECESSARY APPROPRIATIONS TO AID IN A SIMILAR ACCIDENT. INSTEAD UNITED STATES NAVY DESTROYERS ARE TURNED OVER TO EVIDENTLY INCOMPETENT PERSONS WHO RUN DOWN A NAVY SUBMARINE AND NO PROVISIONS SINCE THIS FORMER DISASTER HAVE EVIDENTLY BEEN CONSIDERED, DEVISED, OR PREPARED FOR IMMEDIATE RESCUE OF THE MEN WHO HAVE GIVEN THEIR SERVICES AND LIVES TO THE UNITED STATES GOVERNMENT.

The Associated Press interviewed Commander Kenneth Whiting, executive officer of the *Saratoga*, who said that the men could escape by exiting through the torpedo tube. Whiting claimed to have done it himself when his submarine was stuck on the bottom in 1909. "With the *S-4* on the bottom on an even keel . . . torpedoes might be ejected from the tubes to permit men to shoot to the surface.* All but one man could escape. He would have to remain behind to manipulate water and air valves." Whiting did not know that the *S-4*'s torpedo tubes had been buried in the mud.

But the most press coverage on December 19 was given to the burning question of how long Fitch and his men could survive. Reporters interviewed Lieutenant Charles Momsen, a submarine officer who was assigned to the Bureau of Construction and Repair. Momsen said:

> It all depends on how many men are alive and who are with them. If an officer is with them and forces the men to lie perfectly quiet which would lessen the discharge of carbon dioxide from their bodies, or if a torpedo man is there and knows how to get air out of the torpedoes they will have sufficient oxygen to keep them alive for 150 hours. But the normal discharge of carbon dioxide under the most favorable conditions would overcome the men in 87.7 hours, which would bring them to early Wednesday morning.

Momsen added that the quickest time a submarine had been raised was ten days under optimal conditions. But even the salvage pontoons were having trouble getting to the scene. It was reported that the *Iuka* had lost one of the three pontoons it was towing to Provincetown. When the sailors aboard the tugboat realized that a pontoon had broken off, fourteen of the crew jumped in a small motorboat to secure it. However, due to the weather, the boat capsized, forcing the sailors to swim back in the cold water to the *Iuka*. The pontoon

---

*It is highly unlikely that Whiting actually meant that he *shot* himself to the surface through the torpedo tube but rather swam out. If a man was to be shot out of a torpedo tube, he would almost certainly be killed by the overpowering compressed air used to fire a heavy torpedo.

was later found on a beach on eastern Long Island. The *Iuka* carried on the journey with its sister tug, the *Sagamore*, minus one pontoon. Other pontoons were being hauled up from Virginia by the *Wright*, Captain King's ship, but the *Wright* was not expected to arrive until at least the next day.

Then there was the question of the crane derricks, which were chartered by the navy from the Merritt-Chapman & Scott Corporation. It was reasoned that since the *S-4* was lighter than the *S-51*, they might have more success in raising the boat than they did in the previous disaster. Still, the cranes were unusable while the storm lasted.

So there was a general feeling of pessimism and helplessness that was generated by newspapers. The country was simply shocked. It is no wonder that when the *Falcon* left Wood End to bring Michels to the Navy Hospital, the shock turned to anger as the impression grew that the navy was giving up on the crew of the *S-4* for dead.

21

"Is There Any Hope?"

THE *FALCON'S* STOP AT BOSTON was brief. They lingered for a half hour while Fred Michels was offloaded, stores were brought on, and personnel exchanged. Important among the new men was Chief Gunner Clarence Louis Tibbals, a veteran of the *S-51* salvage. Tibbals was an expert at supervising diving and decompression. His addition would enable Hartley, who was the only one aboard the *Falcon* with approaching skill, to be free to pilot the ship.

Admiral Brumby was able to hold a brief meeting with Admiral Philip Andrews, the commandant of the Boston Navy Yard, during the stopover. Brumby needed all the advice he could get, as the long odds against the men of the *S-4* grew even longer.

There were two dilemmas. First, the weather was beyond anybody's control. All the navy could do was watch the weather reports and hope that the storm would subside enough for them to continue diving. The second dilemma was to figure out a way to get air into the torpedo room. Since Fitch had communicated that the compartment air salvage line had been flooded, they needed an alternate way to deliver air.

For both of these problems there was no shortage of advice from those inside and outside the navy. Most of these opinions came in the forms of telegrams sent to the Navy Department by concerned individuals. These individuals were generally aware of the problems of the storm and getting air into the boat.

Some, such as William H. MacKay, the former chief engineer of the liner *Leviathan*, suggested using ships as a breakwater for the storm: IF A FLEET OF SHIPS ANCHORED STEM TO STERN AROUND THE S FOUR THEY WILL BREAK THE WIND AND SEA AND PERMIT RAPID RESCUING WORK.

IF ROUGH WEATHER PREVENTS DIVING, telegrammed Harold Wesson, a retired lieutenant commander from the Naval Reserve, WHY NOT TRY OIL TO CALM SURFACE? This suggestion was a common sailing technique to smooth out the breaks on the surface of the water. This advice was repeated in multiple telegrams to the navy. The problem was not so much breaking up a choppy sea, but the deep swells that drew in and slacked out the lines connected to the divers.

Gladwin Bonton, from Tenafly, New Jersey, telegrammed the secretary of the navy: CANNOT CHAIN BE MADE FAST TO S-4 AND TOW TO SHALLOW WATER BY OTHER SUBMARINE OR SURFACE VESSEL? Herbert Griffith of Reading, Pennsylvania, suggested to the secretary, SUNKEN S-4 BEING ONLY 1800 YARDS OUT BY CABLE ATTACHED TO POWERFUL SHIP DRAG AS FAR AS POSSIBLE. COMPLETE OPERATION BY LAND POWER PREFERABLY RAILROAD ENGINE. Bringing the submarine to shallower water would be preferable, but to set up a proper tow would require diving, which was then impossible. Also, these suggestions did not realize that to actually haul a submarine like this would necessarily mean dragging it against the bottom, thus breaking it up.

John Weymouth of Baltimore, Maryland, sent to the Navy Department: DRILL HOLES IN SIDE OF HULL. CONNECT HOSE OR TUBE AND PUMP AIR FROM SURFACE. This type of suggestion was often repeated, and called a "drill and tap" method. This was the best option for the rescue force.

The drill and tap method had been an operation that had been done before on the *S-51*, something that Edward Ellsberg himself had done. The question was where to do it. But then, when the navy asked a commander of one of the *S-4*'s sister boats stationed on the West Coast, he suggested that it would be more efficient to use the SC tube.

The SC tube was a listening device shaped like a letter T that was set on the forward deck. Inside the tube were two rubber balls that were filled with air, and a microphone. The microphone was hooked up to a set of earpieces used by a listener inside the submarine. The crew member could then rotate the tube to try to have noise become apparent in both earpieces. Based on the direction that the tube was turned, the listener could figure if the noise was coming from ahead of or behind the submarine. The distance of the noise source could only be estimated by the intensity of the sound.[*]

Removing the balls and connecting the tubes to air hoses seemed to be the most expeditious way to deliver air to the *S-4*. It was an idea that the officers aboard the *Falcon* had not considered. Immediately, orders were sent to the *S-3* and *S-8* to measure their own devices. On the *Falcon*, they used their lathe to make a dummy model of the SC tube. The rescue force prepared short lengths of hose to cover the tubes and prepare it as the means to vent the torpedo room. The only necessary thing to be done was for the men inside the torpedo room to open up an interior valve so that air could be pumped in.

By the time the *Falcon* left Boston at 1:40 PM, a plan was in place. In the meantime, communication had continued between the *S-4* and the *S-8*, which had remained off Wood End. At 9:38 AM Fitch tapped out a message:

Oxygen bottle empty. Can you send down a couple?

The message was somewhat garbled and the *S-8* requested that Fitch retap the signal.

Can you send down a couple?

In the meantime, the rescue force made plans to send supplies through the torpedo tube. It was the most logical method to deliver supplies to the *S-4*. Despite Eadie's reports that the *S-4*'s bow was buried in mud, if the team could manage to get a diver down after they delivered fresh air through the SC tube, they could then wash out the mud at the bow, which would allow access to the tubes. Divers could

---

[*]It is uncertain the exact etymology of the acronym SC. It may be related to its technical predecessor, the "C-Tube," which was named after its inventor, a man named Coolidge, or be derived from the fact that the SC tube was first used on vessels known as "Submarine Chasers."

then insert survival packages into the tubes that could be delivered to the men inside. To do so would require a tremendous effort from the men inside the *S-4*. After the diver delivered the package, the submariners would need to close the tube from the inside then open an inner lock, which would release more than three hundred gallons of cold seawater into the compartment. Then one of the men would need to crawl into the narrow tube to retrieve the package.

Immediately, Commander Harold Saunders oversaw the preparation of packages. Men took automobile tire inner tubes and sealed in canisters of oxygen, cans of freshwater (which had to be filled completely in order to avoid being crushed by the water pressure), flashlights, chocolate, and cans of soda lime—which has the ability to absorb carbon dioxide from the air. The packages were made watertight and tested so that they resisted pressure of up to 115 feet of water. Meanwhile, as divers would work on clearing the torpedo tubes for the delivery of these packages, the rescue force planned on pouring hot soup down the hoses that were to be connected to the SC tube. While not palatable, it would sustain Fitch and his men until the torpedo tubes could be cleared.

As plans were being laid and all prayed that the gods would moderate the weather, the *S-8* carried on its conversation with the *S-4* throughout the day of December 19 in the hopes of improving morale—or at least to show the survivors on the *S-4* that they were not alone. The *S-8* messaged:

Two floating cranes are on their way now.
Where are the cranes coming from?
New York.

These were the two cranes being sent by the Merritt-Chapman & Scott Company.

Then, later, the *S-8* messaged: *Will the air last until tonight?*
It will last until six tonight.

As the day progressed, there were no signs that the storm would relent. The slosh of water made it difficult to hear Fitch's signals. Finally, the *S-8* signaled: *Much noise. Will call you in ten minutes. Time is now a quarter of eleven.*

Fitch then asked: *How's weather?*

Choppy. Force four.

By 3:00 PM, the *Falcon* was on its way back to Wood End in a heaving sea. All day they had been forwarded the messages from the *S-8*, to which the senior officers drafted replies. Then one was radioed in from the *S-8* that was immediately taken to King, who was conferring with Ellsberg.

Both men read the message.

Is there any hope?

It was the irascible, tactless King who composed the reply.

There is hope. Everything possible is being done.

Even King felt the raw emotion of Fitch's plight. Everything humanly possible *was* being done. The navy had managed to assemble the best possible team to effect a rescue. The rescue force had the best divers in the country, and they had the *Falcon*. But they could not control the weather.

At 5:00 PM, the *S-8* signaled a message to the *S-4*: *How many torpedoes and where stowed?* The rescue force wanted to get an idea of how much air they had available.

But there was no reply.

Forty-five minutes later the *S-8* signaled again: *There is hope. Did you get last message?*

This time there was a reply of taps. But they could not be made out. The *S-8* signaled: *Will call you in a few minutes. Water splashing against boat drowns out our taps.*

A few minutes later the *S-8* asked: *Can you hear me now?*

They received back a few taps, but again they could not make them out. The rescue force signaled:

Everything possible has been and will be done.

No clear message could be made out from the *S-4*. To encourage Fitch, the *S-8* sent down: *S-51 pontoons have arrived.*

Then the rescue force heard taps again. It was three groups of three taps. The *S-8* signaled:

Have you a message?

No message came. Instead, to the listener at the phones aboard the *S-8*, it sounded like some piece of equipment was being moved around inside the submarine.

Then at 9:59 PM, the *Falcon* received a message from the Navy
Department:

ADVISORY NORTHWEST STORM WARNINGS ORDERED NINE THIRTY
PM DELAWARE BREAKWATER TO PORTLAND MAINE. DISTURBANCE
OF UNUSUALLY GREAT INTENSITY OVER NEWFOUNDLAND WILL
CAUSE STRONG WEST WINDS TONIGHT SHIFTING TO NORTHWEST ON
TUESDAY. WINDS WILL REACH GALE FORCE AT TIMES.

Then on the *Falcon*, Brumby received a message from shore. He
then sent an order to the *S-8* to send a transmission directly to Lieutenant Fitch:

Your wife and mother are constantly praying for you.

The sea raged through the night, and the *S-8* kept sending the
message. There was no response. The *S-8* asked the *S-4* to signal with
three taps if they received the message. There was no response.

But the *S-8* kept sending the message anyway.

Your wife and mother are constantly praying for you.

At 6:20 AM on Tuesday, December 20, the *S-8* picked up a signal:

TAP-TAP-TAP

TAP-TAP-TAP

TAP-TAP-TAP

22

"Y-E-S"

THE THREE SETS OF TAPS made by the *S-4* brought new life to the rescue force. Fitch had proclaimed that their air would run out at 6:00 PM on December 19. But they had made it twelve hours past that deadline. The *S-8* immediately sent a new signal to Fitch and his men:

Diver will try to connect air to SC tube. Three taps for yes; five for no.

TAP-TAP-TAP

Then, in order to give confidence to the *S-4*, the *S-8* signaled at 7:40 AM: *Weather slightly calmer than last night. Force four. Still choppy, but calming down slowly.*

But there was no response.

At 8:15 AM, the *S-8* thought they heard taps, but it was uncertain.

At 10:15, the *S-8* signaled: *Cranes are here.*

No response.

There was no word from the *S-4* throughout the day, and no work could be done since the storm was still underway. At 4:05 PM, The *S-8* signaled:

Are you all right? OK?

TAP-TAP-TAP

They sent the same signal again at 4:30 PM. Again, three taps were heard.

But there were no other signals. Because of the storm, at times the listening operators aboard the *S-8* thought they made out taps, but were not certain. This was the case at 6:30 PM, when there seemed to be random taps coming from the stricken submarine. The last coherent message from the men in the torpedo room had been *Is there any hope?* But these random taps indicated that either Lieutenant Fitch had succumbed and somebody else of lesser skill was tapping, or that Fitch himself was simply too weak to message anything more elaborate.

Divers were dressed, ready to go down at a moment's notice. But that moment never came on December 20.

In the meantime, the press had not been idle. Headlines of all the major newspapers talked about the fading chances of the *S-4*. The *Boston Globe's* read, MEN IN *S-4* BEAT ON THEIR WALLS FOR RESCUERS WHO DO NOT COME.

In describing the conditions inside the torpedo room the newspaper wrote:

> The heating and regular lighting systems were undoubtedly put out of commission by the crash which sent the submarine to the bottom Saturday, yet there was a possibility that faint battery lamps, attached to the bulkhead at either end of the chamber, were burning. A penetrating chill was thought to pervade the chamber. The cold of the water which numbed and hampered divers would pass quickly through the steel walls of the *S-4* and in time to penetrate to the very bones of the six men still living.

Press boats circled the rescue flotilla. They wanted to know if it was over. There was a creeping cynicism on their part. Criticism emerged stating that the *Falcon* abandoned the scene of the collision the day before.

"We went to Boston to save a man's life," said Brumby to the reporters, referring to Fred Michels. "If he had been exposed to air at normal pressure after he ballooned to the surface, he would have caught pneumonia instantly, and with his severe attack of the bends he probably would have died. The *Falcon* was the only vessel with a compressed air chamber and the *Falcon* had to leave."

Since there was no diving to be done, reporters' attentions naturally gravitated to the *S-8*, which had been sending and receiving messages. As press boats neared, an officer on the submarine's deck, using a megaphone, shouted out the latest correspondence from the submarine.

The officer on the *S-8* said to reporters that he believed the men in the *S-4* to be still alive.

"What makes you think that?"

The officer took the megaphone and converted it to an earpiece to listen to the query. He then turned it to his lips. "They were alive this morning."

"Do you think they are unconscious?"

"The absence of rapping would indicate that they are."

"How long after they lost consciousness do you think they would be dead?"

"I don't know."

"Can you guess?"

"Yes. So can you."

"Can you make any estimate as a submarine officer?"

The officer conferred with another officer. The *Boston Daily Globe* reported that the officer said that "because of the three raps which were intended to mean 'All's well,' he believed that Lieutenant Fitch's message was received and understood. Newspapermen were not wholly in accord with this belief, considering the matter later."

The relations between the rescue force and the press, if strained before, had now reached a breaking point. That same day, a reporter attempted to board the *Falcon*. He was pushed back by an officer, "Get out of here; I don't come into your house without knocking, and you can't come into mine."

Another person from the reporter's boat shouted, "Who owns the navy anyway?"

The officer took a match from his pocket, broke it, then tossed it into the press boat. "I'm a taxpayer," he said. "Here's my share."

"But we've got to get the news," another reporter yelled.

"Oh, go to hell," replied the officer.

Then, at about 3:00 PM, one of the press boats drew close. Reporters had aboard Joseph J. McGinley, the father of Lieutenant Joseph A. McGinley, the *S-4*'s executive officer. But as they approached, the *Falcon* lifted its anchors and headed toward Provincetown Harbor.

One newspaperman shouted, "Why are you leaving?"

Admiral Brumby, completely irritated, shouted back, "Because we want to."

The press boats trailed behind. When the *Falcon* arrived, the small boats pulled up next to it. Then one of the reporters, seeing Admiral Brumby, shouted, "Have you quit?"

The admiral became furious and explained that they had come to get more men. Brumby did not know, but found out later, that McGinley's father was on one of those boats. Reporters, who were overworked and tired of obstinacy, wrote a story of the *Falcon* running to shore, ignoring the father who had come to look on the likely grave of his only son.

This trip to Provincetown had been at the suggestion of Henry Hartley to deal with the cramped conditions aboard the *Falcon*. Hartley had related to Brumby and King, "We have normal quarters for five officers and 61 men. Have aboard fifteen officers and 150 men. It is too rough out here to send any of them to the *Bushnell* and will certainly be more dangerous after dark. I recommend that the *Falcon* and *Bushnell* proceed into the harbor where *Falcon* can transfer some of her surplus officers and men to the larger vessel until we need them."

The admiral consented and so they went—but it was a public relations disaster.

By now the *Falcon* had at least twenty deep sea divers ready to descend to the wreck. Aside from Eadie and Carr, other men had been assembled from across the country. Among these were Joe Eiben, Bill Wickwire, John Kelley, Daniel Burd, F. W. Crilley, Raymond C. "Tug" Wilson, and James R. Ingram.

Bill Wickwire and John Kelley were Brooklynites. When Ellsberg left New York on December 18, he made a public plea for these two *S-51* veterans to come to the scene. The New York City Police Department was on the case. On December 19, they had located the pair and got them on an overnight train to Boston. John Kelley was considered particularly valuable because he was adept at using an underwater torch—a difficult tool to use. They boarded the *Falcon* when it had dropped off Michels at the hospital on December 19.

The *Falcon* left Provincetown Harbor at 4:04 PM to return to its miserable vigil. The press boats returned, peppering the *Falcon* with questions. One reporter on a fishing smack called for Lieutenant Commander Ellsberg. A sailor fetched him.

"Are you going to try to send divers down to the *S-4* today?" screamed a reporter against the howling gale.

"Can you come aboard in your dory?" Ellsberg called back.

The reporters tried to launch the dory in the storm, but Ellsberg halted them. "Don't try it," he shouted. "I mean that when you get us weather that a dory can live in we'll begin to work."

Captain Ernest King joined Ellsberg to entertain the reporters across the chasm of sea. One asked him, "What chance is there for them now?"

"Very little," replied King.

"Do you think it will be a matter of days or hours?"

"We can't tell. It all depends on the weather."

"What is the first thing you'll do?"

"Get oxygen into that compartment."

"How? Through a torpedo tube?"

"We will use a listening device, the SC tube, to put oxygen and condensed food into the compartment," said King.

"Has that ever been done before?" called the reporter.

"No," replied King, "but it can be. We've got lots of bright ideas if we could only use them."

"Will you have to use divers?"

"Yes, the whole thing depends on divers."

By midnight of December 20, gloom held sway. Admiral Brumby was obviously exhausted as he sat in a chair and conferred with the *Boston Daily Globe*'s Joseph Ward Jr., one of the selected reporters.

"How long it will take us to get the men out of the submarine after we're able to reach her, I can't say," said Brumby. "Anything like that would be a guess."

• • •

In the meantime, thousands of suggestions flooded the Navy Department.

Most of these suggestions were reiterations from the day before. There were comments that the men inside could use the torpedo tubes in a desperate attempt to launch themselves to the surface. Others again continued to suggest towing the submarine or using other ships as a breakwater.

This last type of suggestion was made by Marion Weller, the wife of engineering officer Donald Weller. She had placed a call to Rear Admiral Philip Andrews and asked if all the nearby vessels could be ordered to form a circle about the *Falcon*.

It was reported by the *Boston Daily Globe* that Mrs. Weller said to Andrews, "I am strong, and I am just going to fight to help get those men out. It's not a question who is in that compartment. The thing is to get them out."

Andrews commented, "There's a fine example of stalwart courage and faith. That woman was not crying or bewailing her fate. She is still buoyed by hope, and her first thought is of the living, whether or not the living includes her young husband."*

Some suggestions were unorthodox. Secretary of the Navy Curtis Wilbur received this telegram on December 20:

ADVISE MEN CONFINED WITHIN S-4—THEY HAVE A THIRTY DAY
SURVIVAL CHOICE AGAINST CONDITIONS. ANY SIMPLE DEVICE OF
THEIR CONSTRUCTION FOR THE PURPOSE OF GIVING THEM IN THEIR
CONFINEMENT EQUATORIAL OR CENTRIFUGAL MOTION WILL TRANS-
FORM THEIR NATURAL EVACUATION INTO A FILTER FOR THE PUR-
POSE OF RENEWING THEIR WITHIN LIFE SOURCE AND FILTERING ITS
USAGE.

    LEWIS BLYDEN

    ATLANTIC CITY, NJ

---

*The admiral had explained to Weller that using ships as a breakwater would not work because of the depth of the water. The water swells from below would negate any positive impact the ships would have.

Wilbur received another telegram the next day:

HAVING THOROUGHLY INVESTIGATED THE LIVING BURIAL IN INDIA
HAVE DISCOVERED HITHERTO UNKNOWN METHODS OF CONSERVA-
TION OF OXYGEN IN SMALL AIRTIGHT COMPARTMENTS. BY THESE
METHODS THE HINDU YOGI REMAIN ALIVE FOR LONG PERIODS OF
TIME WITH VERY LITTLE AIR. I OFFER MY SERVICES TO IMPART AND
DEMONSTRATE THIS KNOWLEDGE TO NAVAL AND SUBMARINE OFFI-
CERS RESPECTIVELY.
        HOWARD THURSTON
        GARRICK THEATRE, PHILADELPHIA

One woman entered the Boston Navy Yard and suggested using a giant magnet to haul the submarine from the bottom. Another telegram suggested forcing flowering plants through the torpedo tube that had been first subjected to strong light in order to provide oxygen to keep the survivors alive.

· · ·

Meanwhile, on the *Falcon*, Lieutenant Henry Hartley had noticed that the two buoys that the rescue force had attached to the *S-4* were missing. However, the air hose that Carr had connected to the ballast salvage line was still attached, as shown by the two cork buoys nearby. The divers could use that as the descending line. The *Falcon* itself was ready, and they had a plan. They would drop two heavy mooring anchors behind each quarter of the submarine, attach these to long cylindrical log buoys, then drop the *Falcon*'s bow anchors at a 15-degree spread. Then, they were to run lines to mooring anchors from the *Falcon*'s quarters. The *Lark* and *Mallard* would move forward of the *Falcon*, anchor, and run nine-inch hawsers to the salvage ship from bow to bow. It would be stable enough then for them to dive.

But no diving could be done for the entire day of December 20, and no further signals had been heard from the *S-4* since 6:30 PM that evening. Fitch and his five companions had lapsed into unconsciousness.

Then on December 21, the barometer rose. The storm was finally subsiding. As daylight broke, all hands could see that the buoy was still there, but it seemed out of position.

At 8:05 AM, the *Falcon* dropped the heavy mooring anchors near a marking buoy that had been planted near the wreck. This was a safety precaution, since Hartley did not want to land an anchor right on the *S-4*. Almost another hour and a half was used to move the ship into the right position using the marker buoy and sextant angles that had been taken on December 18.

Once the *Falcon* was in position, men reached over with a hook and caught the air hose marked by the buoy. Immediately, Captain King, who was present, knew something was wrong. It was coming up too easily. Sure enough, the men dragged up the hose and found that the end was chaffed through. It was by some freak accident that the buoy was even close to the collision site at all, unlike the other lost buoys that were found washed up on the shore near the village of Truro. It may have been that the air hose line was finally cut through at that last instant.

The *Falcon* sounded with the lead.

The *S-4* was missing.

Hartley checked and rechecked his instruments. They were exactly in the same place as before.

Immediately, the *Falcon* lowered boats to begin dragging grapnels. At the same time, Hartley figured he must have made some mistake in his measurements. He maneuvered the *Falcon* forward by hauling in on the forward anchors and paying out the line to the moorings. The *Falcon* sounded again and searched.

No luck.

By 1:00 PM, the sea had calmed enough for diving. Divers, starting with Bill Wickwire, were ordered over the side either singly or in pairs to try to find the submarine. Instead, they found themselves buried in mud, although they were supposedly within feet of the *S-4*.

"It was like a fog," Wickwire said. "Nothing like the water around the *S-51*. We had a twenty-foot visibility there. Down here the visibility was only about four to seven feet."

The frantic searching continued. James Ingram was to follow Wickwire, then John Kelley. On the positive side, the temperature of

Two divers preparing for descent from the *Falcon*.
Courtesy of the Library of Congress, Papers of Ernest J. King

the water had increased from the 34 degrees it had been on the night when Eadie cut Michels free to 51 degrees.

Despite the warmth of the water, a cold silence had settled on the *Falcon*. Doors that might slam were closed, cooks were ordered not to rattle the dishes, and the men were ordered to speak in whispers. Even Hartley's pet dogs lay face down, unmoving. The only voice that was loud and clear was Ellsberg's. The salvage expert was at the telephone with an earpiece strapped to his skull. He alternately sat and then stood rigid as he spoke with the divers.

At this hour, it was obvious to the reporters aboard the *Falcon* that Ellsberg was the man in charge. He "gave out his orders with an assurance that showed expert knowledge of the work and assurances of purpose that was unequaled by anyone else aboard. And the score of divers, the best in the navy, showed their devotion and admiration of Ellsberg by their air of easy friendship and earnest efforts at cooperation."

Meanwhile, Brumby and King had given strict orders not to speak to reporters about the submarine being lost. But in their eagerness to find out what was happening, the reporters on the rented fishing boats threatened to hamper grappling operations. Everybody's patience had gone.[*]

Hartley wrote that at one point he called out to a press boat, "Please move so our boat can drag its grapnel there."

A reporter then shouted, "What in the hell is this? A naval secret?"[†]

To the reporters, the entire experience was frustrating.

"What are you dragging for?" came a question from a reporter through a megaphone.

The query was ignored.

"Have you lost the sub?"

No response.

"Do you refuse to answer questions?"

It was unanswered.

"Is this a naval secret?"

This was the nadir of the relationship between the press and Brumby's rescue force.

On one of these press boats was Mark McIntyre, the reporter who first broke the story of the *S-4* by semaphore. It just so happened that at that moment James Ingram was preparing to dive. Ingram and McIntyre had been friends when McIntyre was in the navy, and they had met again when McIntyre was covering the *S-51* story. Just before Ingram's helmet was put on, McIntyre caught his eye.

The reporter began making motions with his hands. It looked like he was adjusting his coat or putting on mittens. But these movements had meaning. They were signals.

Is she lost?

McIntyre did this over and over again.

---

[*]It is unlikely that, at this moment, many would have noticed the *Paulding* being towed stern first out of Provincetown Harbor just then. But its flag was set at half-mast as a sign of respect from Lieutenant Commander Baylis.

[†]It might be suspected that Hartley himself was not quite as polite as he made out.

Ingram did not respond. Then there was a cry from the deck, "Down stage!"

Ingram's helmet was screwed on and he was brought to the water. But before the diver entered the cold sea, he seemingly stretched his arms, kicked his legs, and lifted his hands high above his head several times. Each time, the movements spelled:

Y-E-S.

Ingram's *Y-E-S* may have been simply to indicate that the submarine was missing at the moment, and that they would soon find it. McIntyre saw a deeper meaning. He thought it was the clearest indication that there would be no survivors aboard the *S-4.*

Word soon spread. The *S-4* was lost. Just before 1:00 PM, one of the navy boats that was grappling for the submarine broke down. A boat, owned by a Provincetown fisherman named Mike Volton, came by and asked if they needed assistance. The navy boat accepted the help and took a towline. The reporters on Volton's boat shouted, "Is she lost?"

"Yep," was the reply.

The strain and criticism was wearing on Admiral Brumby. He was visibly tired. During this time he held an impromptu news conference with several reporters who finally managed to get aboard. He was hesitant to deal with them and made it clear that he only wanted one reporter to stay to represent all of them. He then showed them a clipping from a local newspaper that read that he "had been driven into the harbor yesterday by gentle winds."

"That got me mad," said the admiral to the reporters. "Why, I'm not afraid of any wind at all. I went in to make some changes to the men. No wind drives me into any harbor."

The reporters, however, did not care about yesterday's news. One asked, "Do you believe any of the men who went down with the *S-4* are alive?"

"No I don't," said the admiral in a sharp tone. He then added quickly, "Of course, that is only my personal opinion."

"And you have lost the submarine?"

"Yes," said Brumby. "Yes we've lost her. But we are within fifty yards of her."

This was all true, and it shows the difficulty of locating a submarine even when the general position is known. Submarines were designed to be smooth and to repel grapnels, and the muddy conditions were of no help to the divers.

It was only at almost 5:00 PM that Chief Boatswain Hawes, grappling from one of the *Falcon*'s surfboats, made a heavy strike.

Immediately, diver Daniel Burd was dressed even as the line was brought close to the *Falcon*. The men aboard tossed Hawes a rope to hold the grapnel line and bring it aboard. Burd was given a submersible lamp and sent to the bottom. On the *Falcon*, Edward Ellsberg was operating Burd's telephone.

"I've landed on the sub," said Burd.

"Where are you?" called Ellsberg.

"I'm on the conning tower," Burd reported.

"Thank God for that," said Captain King. It was 5:08 PM.

Burd remained on the bottom for about forty minutes. He fastened a descending line at the conning tower, then groped ahead in the dark. He came to the torpedo room hatch. He banged the hatch with his hammer.

There was no reply.

Next up was Bill Carr. He went down at about 7:00 PM. He spent thirty-five minutes on the submarine, moving the descending line closer to the torpedo room as well as doing other work. He heard no sound either.

Next was "Tug" Wilson followed shortly after by Joe Eiben. They carried the line to be attached to the SC tube. Upon landing on the *S-4* they began work. Wilson and Eiben first cut the caps of the SC tube then covered it with hoses. They clamped these on then attached another hose that would deliver air. They were almost ready.

The only possible flaw in the operation would be if the men inside the torpedo room did not open the flapper valve for the SC tube leading into the interior of the compartment. However, since the rescue team had messaged that they were going to hook up the SC tube while Fitch and his men were yet cognizant, they expected them to do it. King himself was doubtful. In order for the SC valve tube to be opened, the tube's listening devices needed to be mounted, which was a somewhat complex operation. It was unlikely that Fitch would have found the strength to do so after the collision. If the gear was mounted before the submarine went down, however, this maneuver would work. If the attempt failed, the rescue force would employ the drill and tap operation. As Wilson and Eiben worked, King was preparing the men for this eventuality. Two men would go onto the submarine, drill a hole, and follow it with a thread. Then one of the men would plug the hole to keep out the water. Then a valve would be swapped for the plug to allow air to enter.

Tom Eadie was on the deck, practicing with the drill.

Wilson and Eiben continued the work and noticed that water started to rush into the tube. The valve seemed to be open. However, they ran into technical trouble and could not quite finish the job. They were quickly hauled up, and Tom Eadie went down to make the final air connection to the torpedo room.

At 10:05 PM Edward Ellsberg ordered on the compressed air to the SC tube.

Immediately, the *Falcon* knew that the SC tube was open, because the pressure readings on the air compressor dropped. Ellsberg halted the compressors for a moment, got a reading, and figured the pressure inside the torpedo room to be about the same as the air at sea level. This meant that there had been little flooding inside the compartment, since if water had flooded the torpedo room it would compress the air.

The *Falcon* then desperately pumped air into the torpedo room, built up the air pressure to seven pounds per square inch, then turned off the compressor to let the bad air vent until the pressure was at four pounds per square inch.

Originally, they had planned to hook up the two tops of the T shape that made up the SC tube and use one for venting and the other for the intake of new air. But since the tube outlets were so close on the inside (one half inch apart), it was thought that the air would simply short circuit, flowing directly from intake to outtake without ever making it to the men inside the torpedo room.

The new plan was doing the job. The bad air was coming out. Captain King smelled it. It was nasty and rancid with the odor of oil.

The *Falcon* gathered a sample of air by inserting the venting hose into a gallon-sized bottle underwater, so as not to pollute the sample. The ship's doctor, Camille J. Flotte, then tested the air for carbon dioxide content. He had a set of four flasks filled with liquid that were exposed to the air. These turned brown. He held these up to the light and consulted a chart.

The carbon dioxide level was at 7 percent. Typical levels of air had less than 0.5 percent. It would take a while to fully vent the compartment. It was anticipated that if any of the men in the torpedo room were to wake, it would happen in several hours.

Admiral Brumby, at the beginning of the rescue mission, had said that the outside limit that the men could survive was one hundred hours. By the time the air was flowing into the SC tube, over 102 hours had passed since the *S-4* first collided with the *Paulding*.

Brumby said to reporters, "We have no hope that any men are still alive on the *S-4*, but we must proceed on the theory that they are."

The airing and venting continued. In twelve hours they got the carbon dioxide levels down to 2 percent and in twenty-four hours to 0.5 percent.

But Graham Fitch never awoke.

Nor Russell Crabb.

Nor George Pelnar.

Nor Robert Short.

Nor Frank Snizek.

Nor Joseph Stevens.

23

Carr's Cross

CHRISTMAS CELEBRATIONS WERE CANCELED IN Provincetown. From all across the country, people who were touched by the tragedy of the *S-4* came to the village. Of these, one of the most prominent was Joseph J. McGinley, father of the *S-4*'s executive officer.

The elder McGinley received more attention from the press than other relatives of the victims. This was because he was a former newspaper publisher. Feeling comfortable among the newsmen, he situated himself at the Provincetown Town Hall, where he mingled with the reporters. "I am right at home here," McGinley said. "I know you people. I don't know what I would have done if I had not been able to come here and be with you. I would have been all alone. It would have been horrible."

McGinley, in his grief, was understandably critical of the navy. He said, "My son loved the navy. It is too bad the navy did not love my boy enough to take better care of him."

McGinley became a source of comfort for the grieving. He spoke on the telephone to Marion Weller, who asked him when the bodies of her husband and his crewmates might be recovered. McGinley told her it wasn't likely until after the winter. McGinley also met Mildred, the twenty-year-old wife of Russell Crabb, one of the torpedo room six. She had arrived in Provincetown on December 21, just as the *Falcon* struggled to relocate the *S-4*.

86 SEVENTEEN FATHOMS DEEP
Mildred Crabb wanted to go to the *S-8*, to find somebody who might have known her husband. The *New York Times* described her: "A slight woman, she was bowed so deep in the collar of her coat that her face seemed only an enormous pair of tear laden eyes."

Mr. McGinley introduced himself to Mrs. Crabb. He said, "I had a son on the submarine."

Mrs. Crabb, sobbing, said, "I'm glad I haven't a son to bring up to go in the navy." She added that she urged her husband to leave the navy and enter what she considered to be the less dangerous field of aviation.

On December 22, the elder McGinley made his way back to Boston and came to the Navy Yard, where he was to have dinner with Admiral Andrews. McGinley had been insulted when, after he had been brought to the *Falcon* by reporters, Admiral Brumby, unaware of his presence, steamed off suddenly to Provincetown Harbor to change crews. The navy was now trying to mend fences. Brumby met with McGinley and apologized. At the Navy Yard, McGinley met Lieutenant Commander John S. Baylis. The two looked at each other sadly before McGinley said, "Sorry you weren't five minutes later."

"Please accept my sincere sympathy," said Baylis.

The two clasped hands in silence. Then McGinley asked, "Was it a tremendous crash?"

"Just like hitting a stone wall," said Baylis. "It was only a miracle that both ships did not go down."

"I am sorry, so sorry," said McGinley, wiping away tears. "But I am sure this tragedy could not have been averted."

But others were not so sure if the disaster could not have been prevented. The deluge of criticism against the navy was only beginning.

. . .

Meanwhile, off Wood End, the only noise that stirred from the *S-4* was that of the air being sucked in and ventilated out through the SC tube. Few aboard the *Falcon* admitted the failure of the rescue operation since the team had not ceased pumping air into the torpedo room. In fact, the rescue operation had not officially ended, but all hands knew it was in reality over. It was like the *S-51*—but worse.

Brumby, King, Hartley, Ellsberg, and Saunders had done all they could do—all that was humanly possible. Yet aboard the *Falcon*, a gloom cascaded over the officers and men. There was no weeping or sobbing. They simply kept venting the torpedo room while they prepared for the eventual salvage of the *S-4*.

Meanwhile, Edward Ellsberg donned the diving suit. Ellsberg was tired. He hadn't shaved for days. While there were no survivors, the least Ellsberg could do was to help start a successful salvage operation so the bodies of the dead could be brought home. To do this, the *Falcon* needed to know the extent of the damage done by the *Paulding*. They had the reports of the divers, but it was considered better if an expert naval constructor could assess the damage and see if there was a risk of breaking the *S-4* in half if they lifted the submarine by pontoons. In essence, Ellsberg needed to find the hole and make sure it wasn't too big.

In the eyes of the press, Ellsberg was one of the heroes of the *S-4* salvage. He was not hesitant to speak with reporters, and he made a compelling story—the retired navy officer who donned his uniform to rejoin his old shipmates in a moment of crisis. He was the miracle worker who raised the *S-51*. He was the man who prophetically warned the navy about future disasters if they did nothing. While Tom Eadie was the hero on the frontline, Ellsberg was the strategist and prophet. Eadie was Achilles, but Ellsberg was Odysseus.

In many ways Ellsberg overshadowed his counterpart, Commander Harold Saunders, who was equally if not more knowledgeable about submarine design and construction. In fact, when Ellsberg had arrived on the *Falcon* during the height of the storm, he did become the rescue mission's salvage officer in lieu of Saunders. The newspapers amplified Ellsberg's role. Some accounts seem to imply that Ellsberg, upon arrival at Wood End, became the man in charge. However, Ellsberg was one of several senior officers who reported to Brumby and King. But Ellsberg was a strong character—brilliant, intense—a man who thrived on attention with a sense of righteousness, and he could tell a masterful story.

So Odysseus himself was going to the bottom. This was something, the press emphasized, that no other officer had done. In the meantime, salvage work had commenced. Bill Carr was already on the bottom, washing a tunnel beneath the *S-4*, preparing it for a lifting chain to be attached to a pontoon. Ellsberg would not join or see Carr; he would be on another part of the submarine.

Despite the rescue mission's failure, Ellsberg must have been excited while he was seated on the bench of the *Falcon*'s fantail. Even though he was, as Tom Eadie put it, a "novice" whose skill on the bottom was dwarfed by the other seasoned divers, his eagerness made up for his lack of experience. The bears helped Ellsberg slide the diving suit over multiple layers of clothes. He was grateful for the heavy diving suit. It was cold and blustery, even with a heavy canvas rigged to break the wind. After a check of the telephone he was lifted by the dressers and brought to the steel diving platform. Ellsberg was hauled over the water, and lowered in as a signal was piped. The seas, while much calmer than they had been in the past few days, were still rough. The suit, which had billowed out from compressed air, was flattened by the water pressure. He looked about and saw barnacles decorating the red hull of the *Falcon*.

"Topside, there! All ready! Lower away!" Ellsberg telephoned.

"OK. Step off the stage!"

Ellsberg stepped off as the stage was hoisted upwards. He dangled in the sea with three lines to contemplate: his lifeline, his air hose, and a long manila line that slithered into the deep. This was the descending line to the *S-4*.

He grabbed it and slid down. The faint light of pre-winter almost vanished completely. There was only him and the line that slid down into nothingness. Above him, a trail of his own bubbles spiraled upward.

As Ellsberg descended, his eardrums popped with pain, causing him to swallow hard. Then he saw it. The *S-4*. It was large, and to his mind, imponderable. He landed safely.

"On the bottom!"

Ellsberg swayed—he was slightly dizzy. He clung to the descending line. He had landed on the *S-4*'s bow. He could see maybe ten feet ahead. He could see the SC tube connection. It appeared to be in good condition. The deck was level, so after some quick adjustments to his air, Ellsberg plodded aft. The loud ringing footsteps of his boots went unanswered.

Ellsberg was struck at how undamaged the *S-4* looked. The bow diving planes looked shipshape, and there was no apparent damage by the bow. In fact, Ellsberg could say that the *S-4* seemed fine, as if it were resting on the bottom and just waiting to pop up. The only telltale sign of how long it had been on the seafloor was a fine film of slimy mud that covered the submarine. It kicked up in fine misty clouds as Ellsberg walked along.

The deck widened, and after about seventy feet he saw it—the cut. The deck below him, like a chasm, opened. The superstructure had been gouged away. Yet this type of damage was only superficial. He needed to locate the breach in the double hull.

Ellsberg dropped into the cut superstructure carefully so as not to compromise his diving suit against the wreckage. He looked about, but he could find no opening. All he saw was the rounded hull—smooth plating with the superstructure torn off it.

He looked to port. It was uglier there. A tangle of twisted remains showed him that there was the place Michels had been caught.

Ellsberg kept on for about twenty more feet, navigating in the wreckage. Then, out of the gloom, the deck emerged again. Beyond was the conning tower. He could see the *S-4*'s gun, horribly askew, its muzzle down to port and its breach high to starboard. It must have been struck a glancing blow by the *Paulding*.

Ellsberg climbed out of the cut and onto the deck. He crawled aft, carefully carrying his hoses upward to make sure they did not get caught. He did not wish to get into the same predicament Michels had been in.

He made it to the conning tower and, looking aft, he saw no further damage. He could not find the hole. Idly, Ellsberg mused that he must have missed it.

He turned about and headed back the way he came. He saw his lifeline and air hose slacken, so he ordered the topside to haul in some of the slack. Then he dropped down into the cut again. He turned his faceplate down to the hull, studying it.

Then, suddenly, he could see nothing at all. A cloud of fine silt had rolled in and covered everything below him from the waist downward. It seemed to him that in his original passing, he had kicked up

This photograph of the *S-4* shows clearly the cut across its deck and what divers had to contend with while performing operations on the bottom.
Courtesy of the Stephen B. Luce Library Archives, SUNY Maritime College

a cloud of the mud that caked the *S-4*. Now it obscured everything,
making it impossible for him to find the hole.

Yet this was not Ellsberg's immediate problem. Since he could not
see the *S-4*, he dared not move. He could fall into the hole that he
hadn't found yet or bump into the wreckage and tear his suit open.
Or he might simply blunder straight off the submarine and onto the
ocean floor. He could not make out where the conning tower was since
it disappeared into the gloom. He knew the submarine lay roughly on
a northwest line, but looking up he couldn't discern which way the
cardinal directions were. Nor could he see the *Falcon*.

Ellsberg cursed, and he began to rue his decision to volunteer for this duty. He leaned over, trying to figure out which way was forward on the *S-4*.

Then the *Falcon*, one hundred feet above him, yawed.

Ellsberg's lifeline snapped taut and jerked him. He stumbled sideways, then fell on his face. In an instant, he was rolling off the starboard side of the submarine. Quicker and quicker he slid down the hull. Ellsberg grasped in vain, trying to find something to hold on to. But the weighted suit carried him down as his helmet banged into the wreck.

Then in front of him something flashed before his face. Ellsberg grabbed it. It was part of the steel stem of the *Paulding* that had lanced through and into the *S-4*.

As he dangled there by one arm, he stared into the hole. For a moment, Ellsberg forgot his plight. He found the object of his mission. It was a small wound, perhaps twelve inches high and two and a half feet long. This was the nick that ended the lives of forty men.

In an instant, Ellsberg's examination was over. The damage was minimal enough that if they tried to lift the boat by pontoons then there would be no danger of it snapping in two.

But he was still dangling off the side of the submarine. He tilted his head back and looked through the top port of his helmet. He saw the stem of the *Paulding*, his glove grasping it. A trail of bubbles wafted out of the glove.

His suit was cut.

What made this worse, and filled Ellsberg with dread, was that the cut was currently situated in the highest possible position. He was losing air. The sea pressed against him in every direction as the pressure of the air in his suit became less than that of the water about him. He was facing another of the great dangers of deep sea diving, the so-called *squeeze*.

He needed to get the glove below him in order to mitigate the damage.

Ellsberg could not physically pull himself up, since cold water was seeping down through his sleeve and numbing his arm. He flailed his legs about and tried to find a place to stand. Then he felt the squeeze as his suit lost more air and the pressure of the sea bore down on him. Breathing became difficult. He had no choice but to let go.

Ellsberg spun downward, the *S-4* passing swiftly before his face-plate. There was no way to slow himself, much less stop. He did not have enough air left in his suit to give him any buoyancy.

In an instant, any faint light that was about him shut out. He had reached the bottom of the sea and had sunk on his right side into a quagmire of oozy mud. The mud was gelatinous, like quicksand. Ellsberg thought of the forty dead men close at hand.

Then water poured into his suit through the cut glove. It began to work its way into his helmet. Instinctively, desperately, Ellsberg tried to stand, but there was no bottom. Every movement dragged him deeper until at last he reached something hard and the sinking stopped. He lay on his right side. Quickly, Ellsberg took his arm and pushed it below him, to try to push himself up.

But his arm, even extended fully out, could find nothing. Only his hips downward seemed to rest on some sort of precarious shelf.

Instinct took over. Ellsberg wanted to get entirely on the shelf so he could somehow push himself up to standing. He wriggled back. Then he felt the pinpricks of tiny pieces of jagged metal, resting against his diving suit. He froze. The slightest movement against the metal would saw his suit open. Ellsberg supposed that he was lying on a piece of the *Paulding*. Ellsberg tugged on his lifeline then tilted his head back and yelled into his suit's telephone. "Topside there!"

"Topside. What is it? Do you need any help?"

"You're damned right I do. I'm buried in mud. Heave in on my lifeline!"

"Aye, aye. Right away!"

Ellsberg waited for the heave on his lifeline that would straighten him up and out of the mud.

He waited for what seemed an eternity, but the pull never came.

"Topside there! Are you heaving yet?"

"Yes! Four men are heaving hard on your lines but they can't get an inch of slack. What's the matter down there?"

A panic gripped Ellsberg.

"Avast heaving! Slack off! Slack off, for God's sake!"

Ellsberg's lines had become foul. If the top pulled too hard, they might sever his air hose against the wreckage.

The topside called down. "We're slacking away! Do you want any help down there?"

Ellsberg didn't respond. For some reason, he knew they'd send some sort of help anyway. Perhaps Tom Eadie himself would come down to fish him out. Then the topside told Ellsberg they would send Bill Carr, who had been busy digging a tunnel on the other side of the boat.

Ellsberg held the cut glove under him, which kept the air in the suit. This gave him time to think in the mud. Ellsberg turned inward. He did not think of his wife or daughter. All he thought about was, "How in the hell am I going to get out of this? This would be a hell of a place to stay forever." He was seventeen fathoms deep, buried in mud.

Ellsberg calmed himself and thought about what he had at his disposal. He recalled his training as a diver. He had air—he had an air valve. Then, in a sudden epiphany, Ellsberg thought of the answer. He reached for his air intake valve and turned it open.

Immediately, compressed air roared into his suit. The canvas, which had pressed tight against him, pushed out like a balloon. Then, inch by inch, the air made Ellsberg buoyant, and lifted his helmet upward. In another moment he was upright. Then he drew himself straight up from the mud. Light came through his faceplate, and even the dim radiance found on the sea floor was gladly welcomed by Edward Ellsberg.

He released some air and eased off the intake. If he suddenly burst out of the mud, he might just pop right to the surface and suffer a blowout, or slam into the *Falcon*'s keel, or get the bends. Or all three.

Carefully, he adjusted the valves on and off until he was upright and only waist deep in the mud. Then looking upward, Ellsberg saw his air hose and lifeline, floating freely and vertically above him. They did not look foul. He figured that when he turned up the compressed air entering his suit they must have slacked free.

"Topside there!" he called. "Take an easy pull on my lines!"

In a moment he felt a tug on his breastplate. His lines were indeed free. He released more air, and then gave the order to haul him up ten feet. Ellsberg slid out of the mud. Then, free-floating in the water, he looked about for the *S-4*. But it was lost in the gloom. He gave the word that he was ready to go up.

Ellsberg reached the surface and was hauled onto the diving stage. Reporters aboard the *Falcon* wrote that Ellsberg "swayed as though he was going to lose his hold and fall back into the ocean. Then when they placed a chair under him and tapped his helmet to know all was ready, he slumped down as though exhausted." In a few minutes, they removed his diving gear. The tenders got him up and led him to the decompression chamber. Ellsberg's unshaven face was drawn. He then blurted, "Eadie should have got fifty medals for bringing up Michels safe Sunday night."

As Ellsberg stepped through the inner lock of the decompression chamber he saw, to his surprise, Bill Carr and Tom Eadie. Eadie was massaging Carr, who was half undressed from his diving suit. His legs looked blue and cold. Eadie offered Ellsberg a drink. It was one of those submarine cocktails made from the illegal booze confiscated and brought to the *Falcon* by the Coast Guard. Ellsberg drank it and eyed Carr.

Carr then began to curse at Eadie, who had evidently been needling him.

After Carr calmed down, Ellsberg found out what happened. Carr had been on the bottom on the port side of the submarine at work. He then received a message from the *Falcon*: "Commander Ellsberg's in bad trouble somewhere on the sub. Leave what you're doing, Bill, and go over and help him!"

So Carr left what he was doing and while plodding through the mud to find Ellsberg, he could not help but think that here, at last, was his chance to earn that Navy Cross that had been denied to him during the *S-51* job. The irony was that it would be Ellsberg, the man who had refused him the Cross, who would be the one he rescued. Then William J. Carr could stand equal with the likes of Tom Eadie. "Here's my chance to get a Navy Cross!"

Then he got a message from the topside calling him off. Ellsberg was safe and Carr should come to the surface.

"Commander, why didn't you wait till I got there to rescue you?" asked Carr.

24

Christmas Eve

IN THE EARLY MORNING HOURS of Christmas Eve 1927 the Union Station at Providence, Rhode Island, was mostly deserted. On a normal day, hundreds of travelers shuffled through the wide halls of the railway hub. But either due to the cold, the holiday season, or simply the early hour, the large halls were devoid of people except for a solitary, disheveled woman, perhaps in her forties, who stood staring at the arrivals board.

Mrs. Maude T. Stevens had been waiting there for hours. In her pocket she carried the photograph of a seventeen-year-old boy that she frequently glanced at. Seaman Joseph Stevens was a few years older now and taller, at six foot two.

Mrs. Stevens had hardly slept or ate since she had received news of the disaster off Wood End. When reporters found her at Union Station and asked how long she had been waiting there, she shrugged it off. "It's only been four hours," she said. "My Joseph has been waiting for 148 hours under the sea." She was convinced that her son would be the last one to succumb, since he had so much stamina.

The train that Mrs. Stevens had been waiting for arrived at 7:30 AM. Out stepped two men. The first, Curtis D. Wilbur, looked more like a banker than the secretary of the navy. He wore simple wire-framed glasses and had tightly parted, pomaded hair. That might be expected from a man whose boss was known for saying, "The chief business of the American people is business."

The other man was dressed in an admiral's uniform. His most dominating feature was a thick walrus mustache. Charles Frederick Hughes, chief of naval operations, was in looks, demeanor, and position, the navy incarnate.

Mrs. Stevens approached the duo and said, "I am Joe Stevens's mother." Curtis Wilbur, without saying a word, took her by the arm.

Since the *S-4* went down on December 17, there had been growing criticism against the rescue mission, the navy in general, and Wilbur in particular. This reaction, in turn, led to a bipartisan political roasting of the US Navy.

"The navy is plainly not doing what it could," said Charles L. Gifford on December 21. He was the Republican representative of the Sixteenth Massachusetts District, the district that included Provincetown. "The officers should be reported to Congress for withholding news from the newspapermen, and therefore from the American public." He said that he had talked to the fishermen in his district. "They know this sea and they can tell me if weather conditions were too severe for the navy to work."

Representative James V. McClintic, a Republican from Oklahoma, demanded that the salvage work be continued despite the winter weather. "Down in that dark hull of steel are the remains of . . . brave men who went to their death in the performance of their duty. Loved ones whose hearts have been broken by this disaster are entitled to human consideration."

Representative Anthony Griffin, a Democrat from New York, called for the appointment of a special committee to investigate not only the *S-4* tragedy, but the *S-51* disaster as well. Griffin said the rescue was a failure because of "red tape." Representative George Seger, a Republican from New Jersey, called on the secretary of the navy, Curtis Wilbur, to provide full information about the condition of the submarine fleet. New York representative, Democrat Loring Black Jr., demanded Wilbur resign, and he called for a committee to be formed that dealt with all submarine matters.

The navy, however, was planning to hold its own Court of Inquiry in January. Admiral Charles Hughes said, "It appears to me to have been an unavoidable accident and one that is to be expected from a hazardous service like the navy. The Court of Inquiry will make a sufficient investigation and there is no need for a Congressional inquiry."

Hughes was derided, and some politicians declared that a navy Court of Inquiry would whitewash the entire matter. All this pressure led Speaker of the House Nicholas Longworth to state, "It may be necessary to have a Congressional investigation of this tragedy. That will be determined by developments in the next few weeks. There must be a thorough investigation to get all the facts by some public agency."

President Calvin Coolidge directed that an independent committee be established to investigate the matter, made up of men he himself selected. William Saunders, the chairman of the Naval Advisory Board, of which the famous inventor Thomas Alva Edison was a former president, recommended his board members for the job. Saunders said, "Its members are civilians who have no ties or commitments with the navy and their impartiality in an inquiry of this character would be unquestioned."

The fires of political heat were stoked by the criticisms from the relatives of the *S-4*'s officers and crew. In most cases, these relatives were unfamiliar with submarines and could not imagine how mere weather could stymy a salvage operation to which the US Navy purportedly threw all its resources. Nor was this helped by the fact that Brumby and King were so closed-mouthed to the press. The aunts of Lieutenant Graham Fitch sent an open telegram to the navy that reflected the misunderstandings of the public on what really occurred:

- PLEASE EXPLAIN WHY THE *FALCON* LEFT THE SCENE OF RESCUE SUNDAY, ALSO WHY THE DRILL SHIELD, SUCCESSFULLY USED TOO LATE ON WEDNESDAY, WAS NOT USED SUNDAY WHEN SIX MEN WERE ALIVE AND LIEUTENANT FITCH TAPPED HIS PLEA FOR AIR.

- WHY DID ADMIRAL BRUMBY STEAM AWAY SUNDAY, WHEN EVEN HE COULD NOT THEN OFFER THE WEATHER AS AN EXCUSE FOR STOPPING THE RESCUE OPERATIONS?

Jacqueline Jones, the widow of Roy Jones, also made a series of inquiries that were perhaps more constructive:

- WHY DOES ADMIRAL HUGHES CALL THIS TRAGEDY A LEGITI-MATE ACCIDENT WHEN THE *PAULDING*, A DESTROYER ESPECIALLY BUILT TO CUT SUBMARINES IN TWO BY RAMMING DURING WAR-TIME, WAS PERMITTED TO OPERATE IN AN AREA WHICH HAD BEEN DESIGNATED FOR SUBMARINE MANOEUVRES?
- WHY WAS THE *S-4* ALLOWED TO SET OUT TO MAKE A DEEP SEA TEST DIVE WHEN THERE WERE NO MEANS OF RESCUE AT HAND SHOULD SOMETHING GO WRONG DURING THE DIVE?
- WHY DIDN'T THE NAVY DEPARTMENT HAVE PONTOONS AT PROV-INCETOWN WHEN THEIR IMMEDIATE AVAILABILITY WAS VITALLY NECESSARY IN JUST SUCH AN ACCIDENT AS SANK THE *S-4*?
- WHY IN PEACE TIMES, WITH THE WHOLE ATLANTIC COAST TO CHOOSE FROM, WAS PROVINCETOWN, WITH ITS COLD, STORMY WATERS, SELECTED AS THE SCENE OF THE MANOEUVRES?

The situation threatened to become a fiasco as the rescue operation had plainly, but not officially, turned into a salvage operation. Reporters had a field day interviewing local residents who insisted that the navy brusquely refused any help they offered.

The *Hyannis Patriot* editorialized on December 22, "The submarine tragedy that has been and is being enacted down in Provincetown Harbor suggests that the Navy of the United States is woefully lacking in adequate appliances for the rescuing of disabled undersea craft when trouble overtakes them. Trouble has overtaken altogether too many of them in the 'piping times of peace.' A continuance of such conditions will be nothing short of disgraceful. . . . It is no credit to our government to be compelled to go into a helpless panic every time a submarine disaster occurs—and there are more than plenty of them."

Reporters had also found inventors and engineers who were critical of the rescue effort. Elmer Sperry, co-inventor of the gyroscope, and Simon Lake, a brilliant but eccentric designer and builder of submarines for the navy, both made armchair pronouncements on what the navy could have done. Lake had suggested sending a box, similar to a diving bell, with diving suits that could have been given to the trapped men.

The most vocal critic of the navy was ironically Reginald Fessenden, the inventor of the oscillator. "The sinking of the S-4 was more than avoidable, it was criminal," Fessenden said. He went on to list several devices that could have been used to avert the disaster or aid in the rescue effort. First there was the oscillator itself, which if used properly on the submarine or destroyer would have told the other it was present from miles away. When discussing the difficulty of finding the S-4, he said that "if any of the vessels had been equipped with a fathometer or echo sounder, such as is used on transatlantic liners and many European war vessels, the submarine could have been located within fifteen minutes. The fathometer gives an indication when the vessel passes over a submerged ship." He also asserted that the navy failed to install submarine telephones, something that had been successfully tested since 1920.

So much misinformation was circulating that *Scientific American* commented, "Not, we hazard, since the Peary-Cook controversy[*] was waged in the press has such a mass of uninformed comment filled the columns of responsible newspapers as that which the deplorable loss of the United States submarine S-4 has brought forth. Members of Congress, seeking as usual to make political gain, have displayed as perhaps never before their ignorance of naval matters; editors have printed letters which, had they shown a like want of understanding upon any other conceivable subject, would have found their way to the yawning maw of the nearest trash basket; no bit of freak advice has been too wild to publish, and even the editorial articles themselves have in most cases displayed a sad lack of comprehension." The Provincetown Western Union office estimated that in the week after the collision almost 520,000 words of news coverage had been sent out from Provincetown. The events of the past several days and the news coverage that emerged resulted in a tough week for Curtis Wilbur.

---

[*]This is in reference to a debate waged as to who reached the North Pole first: Dr. Frederick Cook in 1908 or Robert Peary in 1909.

Wilbur had become secretary of the navy on March 11, 1924, when his predecessor, Edwin Denby, was forced to resign the office due to blowback from the Teapot Dome Scandal of the Harding administration. Wilbur was an amalgam of navy man and jurist. He graduated third in his class at the US Naval Academy in 1888, but shortly thereafter he resigned his commission to study law. He eventually became the chief justice of the California Supreme Court; he was then summoned by Calvin Coolidge to take over the navy. He was considered to be a personable, forthright, and honest man who to this point had taken on some controversial positions, such as standing against Prohibition and advocating for the development of naval air power.

The *S-4* incident may have been one of the most tumultuous crises in Wilbur's tenure thus far. It is probable that President Coolidge either ordered or made a strong suggestion to Curtis Wilbur to visit Provincetown on Christmas Eve.

The *Brooklyn Daily Eagle* noted:

> There is nothing that either of them [Wilbur and Hughes] can do except the all-important function of attempting to dissipate the impression that the navy has been lax or callous. That is the purpose of the visit, which is almost without precedent. Not in years has a naval disaster brought such a flood of censure upon the Navy Department as the *S-4* tragedy. The attitude of the department during the first few days was rather resentful of this criticism, and very impatient at outside suggestion or advice. During the past 48 hours, however, this attitude has changed. But so general and so biting has been the public criticism which rolled up during the past week that the Navy Department finally realized that the *S-4* disaster was very much the public's business.

So while Wilbur was certainly courteous to Mrs. M. T. Stevens when she intercepted him at Union Station in Providence, meeting a grieving mother of one of the *S-4*'s victims was likely the last thing he wanted to do. But there were the reporters present, and Wilbur would not dare to be anything but kind and gentle to Mrs. Stevens. He offered her a lift to Provincetown.

As Stevens walked with Wilbur and Hughes to a waiting car she asked, "Is there any hope that the men are alive?"

Hughes, who did not have the tact of the secretary of the navy, replied, "Not a chance."

"Then why does the navy continue to pump air into the submarine if there is no hope?"

Hughes, contradicting himself, said, "We can't afford to take that chance. There might be a faint spark of life."

Wilbur, Hughes, and Mrs. Stevens talked, but whenever she asked about the S-4, they changed the topic. At one point, Admiral Hughes expressed concern for the health of Admiral Brumby and was afraid that he might overwork himself and get sick.

But Mrs. Stevens was concerned about her boy.

After the three-hour ride, the car rolled up to the Coast Guard office at the west end of Provincetown. The town itself seemed indifferent to the arrival of the secretary of the navy. The people in Provincetown had just undergone a week of tension that culminated in heartbreak.

Wilbur stepped out of the car, a worried look on his face, Hughes in his wake. Mrs. Stevens, however, was quickly hustled into the Coast Guard office. She spent five minutes talking to Coast Guard officers before being taken to the local Red Cross. She would return home that night, thinking her whole trip was worthless, but not before speaking with reporters and stating that "the navy cares nothing for life."

As for Wilbur and Hughes, they headed into the Coast Guard office and had a private meeting with Howard Wilcox, the commander of that district. Meanwhile, on the first floor of the office, reporters milled about, waiting for the secretary to come downstairs.

Wilbur soon did, and positioned himself before an old-fashioned stove that gave off a much-welcomed heat, since the temperature outside had plunged again. It was now below 20 degrees with high winds. Hughes stood off to the side.

Wilbur agreed to take questions. One of the first questions asked was, "Is there any significance to your visit on Christmas Eve?"

Wilbur replied, "There was not. I merely came down to see how things were going with the salvage fleet."

Another reporter queried, "What do you think of the *S-4* situation?"

At this point, Hughes interjected: "I believe the secretary is perfectly satisfied."

Another reporter then asked about criticisms concerning the rescue operations.

Wilbur said, "The men have done their job. They have done all it was humanly possible to do. Captain King and Lieutenant Commander Ellsberg and others have had previous experience in this kind of task. They were on the job when the *S-51* was raised. A number of divers here were also working on the salvaging of the *S-51*. I have the utmost confidence in the men on the *Falcon*."

Wilbur went on. "We will continue with the salvaging work with the idea of getting the ship up as soon as possible. Of course we will be governed by the weather conditions and all decisions are only tentative. We plan to use every resource of the government to do all that can be done."

Wilbur's news, that the salvage operation should continue, was somewhat surprising. The reporters knew that the officers of the *Falcon* had told them that the salvage should continue in the spring when the weather was calmer and warmer. Some of the officers had even packed their bags. The tip of Cape Cod offered some protection from the worst of the Atlantic's elements, particularly easterly gales, but still the conditions would be miserable, if not dangerous, for the divers.

Then another reporter asked, "What everyone here is anxious to know, is why the operation by which the air was pumped in through the SC tube on the side of the of the submarine from Wednesday night to last night could not have been done Sunday night when divers were going down and the men in the forward torpedo compartment were calling for help?"

Wilbur replied, "As I understand it, hose lines were attached to the salvage line of the submarine on Sunday. At that time and up to early Monday morning there was every reason to believe the air was getting into that compartment. Then when it was discovered that the air was not getting in because of a broken line in the submarine and that a small amount of water had come in instead, the storm came and no more divers could go down." Even Wilbur was confused by what had happened.

Then Wilbur was asked, "What is the explanation of the delay in rescue operations from Sunday morning to Wednesday afternoon?"

Wilbur answered, "The weather conditions would not permit diving."

Then another reporter asked, "Why doesn't the navy have a salvage ship like the German *Vulkan*, which is reputed to be able to raise a submarine quickly?"*

Wilbur made no reply to the question. He was probably unfamiliar with the *Vulkan*, but somebody like Edward Ellsberg could have answered this question as he did to reporters the next day, explaining that the submarines that the *Vulkan* salvaged were much lighter than S-class submarines.

The reporters turned their attention to politics. "What do you think of the resolution which Congressman Gifford of Massachusetts proposes to introduce in Congress concerning the withholding of news of the disaster by the navy from the American people?"

"I won't answer that question," replied Wilbur. "I have no comment to make."

Admiral Hughes headed toward the door, "I think we had better get out there. They are waiting for us with the boat."

Wilbur followed Hughes but stopped, turned to reporters, and said, "I am not here to answer criticisms or to be catechized."

Wilbur and Hughes headed outside, where a gang of photographers and newsreel men filmed the pair as they boarded a Coast Guard patrol boat. A couple of representatives from the press went with them.

The boat headed into Provincetown Harbor. It was cold and windy. A new gale had come, a nor'easter with upwards of fifty-mile-per-hour winds. It threatened to hamstring the salvage effort—the *Falcon* had been torn from its moorings the night before. The waters grew rough as they rounded the hook of Long Point and headed toward Wood End.

Wilbur looked at the land and said to Hughes, "If the submarine was inside of that hook she'd be much better off, wouldn't she?"

---

*The *Vulkan* was a former German salvage ship that recovered some U-Boats during the 1910s and World War I. At the end of the war it was given over to the British, who promptly sank it in 1919.

Hughes agreed. "It looks pretty bad out there. There's one thing about it. You can't hold a ship steady in this weather and you drag the diver too."

Soon enough, Wilbur and Hughes came to the salvage fleet. First they saw three sister vessels of the *S-4*: the *S-3*, *S-6*, and *S-8*. These were standing by to be used by the salvage team's divers to rehearse before going down to the wreck. In the midst of the submarines was the *Falcon*. Since the wind was high, no diving was being conducted.

The Coast Guard boat came alongside the *Falcon* and latched on. The secretary of the navy boarded the ship with little ceremony. Waiting for him was Rear Admiral Frank Brumby. Brumby looked tired and disheveled, as if he had not changed his clothes for several nights.

Wilbur extended his hand. "Hello, Brumby. How are you?"

● ● ●

Work on the wreck had been frantic. On December 23, three divers had suffered mishaps. Frank Crilley suffered a blowup when his air valve malfunctioned and blew in too much air. When Crilley popped up at the surface, six tenders leapt onto the diving platform to haul him aboard and then into the decompression chamber.

Frank Mattox's suit was cut among the wreckage. The winter water filled his suit from his feet to his shoulders, but he kept on working for an hour. Joe Schaddt injured his ears while on the bottom. Despite the injuries, the divers had completed one tunnel for the pontoon chains and were working on a second.

For the reporters, there was more positive news. The drubbing the newspapers had given the rescue effort, particularly after the story about Brumby leaving McGinley's father at the scene had been published, made the navy realize they needed a public relations manager. They assigned an officer to do the job.

The meeting with Wilbur and Hughes aboard the *Falcon* lasted two hours. Brumby, King, Hartley, Ellsberg, and Saunders were present. The officers related to Wilbur and Hughes all that had occurred over the past several days. They told them about the failed attempt to blow the ballast tanks, the desperate effort of Michels to hook up the compartment salvage line, and Eadie's heroics. Then they spoke of the trip to Boston and the continued storm that finally defeated the rescue mission.

Eadie was called in to meet Hughes and Wilbur. Wilbur told Eadie that "further recognition of the deed" was forthcoming.

Then they turned to the question of whether or not to continue the salvage. Wilbur and Hughes made the case to carry on salvage. First, they said that it was necessary because of the public sentiment about the disaster. Second, Provincetown was more sheltered than Block Island, where the *S-51* went down. To Wilbur and Hughes, it was plausible to raise the *S-4* in winter.

A winter salvage operation was something that had never been tried before. Indeed, all the officers who were present at that meeting who later wrote anything about the matter wanted to halt operations until spring. But Wilbur had made the directive, and it was to be done.

Wilbur then addressed the crew of the *Falcon* and thanked them for their efforts. According to Henry Hartley, Wilbur's Christmas Eve message had "exceptionally kind, sympathetic and encouraging words [that] were highly appreciated by all hands. We were not unmindful of the fact that the Secretary and Chief of Naval Operations' Christmas Eve were no more cheerful than ours."

Wilbur and Hughes left via the destroyer *Mahan*. According to the *New York Times* they had to leap aboard the *Mahan* as the *Falcon* hit the crest of a big wave. They sailed for Boston. Curtis Wilbur was to spend his Christmas at his sister's in Pennsylvania, where reporters hounded him.

The mission was now officially reorganized as the *S-4* Salvage Force. Men were sent from the overcrowded *Falcon* to the *Bushnell*, which was to become the flagship of the salvage fleet. Christmas dinner was postponed until December 26. There was a certain melancholy on the *Falcon*. The *Boston Daily Globe* reported that even Henry Hartley's dog Pete was downcast. After eating his midday meal, Pete "slunk away aft, eagerly trying to go ashore in the Admiral's launch alongside." But the holiday was not to be a complete loss as the tug *Tuscarora* brought presents and turkeys and other edibles for the salvage workers from their families and friends.

After the rescue mission was officially made into a salvage mission, Ellsberg arranged for his departure. He had reason to resent Wilbur and Hughes for making the decision to continue a salvage operation, though his feelings on the subject are unrecorded. In any event, he left the Salvage Force on New Year's Day and returned to his job at Tidewater. In the meantime, Commander Harold Saunders took up the job as salvage officer.

• • •

At dusk on Christmas Eve, the folk of Provincetown made their way down to the seaside and gathered at Sklaroff's* Wharf. The pier extended far into the harbor and provided a good view of Long Point and Wood End, where the rescue flotilla was gathered. The memorial service was to begin at high tide. The people of Provincetown had kept vigil since the first night. Mary Heaton Vorse later wrote, "I have been in a mining town when men have been trapped in a mine. Provincetown was like this—everyone waiting for word from below, only there wasn't even a pit mouth to wait around."

The people at Sklaroff's Wharf did not carry candles, nor did they sing. The only lights, in fact, were the blinking lights of the *Falcon* and its mates off Wood End. Hundreds of people gathered, but they did not make a noise except for the occasional sob. At 6:30 PM, bells rang in a small church, and when done, bells were rung at other churches.

Out of the darkness came the voice of Reverend C. C. Davis, the pastor of a local Methodist church. He eulogized the men of the *S-4* and ended with "We hope, O God, that the heroic service and sacrifice of these men who are dead will be an inspiration to all the rest of us who are yet alive."

"Taps" played. Then the people of Provincetown went one by one to the water and threw sprigs of evergreen and flowers into the ebbing tide of the sea.

The reporters left the town. By 11:00 PM on Christmas Eve, Provincetown had fallen into a quiet, cold darkness.

---

*Pronounced "Sky-Loft," this pier was a forerunner of Fisherman's Wharf.

25

Bringing Up the Bodies

THE S-4 SALVAGE FORCE WAS forged into a well-organized flotilla of ten vessels, not including the numerous small Coast Guard craft that helped transfer people, stores, and mail between ships. The *Bushnell* served as the base vessel, supply depot, and repair shop. The tugs *Wandank* and *Sagamore* assisted the *Falcon* in maneuvers. The *S-6* was used as a model and rehearsal stage for the divers. During these rehearsals, with their colleagues looking on, divers donned their gear, minus the helmets, and worked their way through the vessel as if on the job. The rehearsals were a serious business. Submarine spaces were cramped. It was too easy for a line to snag, a helmet to catch on a pipe, or a thousand other problems to occur that might kill a diver—not to mention the added complications of a winter salvage.

The navy provided everything that the Salvage Force might have wished. King commented in his memoirs that the navy "provided readily and immediately everything and everyone required to complete the work." This was high praise coming from the irascible King, who, like all the officers of the rescue mission, was doubtful about the possibility of raising the *S-4* quickly.

King, in fact, became the commander of the entire operation shortly after rescue efforts were called off. Admiral Brumby returned to his general command and for some weeks King informally headed the Salvage Force. Then on January 25, 1928, Brumby was officially detached from command, and he joined the fleet on the regular winter cruise. Secretary Wilbur was quick to point out that the transfer was routine and only delayed due to a Court of Inquiry that was being held about the *S-4* disaster. It was a sensitive point, as Brumby had become depicted by some reporters as at best unknowledgeable and at worst foolish.* There were certainly reasons why Brumby would be removed as the head of the salvage operations aside from possible political pressure: there was simply no need for a flag officer on the project, and Brumby did not have a working knowledge of submarines or salvage. But the criticism was still highly unfair, a visceral response to the tragedy. In any event, Wilbur announced that Captain Ernest King would now officially head operations.

The Salvage Force headed by King was composed of a corps of officers, enlisted personnel, and civilians who were the most knowledgeable people in the country, if not the world, in submarine salvage. Many were old hands on the *S-51* job, such as technical assistant J. C. Niedermair, who did much of the calculations and draftsmanship, and Clarence Tibbals, who directed diving operations. Then there were the divers, almost half of whom had worked on the *S-51*. Approximately twenty-four qualified divers were aboard the *Falcon*, divided into three sections. Divers worked for two weeks, then had one week off. In this way, one section was always on leave, with the intent to keep morale high during a hazardous job.

The operation was conceptually the same as that of the *S-51*. Divers would enter the submarine and seal all sealable compartments. Next they would slip a spill pipe with a strainer at the bottom into the compartment at the lowest possible level. Then the divers would seal the hatches with the pipe sticking out and attach an air hose to the pipe. When it was time to rid the *S-4* of water, compressed air would be pumped through the hose and into the spill pipe, which would push the water out of the compartment through one-way outlets that emptied to the sea. Lifting chains were to be passed under the hull,

---

*Perhaps the most biting articles concerned an incident in which Brumby had mistakenly invited a car salesman from Lafayette, Indiana, to visit the Salvage Force and had him presented to reporters as a salvage expert.

A diver being sent down to assist in salvaging the *S-4.*
Courtesy of the Trustees of the Boston Public Library, Leslie Jones Collection

and then divers would attach eighty-ton salvage pontoons to them. The pontoons* would be filled with water so they could be lowered into the sea. Then, after everything was tested and ready, compartments and pontoons would be blown free of water by the compressed air generators aboard the *Falcon.* In theory, the submarine would rise to the surface, where it would be hooked up for towing.

However, several factors made this salvage attempt different than the *S-51* job. First, the location, close to Provincetown Harbor, provided a barrier against some of the worst of the winter elements. But local climate made salvage work unpredictable, as conditions changed hourly. Second, the consistency of the bottom was much muddier than off Block Island, where the *S-51* sank. Instead of coarse

---

*The pontoons were branded with Y.S.P. for "yard salvage pontoon."

sand, divers plunged around in mud, which kicked up fine silt that obscured sight. When the team began to wash tunnels, so much silt was dislodged that a diver could not see his submersible lamp, even when it was pressed against his faceplate. Still, it was easier to dig these tunnels than at the *S-51* site, since the adhesive mud off Wood End held the tunnels together much better. Third, the *S-4* was lighter than the *S-51*, and therefore required fewer pontoons to lift the vessel—six instead of eight. But fourth, and what truly made this job different than the *S-51*, was the season.

Bitter cold plagued the salvage efforts, with the temperature plunging down at times to near zero. Seawater froze over the *Falcon*'s deck and even the hawsers became encased in ice.* Whenever humidity was over 90 percent and temperatures low, which happened often enough, air in the hoses would condense and freeze. On roughly half of all the days in January, there could be no diving because the air supply would freeze. As operations ground to a halt, Saunders and Hartley worked out a schematic for a piece of equipment that would dry the air in the *Falcon*'s air compressors. The plans were sent to the Boston Navy Yard.

In the meantime, diving continued when it could—the immediate work was to clear away the wreckage and thick wires surrounding the *S-4*. This made diving safer. A day or two was spent working on clearing wreckage. To cut wires and lines, divers used a large V-shaped hook with a sharpened edge on the inside. This was lowered to a diver from the *Falcon*. The wires were then fitted to the hook and then the topside would haul the hook up, cutting the wires. Then all of the mess, including a large piece of the *Paulding*'s bow, was hauled to the surface.

Meanwhile, tunnel washing continued. While the mud was more conducive to tunneling than at the *S-51* site, conditions were still dangerous. On December 30, divers Eadie and Mattox were washing tunnels out with high-powered hoses from opposite sides of the submarine—the idea was that the two tunnels would be joined in the

---

*Fortunately, the team learned a trick from the local Provincetown fishermen: dunking the ropes in the water would thaw them out enough to be useful again.

middle. Eadie was practically under the *S-4*'s keel when he got a call that Mattox was in trouble.

Eadie stopped what he was doing and headed over to help Mattox. When he arrived, he found that the high-pressure hose had wrapped about Mattox and was pulling him into the mud. Eadie cleared him and got him on the deck of the submarine. They were hauled up and placed in the decompression chamber.

By the end of that day, two of the three tunnels had been dug and cables had been rove through them. "That's a great relief," commented Captain King to reporters. In retrospect, it was remarkable how quickly the Salvage Force dug the tunnels. It took weeks of work on the *S-51* job.

Next, divers needed to enter the submarine, remove the victims, and start sealing the compartments. The first compartment that the divers were to enter was the engine room. On December 31, divers went down to the wreck and removed the wooden grating that covered the engine room hatch. Then they used a seven-foot-long wrench with a sledgehammer to unscrew the bolt at the top of the hatch. To the divers' surprise, they found that water started to rush into the engine room. Since the failure to blow the ballast tanks during the initial rescue efforts, the Salvage Force had assumed the engine room to be flooded. Divers quickly plugged the hole, and a conference was held on the *Falcon*.

The fact that the engine room was dry, or at least partially free of water, made it clear that the men trapped in the rear of the *S-4* did not drown. What is more, because no air bubbles came out of the engine room hatch at any time, it was apparent that the compartment was always well sealed. However, this brought up the question as to why Jones and those aft of the battery room never responded to any signaling when Eadie first landed on the wreck. The salvage officers supposed the men in the rear of the *S-4* may have been killed by chlorine gas, or perhaps they succumbed quickly to carbon dioxide poisoning. Until they could get a diver into the wreck, this would remain a mystery.

The officers decided it would be better to allow the engine room to flood. Divers would need to enter the compartment anyway to prepare the submarine for salvage, and water had to enter in order to open the access hatch. A diver was sent down that afternoon to remove the plug. A few hours later, water was still entering the compartment.

The Salvage Force never found out how long it took to flood the engine room since that evening, December 31, gales and freezing weather bombarded New England again, driving the *Falcon* from the scene. The ship retired to Provincetown Harbor, where divers conducted rehearsal operations aboard the *S-6*.

On New Year's Day 1928 Edward Ellsberg departed from the Salvage Force. But the *S-4* was constantly on his mind. He turned his able pen to defend the rescue efforts, publishing several pieces in national publications that explained that the navy was only stymied by the weather. He delivered lectures, including one at Harvard University, trying to spread word to the public that nothing could have been done to save the men of the *S-4*.

Commander Harold E. "Savvy" Saunders became salvage officer. He was inexperienced in direct salvage, but he was a submarine expert. He was the officer in charge of constructing newer V-class submarines in Portsmouth, and he had done postgraduate work at MIT in submarine design. Saunders did not quite have the passionate fire of Ellsberg—few men did—but he possessed an integrity and passion for the work that bled through in his writings. Few people in the world knew as much about submarine construction as "Savvy" Saunders.

Ellsberg's departure also coincided with the return of Fred Michels. Michels, who knew personally how impossible it was to save the men in the torpedo room, stated to reporters, "We could not buck the elements, especially with seas running as high as they were. You can't lick old King Neptune." But Michels did not dwell on his near-death experience. He was happy to return to the *Falcon* after spending days at the Boston Naval Hospital.

The wind was too fierce or the water too cold for actual dives, so rehearsals continued through January 3. To test the conditions, the Salvage Force sent a fully rigged dummy diver, nicknamed "Jake," down to the bottom with a thermometer inside the helmet. Those on the surface carefully observed the bubbles coming up from the dummy. If the bubbles stopped, this meant that air had condensed inside the line and frozen, blocking the air supply. Jake was extremely handy in forewarning of when conditions were too hazardous.

On one of these cold, early January days the Salvage Force was visited by Representative Fiorello La Guardia of New York. The diminutive but feisty politician had decided to visit the salvage site to assess whether the navy had truly done all it could. La Guardia was transported to Provincetown on the submarine *S-8*, and then he visited the *Falcon*. Because of the cold, there was no diving, but La Guardia spoke to the officers and divers. La Guardia, aside from gaining firsthand experience in an S-class submarine, probably also witnessed diver rehearsals and saw how the conditions prevented work. At the end of his visit, La Guardia tore up a speech that he had written to denounce the navy. "There is more misinformation loose concerning this accident than anything else I have seen in twenty-three years of public life," he said. "Most of us don't understand what a complicated piece of machinery a submarine is or how difficult it is to rescue when in deep water."

The navy had won an important supporter, who eventually went on to become one of the most famous mayors in New York City's history. King, in his autobiography, credited this visit for helping to turn around public opinion about the navy.

The day after La Guardia's visit, on the morning of January 4, Jake the dummy diver's air hose froze. By the afternoon, however, temperatures had warmed enough for working on the bottom. Divers went down, opened the hatch to the engine room, and for the first time entered the *S-4*.

The water was dark and filled with oil that made it difficult, even with the submersible lamp, to see. But it did not take long to find the first victims of the disaster. Three bodies were bunched together by the foot of the engine room ladder. They were near the dogged door to the control room. These were Machinist's Mate Aron Hodges, Lieutenant Joseph McGinley, and Lieutenant Commander Roy Jones, commanding officer of the *S-4*.

The Salvage Force, in order to do their job and to bring some sense of closure to the families of the *S-4*'s crew, needed to remove the victims. That was the grim reality of the situation. Each diver coped with this task in different ways and to a certain extent, when one reads the recollections of the divers, there was a certain degree of objectifying of the victims.

These three victims were fumbled to the hatch. Another diver tied them to a line by which they were hauled to the surface. It was soon found that the most expedient way to extract the dead was by using lines that had multiple tails on it. That is, divers took a rope and attached shorter lines to it. This line would then be tied to the outside of the *S-4* and passed inside. When the bodies were ready to be hauled to the surface, the divers would then attach this line to another line, which would be hauled upward by men on the *Falcon*.

The dead, inundated with water, were weightless. Tom Eadie wrote, "The bodies were almost the specific gravity of water. You could bring two of them along at the same time; they would swim after you through the water apparently without any weight at all."

Once hauled to the surface, the bodies were not brought aboard the *Falcon* but rather left in the sea for preservation until crew members on one of the *Bushnell*'s motorboats picked them up, put them in body bags, and gave them to a medical team.

Over the next several days, more bodies were recovered as divers went down in teams. On January 6, diver Ingram found two bodies, including that of Lieutenant Commander Callaway from the inspection board. Later that day, divers Kelley, Wickwire, and Burd found two more corpses lying between the engines beneath a canvas sail that the victims had erected as some sort of shelter.

On January 7, Eadie went down with divers Carr and Applegate. Eadie went inside the engine room, Carr remained by the foot of the ladder, and Applegate stayed on the deck. Eadie found a victim's body, which he passed to Carr. Carr got a line on it, but Applegate had trouble pulling the body through the hatch. In the meantime Eadie, not knowing of the trouble, continued to search.

Between the engines, Eadie found more bodies and sent them back to Carr. Every corpse that was found by Eadie and the other divers had its own story to tell. Eadie wrote, "I had found two of them lying cuddled together, and I have always figured they were buddies who simply clung together at the last. One man we found with half a raw potato clutched in his hand, and one more with half a potato in his pocket. We suppose that they had gnawed at them to ease irritation caused by chlorine gas in their throats." One of the victims, found later, was lying in a cot, set up in the motor room. He had burn marks on his face. This man was the one who had been scorched when seawater got into the electrical systems of the control room.

Eadie returned to the foot of the ladder, carefully crouching and backing out of the narrow space between the engines. He then bumped into the floor grating overhead. Eadie became disoriented and found himself surrounded by bodies—the ones he had been sending back to Carr. After regaining his senses, he saw the trouble. Applegate and Carr were trying to haul out the first body, but the victim's neck kept hitting the frame of the engine room hatch. Eadie got them to give some slack on the line, so they could get that body out. Then Eadie had another line passed down. He managed to secure four bodies to a line designed for three.

January 11 started ominously, with Jake's air hose freezing, but the Salvage Force decided to try diving anyway. Eadie, Carr, and another diver went down. Eadie went into the submarine and began to find more victims quickly. These were all along the engine room deck, strung out in an orderly way. Some corpses were over others so that as Eadie started to pull one, the others followed along.

He passed them up to Carr on the deck. Eadie tried to pass up a ninth body, but Carr refused to take it. Eadie came out to the deck of the *S-4* to find that the third diver who went down with them, too squeamish to handle the victims, had retreated to the *Falcon*. About the deck of the *S-4* were five bodies and Carr, with one between his legs and one each under his arms. He had positioned himself so that none of the bodies would float away with the current. As Carr held the bodies, Eadie tied them to lines. Carr and Eadie brought up eight bodies on a single dive—the most during the salvage operation.

When the divers entered the control room, they found no bodies, a surprise to the Salvage Force. It was only then that the Salvage Force began to understand the true plight of the *S-4*. The submariners had been driven from the control room, the heart of the ship, and once they'd abandoned it, they'd lost any hope of helping themselves.

Eventually, divers found that they could not operate the flapper valve for the ventilation shaft between the battery and control compartments. Hartley gave orders to examine the valve and its duct. After many days, they found it—Jones's green curtain—the decoration that killed the men of the *S-4*. After some difficulty and multiple dives, it was removed and the valve shut.

As divers hunted for the victims they found that some of the compartments were not completely flooded. Pockets of air were often trapped inside the submarine, or built up from the bubbles emanating from the divers' exhaust. Divers Campbell, Crilley, and Baker were sent down to the motor room on January 8 to locate more of the *S-4's* crew. They were given orders that the bodies should be passed up through the motor room hatch, which would be more expeditious than passing the bodies along to the engine room. Campbell was given instructions to open the motor room's hatch from the inside, which would be easier than from the outside due to sea pressure. Campbell climbed up to the hatch and found that his heavy helmet emerged in an air pocket. Without the support of the water he became so top-heavy that he could not reach the hatch. The Salvage Force needed to open the hatch from the outside.

Not all the bodies were recovered. Over the course of a week, the divers had recovered thirty-two of the *S-4's* forty men. Six they knew were still in the torpedo room—Fitch and his company. The other two were still unaccounted for. Even though a submarine has a relatively small interior space, there are many nooks and crannies in which bodies could hide. The divers, restricted as they were by their gear and limited in vision by their helmets, could easily have overlooked the missing submariners.

Due to the size and various angles of the other hatches, divers could only safely enter the *S-4* through the engine room hatch. From there, they sojourned to either the motor room aft, or the control room forward. Divers did not dare pass through the battery room, since that is where the cut was—it was filled with debris.

As for the torpedo room, it was physically impossible for a diver to enter. During rehearsals aboard the *S-6*, divers found the entry hatch to the torpedo room had been shaped at an angle to make it easier to load torpedoes. A diver could back down through the hatch and drop onto the torpedo room floor—his belt and boots would keep him upright. But a diver would be hard-pressed to get back out. The bodies of the six men who died in the torpedo room could not be recovered.

This did not mean much to the wife of Russell Crabb, whose husband's body lay in the torpedo room. She sent a telegram to Governor Fuller of Massachusetts: PLEASE DEMAND THAT MY HUSBAND'S BODY IN THE TORPEDO ROOM OF THE S-4 BE RECOVERED AT ONCE BY THE NAVY. I DO NOT FEEL THAT IT IS NECESSARY FOR IT TO BE LEFT THERE UNTIL THE BOAT IS RAISED.

Tom Eadie sympathized and wished to recover the bodies. He knew about the difficulty of the angle of the torpedo room hatch. "You couldn't pull yourself up onto that slide; you had to bend to get there. I volunteered to try it, but they said, 'No—it would only mean seven men in there instead of six.' But I wasn't going it blind; I had figured out a way. I was going to slide a stout metal bar alongside the torpedo slide, and have it long enough to go all the way to the floor on that angle. Then I meant to use it as a trapeze to pull myself up on, taking the proper angle before I started. I could cut off my air supply to make myself heavy, and a man outside would catch my helmet and pull. But they wouldn't let me do it."*

As the dead were removed, the divers also performed the all-important job of sealing the individual compartments by shutting valves and hatches. While making sure valves were closed may seem like a simple matter, each compartment had a large number of them, and winter diving in the dark, oily waters inside the S-4 made it difficult work. The list of valves in the control room, for example, included:

- Voice tube bulkhead valve (two of these)
- Washbasin drain valve
- Main induction valve lever

---

*After diving resumed after the Christmas storm, divers found that the connection to the SC tube had carried away. This had permitted water to partially flood the torpedo room. Later, it was decided to allow the compartment to remain flooded, as the seawater would help preserve the bodies.

- Control room supply ventilation hull valve
- Control room exhaust ventilation outboard valve
- Battery exhaust outboard valve
- Battery exhaust hull valve
- Radio trunk lower flap valve
- Bulkhead valve for battery exhaust
- Main induction trunk valve drain

This compartment alone had a total of twenty valves. Often, the valves were under floor plates, behind machinery, or overhead. Sometimes divers would enter the wreck and not find the valve, despite the rehearsals on the *S-6*. After multiple dives and with some luck, the diver found the valve but then might be stymied because his thick gloves would not allow him to hold a wheel—it was too close to the pipe it was attached to. In these cases, special wrenches were fabricated on the *Bushnell* and given to a diver. Then the diver might lose the wrench as it fell behind inaccessible equipment. To ensure that the diver did not lose the tool again, a duplicate was made and tied to his wrist. Then the valve could be closed in three minutes. But it took six dives to do it over the course of several days.

Sometimes pipes and other outlets could not simply be turned off by a valve. In these cases divers would "blank off" a pipe by sealing it with a cap. At other times, when there was no valve or blanking off was impractical, the divers would seal a pipe by filling it with underwater cement.

Of critical importance was getting a spill pipe into the torpedo room. But the only way they could do it was to cut a hole using an underwater torch. This proved a particular nuisance, as the divers had continuous problems using the torch. It was not until February that the hole was cut.

On the positive side, the air hose icing problem was solved, at least in theory. On January 23, the *Falcon* weighed anchor and made for the Boston Navy Yard, where the navy installed a new air unit that removed moisture from the ship's air compressors. The *Falcon* returned to Wood End two days later. Divers should now have been able to go to the bottom even with humidity at 100 percent and air temperatures at 10 degrees Fahrenheit. But the divers didn't trust the new unit.

On January 27, the unit was tested by Jake the dummy diver. The hose showed no signs of icing. Hartley and Saunders determined it would be safer if the divers did work outside the submarine. Six divers were sent down to work, using the new air system. They then reported their condition.

Tom Eadie, who was the first, reported feeling dazed and having frequent belches. Eadie wrote, "The air had a peculiar smell, and it seemed as though my lungs wouldn't fill with air. All my movements had to be slow. I went forward and secured a new descending line, but that was about all I could do." Carr reported difficulty breathing. Eiben was struck by a bad headache; "Tug" Wilson said he felt fatigued. But then Kelley and Crilley, who went last, reported feeling normal.

Eadie believed the trouble was that oil used during the initial installation of the pump was burning off during its first uses and getting into the compressed air. By the time Kelley went down, the foul air had worked itself off. But Hartley had another notion. "The adverse effect of the partly dehydrated air as reported . . . was mainly the power of suggestion made by an officer who <u>probably</u> did consider that his ideas were correct and who on numerous occasions seemed to lose all sense of loyalty, etc."*

The next day, the Salvage Force held tests of the new equipment in the decompression chamber. All agreed the air was fine. The icing problem was over.

As the winter progressed, the chill of January moderated so that the winter on the whole was calmer and warmer. This allowed for more continuous days of work. On February 1 Michels made his first dive since he was rescued by Eadie. Some crew on the *Falcon* thought he wasn't going to dive again. But Michels pleaded to go down, and when he returned from the bottom he was, as Eadie put it, "as happy as a kid."

Next, it was time to finish digging tunnels so that the final pontoon chain could be readied. Access to the oil tanks was also needed; they had to be drained to prevent potential pollution and to lighten

---

*Hartley never named the officer.

the boat. This task meant that two more tunnels had to be dug—one more than what the Salvage Force initially expected. The first two tunnels, which had already been completed, were washed out for the forward and rear pair of pontoons. These tunnels were considered to be easier to dig since they were toward the ends of the boat, where the submarine was thinner. The central tunnels, however, did cause the divers some alarm, since they'd had substantial problems digging the middle tunnels under the *S-51*.

Saunders and Hartley had given the matter some thought and discussed it with the divers. They had the divers wash their tunnels by first creating a wide hollow that could catch the tunneling refuse. Divers were instructed to begin by standing with their back toward the submarine, and create a wide dish in the mud. Diver Kelley's suggestion to have a diver relieve the man directly at the nozzle proved to be a good one since much time had been lost in one diver trying to pick up the work where the other left off. The water never needed to be shut off; they only needed to telephone to the top to have them reduce the pressure from 150 to 90 pounds per square inch during the transfer. By early March, the two tunnels were completed. The *Falcon* had the fuel inside the *S-4* pumped into its own tanks.

Next, the divers had to make sure that all the outer hatches were fully sealed. Submarine hatches by their nature were one-way doors. They did well at keeping water out, but they were not especially built to withstand strong internal pressure. When the time came, compressed air that would be at a much higher pressure than the surrounding water pressure would be pumped into the *S-4*. The regular hatches by themselves would not be able to stand such pressure. Special salvage hatches were affixed and secured over the old hatches. These were typically equipped with valves for pumping water or air into each compartment as necessary.

Not every hatch could be connected with a salvage hatch due to size, difficulty in disconnecting the old hatch, or any of the innumerable technical problems that plagued a complex salvage mission. When fitting a salvage hatch to the control room proved too difficult, divers weighed down the original hatch using pig lead and sealed it with cement.

As each compartment was sealed and air hoses and spill pipes put into place, each was tested for leaks. The last thing anyone wanted was for the *S-4* to go back down after it was raised. This test was done by turning on the air into the compartments, raising the air pressure, and observing when bubbles came to the surface. When bubbles started coming out, this meant that the compartment was free of water and now the air pressure was overcoming the surrounding water pressure. Saunders, who typically manned the compressors, would then slowly ease back on the air pressure to the point that it leveled out. Meanwhile, while one compartment was blown free of water, others were flooded to make sure the *S-4* stayed on the bottom. Every small detail needed to be perfect.

After sealing was successfully tested, divers were to attach the six salvage pontoons to the submarine. This operation was a delicate business in that the pontoons, while improved from the *S-51* operation,* were still unstable. Even getting the chains through the tunnels was a difficult job, since the divers themselves could not directly handle the massive chains but had to guide the chains through with reeving wire. Two divers were given the wire, which was attached to the chains. Then the divers went to either side of the wreck, entered the tunnel, and met in the middle. The wire was then connected, and the large chain was passed through. Meanwhile, special guards were placed by the other chains to minimize the chance of them slipping off the submarine's hull.

After this step, the divers set up the towing equipment in the hopeful eventuality that the *S-4*, when it came to the surface, could be hauled to the Boston Navy Yard. Again, the operation was delicate and detailed and required many days of work. By the time everything was set, all hands were exhausted.†

---

*These pontoons were of a different design than the pontoons used on the *S-51* salvage. The revised model had three internal chambers to give more control over motion.

†It was even more exhausting after a nor'easter struck on March 9, 1928. The *Falcon* went to Provincetown Harbor to ride out the storm, but then was suddenly called to assist a liner that had struck a set of treacherous rocks in Cape Cod Bay. The *Falcon* went, but found that the situation was under control. The *Falcon* rode out the storm. Hartley remained at the bridge all night. He later wrote, "This had been a rather hectic week."

On March 13, the pontoons were lowered and put into position. On March 16, the last diver to work on the wreck, Bill Carr, came to the surface. All the hoses, all the attachments were ready for hook up at the surface. There was no more need to dive. Everything was ready, as long as the weather cooperated.

Conditions for the past several days had been unpredictable. Forecasts had called for a nor'easter, but none had materialized during the pontoon attachment phase. On the night of March 16, snow had fallen, and it seemed like another blow was coming. Even though everybody was ready to attempt to raise the *S-4*, the *Falcon* was once again at the mercy of the elements.

26

"The Knee of the Gods"

DESPITE ALL PREDICTIONS, THE MORNING of March 17 dawned bright and clear. There was hardly a breath of wind. It was perfect.

Captain King, on the *Bushnell,* invited Lieutenant Hartley and Commander Saunders to breakfast with him aboard the *Bushnell.* The topic of conversation was the weather. The report from Boston looked favorable. Everybody agreed, and King gave the order: "All ships take stations for raising the *S-4.*"

A buzzing excitement filled the Salvage Force. A reporter from the *New York Times* approached Commander Saunders and reminded him that at 3:37 PM it would be three months since the *S-4* was sunk. "I think we can make it almost to the dot," said Saunders.

The *Falcon* moored over the *S-4* at 9:18 AM. By 10:23 AM, all the ships in the salvage squadron were in position.

At 10:30, the blowing hoses were connected to the *Falcon*'s air compressors.

At 11:04, Harold Saunders, seated on a pile of coiled air hoses and wearing a jaunty, striped stocking cap, began turning the spigots.

At 11:23, the control room had been blown dry.

At 11:57, the motor room had been blown dry.

At 1:19 PM, air to the functioning ballast tanks was turned on. They were cleared of water at 1:27.

Then Saunders vented the engine room and torpedo room. He did not completely empty these of water, due to a hunch that if the rooms were completely dry, the submarine would be too difficult to handle.

At 2:36 PM, Saunders turned on the air to the stern pontoons. He carefully monitored the gauges as he made adjustments. Minutes ticked by. Then, from the water there came a great burst of bubbles.

"There she is," shouted one of the divers.

At 2:58 PM, with a great jangling of chain, two pontoons broke the surface. These were the stern pontoons. The submarine's nose was still wedged into the sea floor. The *S-4* would not be considered raised until its conning tower came up and was visible. No part of the submarine could yet be seen. But this had been planned for.

Commander Harold Saunders, turning on the compressed air in order to raise the *S-4* on March 17, 1928. *Courtesy of the Library of Congress, Papers of Ernest J. King*

Saunders turned on the air to the other pontoons. Then more air was put into the engine room. Twenty-four minutes passed before the other pontoons broke the surface in a froth of white water.

A minute later, at 3:23 PM, the S-4's periscope broke the surface, followed by a good deal of its conning tower. Cheering broke out.

After working for more than three months, through 44 working days and 566 dives, the Salvage Force raised the S-4 in a winter operation. It had never been done before.

• • •

For all of a moment, the Salvage Force stared in disbelief at the periscope and conning tower peeping out of the water. The cursed S-4 had been raised in three months, in winter, with no significant injuries. Planes soared overhead, carrying newsmen snapping photographs. In Provincetown, a crowd had gathered on Sklaroff's Wharf to watch the proceedings. Meanwhile small motorboats from the Salvage Force set forth on the glassy water to arrange the twenty air hoses that connected the S-4 to the Falcon for the trip. These hoses needed to remain connected for the entire voyage to Boston.

After adjusting the pontoons, the Salvage Force, flags at half-mast, weighed anchor and set sail triumphantly at 4:50 PM. The Bushnell led the way. The Wandank and Sagamore followed, hauling the resurrected S-4, pontoons and all. The Falcon took the rear guard, holding the air hoses that were aproned from the submarine to the salvage ship. King joined the Falcon for the voyage.

The sea was calm, and the wind light. The salvage fleet, however, moved gingerly—first at 3 knots. King then picked up the pace to 5 knots, since the sea was smooth as they passed into Massachusetts Bay. But King backed off after a while and dropped back to 3 knots, fearing disaster. It was best to be cautious.

All signs showed for an easy voyage to Boston, fifty-four miles away. An easy swell met the flotilla as they said goodbye, at long last, to Wood End. The journey, while short in distance, would still take them overnight because of the snail-like pace. But all hands looked forward to the closure of bringing the S-4 home.

The *S-4*, being towed to Boston. The *Falcon* is on the left side of the photograph and is following the submarine, connected with multiple air hoses.
Courtesy of the Library of Congress, Papers of Ernest J. King

Then at 10:00 PM, a radio message came in from the navy: SPECIAL WEATHER REPORT FOR THE *S-4* SALVAGE FORCE. NORTHEAST STORM OF MARKED INTENSITY EXPECTED TO REACH THE COAST BY EARLY MORNING HOURS.

The message did not specify exactly *when* the "early morning" was, but an acute anxiety filled all hands. There was immediate debate and discussion. They could not stay where they were nor could they turn around and go back. They decided to increase speed to 3.7 knots and try to beat the weather. The *Falcon* radioed ahead to Boston, requesting expert pilots who could bring the Salvage Force into the Boston Navy Yard when they arrived.

By midnight, the wind had turned to a fresh gale from the northeast, and the sea opened into deep swells. Saunders, manning the compressors, blew air into the compartments, seeing that the *S-4* was settling deeper into the water.

At 2:00 AM, the storm struck as they neared the Minot's Ledge Lighthouse on the approach to Boston Harbor.

The wind picked up, and the seas ran. The pontoons thundered about in the water. King gave orders to the accompanying ships to station themselves next to the *S-4* to form a lee to protect it from the worst of the storm. But, as Saunders later wrote, "they were too small to break up the swells, and they could not remain close enough to help very much."

Saunders noted, "The pontoons were now beginning to pound each other, especially the bow and stern pairs, and the middle pontoons whipped back and forth, from port to starboard, like toy balloons with short strings trying to break away in a strong breeze. No one had ever seen a waterlogged submarine, hanging on pontoons, dragged through such waters as was found off Minot's Ledge and no one could say whether the gear would stand up under it or not." They continued on and passed the Boston Lightship.

The Salvage Force drew near the Graves, a collection of rocks about eleven miles offshore of Boston. All eyes, if not on lookout, were staring at the pontoons. The huge and heavy cylinders clashed unpredictably and violently against the outer superstructure of the *S-4*. But there was absolutely nothing they could do except carry on. Their only hope was to get into Boston Harbor before a new disaster struck.

At 5:09 AM on March 18, the Salvage Force passed the Graves. They still had the *S-4* in tow. Dawn broke cold and gray as they turned out of the sea and into the North Channel of Boston Harbor. They were out of the open sea at last.

But there was no solace here either. The long swells of Massachusetts Bay turned to short, high seas. This wreaked havoc on the pontoons, since it made the chains slack. They started to slip. Then, with another turn of the waves, the pontoons were yanked together hard in tremendous clamor. Saunders wrote, "Wave followed wave, with increasing severity, as the shallower water was reached, until it seemed that the pontoon chains could no longer withstand the shock and impact and that the next minute would see the *S-4* go to the bottom."

At this moment, Captain King was on the *Falcon*'s bridge with Lieutenant Hartley. Hartley, overworked, despaired. King wrote that he said to Hartley, "To please not give up since the matter was on the knee of the gods, and to try to help me to be more cheerful about it."

Then, they reached the deep anchorage of President Roads. The water calmed. The *S-4* was still attached to the pontoons. A flag, half-masted, was placed on the *S-4*'s conning tower. Then the submarine was towed to the Boston Navy Yard, and brought into dry dock number two near the *Constitution*, which was undergoing restoration.

The Salvage Force had made it, but now the question became: *What did all of this mean?*

Representative Anthony Griffin read the following ode to Congress on March 21, 1928:

> *Three times the moon the zodiac has strode*
> *And gazed with pity on your dark abode;*
> *The snow, the rain, the winter gales have swept*
> *The sea, 'neath which your tryst with death was kept.*
>
> *Courageous sons, we hail your iron nerve!*
> *You risked your lives Columbia to serve—*
> *And dying, never doubted she would keep*
> *The faith and lift your vessel from the deep;*
> *Whate'er the past that she would make amends:*
> *Restore your hallowed bodies to your friends.*
>
> *Unselfish dead—one promise has been kept:*
> *The sepulcher of steel in which you slept*
> *Is raised at last by faithful comrades' skill—*
> *And your remains a martyr's grave will fill!*
> *'Twas glibly purred: Your death was not in vain—*
> *From your untimely end would spring some gain:*
> *"Such tragedies could ne'er occur again!"*
> *But what's been done to keep the promise true?*
> *What has been done to keep the faith with you?*
> *What has been done to keep the faith with them,*
> *Our cruel neglects to similar fates condemn?*

Shall we forget your sacrifice so great
And shirk our duty in affairs of state?
If there's no pity for your moldering bones
Your death itself our base ingratitude atones!
The age in which we live you have retrieved,
For you have given what you ne'er received—
Loyalty! and thus confirmed the ancient truth:
A nation's honor rests upon its youth!
Posterity will praise and hold you high
When quibbling statesmen shall have sunk in obloquy!

27

"My Body to Pelnar"

THE WATER GRADUALLY RECEDED AT the number two dry dock at the Boston Navy Yard. All about the large basin, curious workers gawked, reporters scribbled, and photographers clicked cameras. The general public, blockaded by ropes and armed marines, could see the slowly emerging visage of the *S-4*. March 19, 1928, was the first time in more than three months that the entire submarine had seen the light of day. There was a grace to the ruined boat that its disfigured decks could not gainsay. Maybe it was the damage itself that gave it solemnity, or maybe it was the dignity of those dead who were still entombed within its hull. The *S-4* had come home at last.

The first person to walk upon the *S-4*'s deck at the dry dock was Commander "Savvy" Saunders. He removed his garish stocking hat and carried a basket of carnations at the request of the divers. He left these as an offering by the torpedo room hatch and backed away. His head was bowed, his job done. Later that day, a huge wreath of flowers from workers at the Boston Navy Yard was set by the submarine's conning tower.

Now was the moment when navy inspectors could attempt to figure out what had gone wrong and perhaps learn how to improve technology to save future lives. To their mind, and to the mind of many Americans, there needed to be redemption so that the *S-4* disaster was not just the senseless death of forty men.

Upon entering the submarine, the first thing inspectors noticed was the oil and slime. It covered the walls of all the compartments. Pits of rust, carved like craters by the salt water, pockmarked the bulkheads. Then, in the control and battery rooms was the blue scorch of acid—the telltale sign of chlorine gas. There were no such marks in the engine and motor rooms.

In those two compartments was evidence of habitation. Food stores had been ransacked and tent-like apparatuses erected. There were also curious marks on the bulkheads, as if a man had been trying to carve his way out of the submarine, or at least had been banging a chisel against the steel walls. The inspectors supposed that the men in these compartments were communicating with Fitch in the torpedo room before they succumbed.

Then inspectors identified unused emergency canisters of compressed oxygen in the motor room. Jones had never tapped into this

The wrecked battery room of the submarine *S-4*.
Courtesy of the Stephen B. Luce Library Archives, SUNY Maritime College

resource. Another riddle. Those thirty-four men had been alive long enough to eat, but they didn't last until the next day when Tom Eadie landed on the submarine. Since there was evidently no chlorine gas poisoning, and the compartments had not been flooded until the divers entered, the only explanation is that they fell victim to carbon dioxide intoxication.

In the deep recesses of the motor room and engine room inspectors found the two unaccounted bodies. Each was behind machinery in spaces that were inaccessible to the divers. Finally, all the men who had been with Lieutenant Commander Jones were accounted for. Now the inspectors turned to a grimmer task as they opened the torpedo room hatch.

There had been much talk in the press, wondering if the men in the torpedo room had died in their bunks. It was expected that Lieutenant Fitch had given orders to the men to lie still—any exertion would have used more precious oxygen. But the inspectors found that the bodies were not in the bunks. Rather, they were strewn about— the compartment had been flooded and aired several times since the men had expired, so it was not possible to know where each man had been exactly at the time of his death.

Among the victims in the torpedo room, Fitch was the easiest to identify. His class ring gleamed, and his sweater was blue, blazoned with "1923," from the US Naval Academy at Annapolis. Next to him was an emergency lantern with a watch tied on it. The inspectors noticed that five of the six bunks available in the torpedo room were unmade. It was supposed that Fitch himself never lay down during the entire struggle. He was the man who was sending the signals. Sure enough, inspectors found a place near the torpedo room hatch that was scarred with marks. Behind the emergency lantern they found a large T-shaped socket wrench that was normally used to assemble torpedoes. This was the tool that Fitch had used to communicate with the outside world.*

---

*It was often assumed until this time that Fitch was using a hammer—this had been widely reported. The wrench was donated by Fitch's widow to the USNA Museum, where it still resides today.

Strangely, as with the men who were aft, inspectors found that the emergency oxygen bottle had not been opened. Yet Fitch had asked the rescue force to send down more bottles of air. But Fitch *had* drained all the air from the torpedoes. This mystery was a source of some conjecture. The *New York Times* speculated, "Intent on conserving it to the last, this [oxygen bottle] had been left for future use. But the six men, overcome with fatigue and the drowsiness of approaching asphyxiation from the exhausted air on the third day, all lost consciousness."

But the biggest surprise the inspectors found in the torpedo room was that the compartment salvage line—the one that Michels had tried to connect in vain, was actually *not* broken as reported by Fitch. It worked perfectly. The only explanations were that there must have been a small leak of water or possible condensation in the line. When Fitch opened the valve and found water coming in, he closed it in an immediate panic, assuming that it was ruptured. This put an exclamation mark on the struggles of Fred Michels, who if he had succeeded, just may have been able to save those six men.

Other evidence was more poignant and needed no forensic examination. On Seaman George Pelnar's corpse was found a note written red on cardboard: "My body to Pelnar 5609 So 19th St. Omaha, NE." A tin box was found containing a note: "In case of my death, please send entire contents of box to my mother, Mrs. M. G. Short, 804 Spring Street, Boonville, Mo. Roger L. Short." The box had fifty-two dollars in cash, American Express money orders, stock and insurance certificates, and some personal items, including a good conduct medal.

The personal effects of the submariners were removed and placed on forty tables—one for each victim—at the Boston Navy Yard for cataloging. Each table told a different story. On some were clothing and uniforms; others had pens, books, watches, and cameras. Photographs of a child, a wife, or other loved one littered the tables next to ruined letters and correspondence. There were collections of foreign coins, a stamp album, roller skates, a baseball bat, and a Shriner's fez from the El Zagal Temple of Fargo, North Dakota. The ceremonial swords of the *S-4*'s officers were found as well as Lieutenant Joseph McGinley's marriage certificate.

The wreck of the *S-4* in drydock at the Boston Navy Yard, March 1928.
Courtesy of the Library of Congress, Papers of Ernest J. King

The remaining bodies were wrapped in flags and removed. No photography was allowed as cranes hoisted them to an ambulance that waited beside the dry dock. The dead men's next stop was the Navy Hospital. From there, the remains were disbursed to their respective families for funerals. But they were kept in metal caskets covered with pine due to the condition of the bodies.

Fitch's remains were sent to Arlington National Cemetery, escorted by six officers and sixteen men. Six of Fitch's classmates served as pall-bearers. Secretary Wilbur and Admiral Hughes were both present as he was buried.

Each of the enlisted men under Fitch was to have an honor guard of a chief petty officer and eight men. But, as ever with the *S-4*, something went wrong.

Many people had come to the railroad station at Ridgefield Park, New Jersey, to pay their respects as Torpedoman Frank Snizek's body was returned to his hometown. To their shock, they found that there was no military escort; the honor guard had never met the Snizek family at New York City's Grand Central Station. As the baggage handlers lowered Snizek's flag-draped coffin to the ground, his sister said, "They died like rats and like rats they send them home."

The mayor of Ridgefield Park ordered the police to guard the body, stating, "We cannot understand why . . . Lieutenant Graham Newell Fitch could be taken to Arlington Cemetery with a fine escort of navy men, and why Frank—being just an enlisted man—got no escort at all." Meanwhile, the local American Legion offered to accompany Snizek's coffin to St. Michael's Cemetery in Queens when it was transported by ferry from New Jersey. The commander of the American Legion Post commented, "We're going to find out why a man who gave his life for his country was slighted so shamefully." The local congressional representative, Randolph Perkins, called Secretary Wilbur to find out why there was a mix-up. Wilbur, trying to mitigate the damage, ordered full military honors given to Snizek, including a firing squad. Thousands of people lined the streets of Astoria Boulevard to send Snizek off.

With the dead of the *S-4* buried, there was some closure for the men and officers involved in the rescue and salvage efforts. The men of the *Falcon* were recognized for their work on the rescue and salvage operations. Distinguished service medals were given to Captain Ernest King and Commander Harold Saunders. Eleven Navy Crosses were awarded, including to Lieutenant Henry Hartley and Clarence Tibbals. Several divers also won Navy Crosses, including Tom Eadie (his second) and Fred Michels. And Bill Carr *finally* won the Navy Cross that he had long coveted.

The greatest honor of all went to Tom Eadie, who in addition to a second Navy Cross was presented with the Medal of Honor by Calvin Coolidge on February 23, 1928—even while salvage operations were still underway. Secretary Wilbur, Admiral Hughes, and a crowd of Eadie's family and extended kin were present. Upon meeting Eadie,

President Coolidge said, "I'm glad to know you, and I thank you for your services."

"I want to assure you, Mr. President," said Eadie. "That everything humanly possible has been done on that job, under the circumstances."

Coolidge nodded. The president then noticed Eadie's family and said, "Quite a large gathering."

Photographs were taken, and newsreels filmed. After they were done, Eadie returned to the *Falcon* to help raise the *S-4*.

• • •

But there were many unsatisfied people.

Since the sinking of the *S-4*, there had been plenty of public outrage and criticism against the navy. The navy, in response, held an investigative Court of Inquiry headed by Rear Admiral Richard H. Jackson and also composed of Rear Admiral Julian L. Lattimer, commandant of the Fourth Naval District, and Captain Joseph V. Ogan, a submarine division commander. The judge advocate of the inquiry, Leslie E. Bratton, stated to reporters, "This is not going to be any whitewashing investigation. We are going to get the facts, no matter whom it hurts."

The court ran from January 4 to January 20, 1928. The proceedings, in which reenactments were conducted and thirty-nine witnesses produced well over six hundred pages of testimony, riveted the nation. All the major figures of the events concerning the *S-4* disaster made appearances, including Brumby, Ellsberg, Baylis, Eadie, Saunders, King, and Hartley.

The court, which published their findings on February 6, laid joint blame for the disaster at the feet of the Coast Guard's Lieutenant Commander John S. Baylis and the *S-4*'s Lieutenant Commander Roy K. Jones. The court wrote, "The collision was caused by failure on the part of the *S-4* to take proper action, after the *Paulding* changed course . . . to clear that vessel; and by failure on the part of the *Paulding* to sight and recognize as a submarine the *S-4* in time to take action necessary to clear her."

Baylis was blamed because he had not stationed a proper lookout. "The inefficient look-out on the *Paulding*, whereby the *S-4* was not sighted till only 75 yards away, was due to the lack of a proper look-out solely charged with that duty, especially at a time when the *Paulding* was approaching at a high rate of speed the submarine course."

Jones was blamed "due either to his lack of vigilance; or to the quality of his observations while the *Paulding* was approaching from 2,000 to 75 yards, from which observations flowed an action which by an error of judgment (possibly as to the speed and distance of the *Paulding*) failed to insure the safety of the vessel."

As for the rescue, the court found no fault with the navy. "Everything was done to save the lives of those on board the *S-4* that could have been done under the weather conditions that existed; but rescue under those conditions were [*sic*] beyond human power." However, the court criticized Admiral Brumby, who by this point was no longer assigned to the command of the *S-4* salvage, writing that his "testimony before this Court showed that he had not the familiarity with the essential details of construction of submarines and the knowledge of rescue vessels, and the knowledge of the actual work being carried on by his subordinates necessary to direct intelligently the important operations of which he was in charge. While the plans he approved, conceived by expert staff of which Captain King was the senior, were logical, intelligent, and were diligently executed with good judgment and in the greatest possible expedition, Rear Admiral Brumby failed to contribute that superior and intelligent guidance, force, and sound judgment expected from an officer of his length of service, experience, and position." The court recommended removing Brumby from his command.

The court had no legal authority to prosecute any person. Rather, the court made recommendations to the secretary of the navy only. Secretary Wilbur passed along the court's finding that Baylis was partially responsible for the disaster to Andrew W. Mellon, the secretary of the treasury.[*] The Coast Guard then set up its own separate board of inquiry to investigate the matter. Their findings were not surprising in that they did not find Baylis to be culpable whatsoever:

---

[*] At this time the Treasury Department was in charge of the Coast Guard.

The submarine is a distinctly unusual type of vessel, and if the person in charge of a surface vessel cruising on the open sea in the daytime in clear weather, with the sea choppy, were held to have incurred serious blame if he fails to sight the periscope of a submarine operating at periscope depth, he not knowing of the presence of the submarine in the vicinity, and there being no warnings displayed of any kind, and collides with such submarine as she suddenly emerges under the bows of his vessel, then, indeed, are the masters of all surface craft subject to unreasonable concern, responsibility, strain, and danger, to which, in the interests of commerce and safety to life, they should not be subjected.

In fact, the Coast Guard board commended Baylis since he "neglected no precautions for rescuing possible survivors of the *S-4*." Mellon completely exonerated Lieutenant Commander John Baylis, and he was not court martialed.

The navy establishment also disagreed with the Court of Inquiry findings. Admiral Richard H. Leigh, the chief of the navy's Bureau of Navigation, criticized the report, writing that while there was a joint responsibility, the burden fell on the *S-4*, since the lookout of the submarine should have more easily seen the *Paulding* than vice-versa. Leigh felt it was the duty of the *S-4* to avoid the *Paulding*.

Criticism was also given to the Court of Inquiry for assigning guilt to Roy K. Jones as commanding officer of the *S-4*. Admiral Leigh opined that there was no "requisite definitiveness that the late Lieutenant Commander Jones was directly and personally responsible for the share in the collision that is properly attributable to the *S-4*." Since there were no direct witnesses as to what occurred inside the *S-4*, all attempts to piece together what happened were based on forensic evidence.[*] Leigh's criticism was sound. As the commanding officer, Jones would be considered responsible for the disaster under the assumption that nothing went wrong mechanically in the submarine or with Jones himself. Jones's body was found right by the door to the command compartment. He had apparently fought to the end—it would

---

[*]This includes the re-creation of the disaster as shown in the early chapters of this book.

be impossible to blame him specifically for what went wrong, and even in reenactments of the collision, assumptions are always made. No one will know absolutely what happened inside the *S-4*.

In addition to criticism concerning Jones, the judge advocate general of the navy, Admiral Edward H. Campbell, noted that since Brumby was never named a defendant and could not defend himself, no action should be taken against him. Admiral Leigh concurred and found it paradoxical that the Court of Inquiry, which praised the rescue effort, could condemn Brumby, the mission's commanding officer.

Secretary Curtis Wilbur agreed and ordered the Court of Inquiry to reconvene on March 27, now that the *S-4* was in dry dock. The court members spent several days piecing together the new forensic evidence. In the end, under probable pressure from Wilbur, the court exonerated Brumby and Jones. Curtis Wilbur said of Brumby that "any errors or oversight or failures in his testimony are insufficient to overcome his splendid record of achievement covering more than thirty-one years of service in the navy." As for Jones, Wilbur said that any evidence was "wholly insufficient to justify a finding of guilt."

No person would ever be found culpable for the *S-4* disaster. But the outrage inspired the government and individuals to take action.

28

Of Lungs and Bells

THE VISCERAL IMPACT OF THE *S-4* disaster demanded action. Political pressure was placed on the government to do something to improve the lot of submariners.

One of the first things Congress did was enact a law in 1928 that doubled the pensions given to men injured or dependents of men killed in submarines. On April 13, 1928, a pay increase for submariners was announced. Officers got an additional 25 percent, and crew received a stipend from five dollars to thirty dollars per month dependent on rank, seniority, and risk of job. On April 27, Congress passed an act that doubled the pensions given to the widows of submariners.

On April 27, 1928, the Senate began to conduct its own separate hearings regarding the *S-4*. Led by Senator Tasker L. Oddie of Nevada, the hearings were relatively inconclusive and focused on improving submarine safety devices. In addition, the submarine safety board proposed by President Coolidge was formed in June 1928. The board reviewed 8,304 letters containing 4,971 plans, ideas, and suggestions of safety devices. This group was important in consolidating plans for new inventions.

During this time, individual inventors began to search for ways to make submarines safer. Inventors tinkered and submitted patents for rescue buoys, telephones, and all sorts of equipment. Simon Lake rebuilt the *Defender*, an old submarine, adding a special door to the sea that allowed divers to leave and enter. Lieutenant Commander John S. Baylis worked on starting a diving school for the Coast Guard and even took some dives himself. But the one person who did the most to harness the visceral impact of the *S-4* tragedy for future good was Lieutenant Charles Momsen.

Momsen was nicknamed "Swede" due to his Nordic heritage, although he was of Danish rather than Swedish descent. He entered Annapolis in 1914, but in response to a cheating scandal, the Naval Academy increased the difficulty of the 1915 midterms. Momsen failed Spanish and lost his appointment. However, after lobbying persistently for reentry, he was reappointed and graduated early, in 1919, due to World War I.

Early on, Momsen fell in love with submarines, despite the crowded conditions of the early pigboats. He entered submarine school and earned his first command, the *O-15*. During this period Momsen became particularly concerned about submarine safety. The peril of the service was shown to him when his rickety craft was caught in a hurricane. The *O-15* barely escaped.

In 1925, Momsen took command of the *S-1*. The S-boats were much better than the O-class but still dangerous, as was demonstrated to him at the scene of the *S-51* disaster. As Momsen held his boat at the surface and tried to contact the submarine in vain, one of his crew stared at the bubbles coming from the deep and said, "Oh my God, oh my God." Momsen sent him below but said to others, "At least it was fast. They probably never realized what happened."

From the *S-51* experience Momsen meditated on how it could be possible to rescue men trapped inside a submarine. During his command of the *S-1*, the navy had installed a small airplane hangar on the submarine's deck with the idea of combining underwater and aerial operations. While this idea proved to be unworkable, Momsen saw the hangar, which was removed, as a potential diving bell that could be locked on to a submarine that would allow crew to escape. After working on the problem with colleagues, he presented the idea to Captain Ernest J. King, who was the submarine base commander at that time.

"Swede," said King. "I think you've got a hell of an idea." Momsen's plan was forwarded to the Bureau of Construction and Repair with King's endorsement.

But the project got pigeonholed, and Momsen only found out about the delay when he was later serving at the same bureau. He found his plan for a diving bell piled in a file titled AWAITING ACTION. His predecessor had left it for Momsen. When Momsen floated his idea to the bureau, they rejected it—not only was Momsen new (it was his second day on the job), but they believed that it was "impractical from the standpoint of seamanship." Despite his pleas, the case was closed.

Then the *S-4* sunk. Only because of the national uproar were ideas for submarine safety now being looked at seriously. Momsen was, in fact, one of the persons who answered correspondence from people who made suggestions to the navy.

As he went through letter after letter, a new idea came to him— something simple that he could develop independent of the Bureau of Construction and Repair. It was a primitive rebreather officially named the Submarine Escape Appliance that became known popularly as the "Momsen Lung." Simultaneously, he pushed his bell idea into development at the bureau. So there were two devices: one that could rescue men trapped in submarines from without, and one that submariners could use from within.

The idea behind the Momsen Lung was simple. A man would strap a mask to his face and breathe in and out of a large bag that was inflated from a flask of compressed oxygen. Then, the trapped submariners would allow their compartment to flood enough that the water rushing in compressed the air and the external hatch could be opened. Then, using the Momsen Lung, a person would swim to the surface, breathing in and out of the device.

To create the rebreather itself, Momsen worked with a civilian engineer from the Bureau of Construction and Repair named Frank Hobson and Chief Gunner Clarence Tibbals. They looked at similar devices in other countries before deciding to start from scratch. Their device had two bags that were about the same size as a man's lungs.

One bag was filtered with soda lime to remove carbon dioxide, and the other was filled with pure oxygen. Momsen estimated that the device would allow a man to ascend about three hundred feet. A nose clip and a valve would be an outlet for excess air, since as the person rose to the surface, the water pressure decreased and the air inside the lung would expand. At the surface, the compressed oxygen had expanded enough so that the device could be used as a makeshift life jacket.[*]

But since the Momsen Lung wasn't formally sanctioned by the navy, Momsen needed to test it himself. He went during off-hours to a model boat basin and submerged himself into a testing tank, Tibbals watching. Compressed air entered the tank to simulate real water pressure. First 50 feet of simulated pressure, then 150, 200, 250, then 300. Momsen wrote:

> There was a hiss of the air and then the intense heat caused by the added pressure. Suddenly the pressure on my ears became almost unbearable and I held my nose and blew as hard as I could. At fifty feet I filled the bag with oxygen and ducked down under the water holding a line attached to an anchor. Tibbals was peering intently through the eyeport watching every move I made from his control station outside the tank. I waved my hand and he threw open the exhaust valve allowing the pressure to fall at a rate approximately equal to the change of pressure that would have taken place had I been rising through the water. While I actually did not move, I had the sensation of surfacing. The bag swelled as the pressure fell and the excess gas escaped through a valve in the bottom just as we planned.

Next, Momsen needed to do some real ascending. Using an old pickle barrel, Tibbals fashioned a makeshift diving bell that fit over Momsen's head. Then Momsen tested the Lung inside a sixty-foot-deep testing tank. This time, he added a line reaching to the bottom

---

[*]Training in using the Momsen Lung was absolutely critical. Two deaths occurred because men held their breath while using them. As a person surfaces, the decrease in sea pressure causes the air in the body's lungs to expand, thus distending the lungs; air then enters the tissues and blood in large bubbles.

of the tank, with stop marks where he would pause for several breaths in order to decompress. It was a success.

Next, Momsen took his rebreather to the Potomac River and went down in a makeshift diving bell. When he reached the bottom, 110 feet below, he smelled the stench of mud and picked up a rock as a souvenir. He put on the Lung and began the ascent. Momsen made all the requisite stops and emerged from the water, rock in hand. Other divers tried it too. All were successful.

News of the Momsen Lung got into the papers, and the navy first learned about it through the press. The day after the testing in the Potomac, Admiral Charles Hughes, with other navy brass, sought out Momsen. Hughes said, "Young man, what the hell have you been up to?"

The navy, however, knowing that it would be impolitic for them to denounce the Momsen Lung, sanctioned more tests—this time aboard the *Falcon*. Momsen went to the Chesapeake Bay and successfully

A Momsen Lung being used in 1930 during training exercises.
Naval History and Heritage Command, Photo Archives, NH-45641

tested the device at 155 feet. Momsen recalled that after the testing, a group of men aboard the ship came up to him. One said, "Sir, we just want you to know that we are proud to have you on board."

Next was to actually test the device aboard a submarine. In this case, Momsen selected the *S-4*.

After the *S-4*'s salvage, Momsen oversaw its conversion into an experimental safety vessel. The submarine as rebuilt was unpowered. Instead, it was towed to where it was needed. The control and battery rooms had been rebuilt to house the testing crew, and the motor, engine, and torpedo rooms were saved for experimental flooding and escape. In fact, the navy, on the second anniversary of the disaster, raised the *S-4* using pad-eyes* and pontoons off Block Island in the same waters that the *S-51* went down.

In the motor room, Momsen had added a metal skirt that extended four feet from the hatch into the compartment. When water entered the compartment, it would flood upward, but leave an air pocket at the top where men could put on the rebreathers. In the meantime, compressed air would pop open the hatch, which would allow an exit for the men inside.

Of course, there was no guarantee that this would all work. There was only one way to find out. On February 6, 1929, Momsen, with a torpedoman named Edward Kalinoski, went down in the *S-4* off Key West, Florida. They landed the submarine on the bottom, at a depth of forty feet. Then, according to plan, Kalinoski unlocked the hatch, and Momsen opened the flood valve. As the water poured in, Kalinoski said to Momsen, "I hope to Christ you know what you're doing."

And Momsen did—both men got to the surface successfully. Momsen tested his invention again, at a maximum depth of 207 feet. It was even tested off Block Island, where the *S-51* went down, in cold January waters. For his efforts, Momsen won the navy's Distinguished Service Medal. Submarines would now be equipped with Momsen Lungs.

---

*Pad-eyes, or rings that were riveted to the submarine's hull, never did quite gain traction since they added weight to the submarine and made it less hydrodynamic. They were installed on the *S-22* in 1929 but not used afterward.

In the meantime, Momsen continued to work on rescue possibilities from outside of the submarine, using his idea of creating a diving bell from the old aircraft hangar of the *S-1*. He developed a prototype that was then refined between 1929 and 1931.

The first field tests of the rescue bell were conducted using the *S-4* off Florida in seventy-five feet of water. Divers went down to the *S-4* and attached guidelines from the *Falcon* to a special collar over the motor room hatch. Then Momsen, with a chief torpedoman named Charles Hagner, entered the pear-shaped bell. Looking downward through the clear water they could see the *S-4* below. Slowly, delicately, the bell eased down, compressed air being pumped inside the chamber so that it remained buoyant. Then it landed right on the submarine's hatch. Momsen and Hagner bolted the chamber to the submarine—so far so good. Then Momsen released air from the bell. This made the sea's pressure greater than the air inside the chamber and pushed it down on the submarine, forming a seal against the hatch. It was a tense moment as the bell became filled with fog due to a drop in pressure from the saturated air. But it seemed to work. There was only a foot of water in the bell.

Nervously, Momsen opened the *S-4*'s hatch. The foot of water inside the bell spilled into the submarine, but no more. Momsen, looking down, saw the commander of the *S-4* staring at him.

"Request permission to come aboard," said Momsen.

The rest of the test went without a hitch. Two of the *S-4*'s crew entered the bell, air pressure was increased, and the bolts that held the chamber in place were removed. The chamber was hauled up the guidelines to the surface.

Tests continued over and over. Not only could the chamber bring personnel out of a stricken submarine, but it could also blow air into a compartment to force out some of the water.

Final adjustments to the rescue bell were made by Lieutenant Commander Allan Rockwell McCann, since Momsen was occupied training men on how to use the Momsen Lung. The final product was named the McCann Submarine Rescue Chamber. There was some controversy over the name. Momsen had apparently stepped on too many bureaucratic toes, and the result was that the device was not named after him, the primary inventor.

Meanwhile, other advances in submarine rescue and safety were being made. Location buoys, complete with telephones,* were affixed to submarines. The buoys could be released in the event of an emergency. Emergency rescue rockets were improved so that submarines could signal their location. Separate air valves to each compartment were built into newer model submarines. Submarines were stocked with soda lime, and divers started experimenting with helium-oxygen air mixtures to reduce exposure to nitrogen, which would allow for faster decompression times. Divers would then be able to work longer on the bottom at greater depth.

Theoretically, if these innovations had existed in 1927, the men on the *S-4* might have been saved—or their odds of survival might have improved. The men may have used Momsen Lungs to escape. The submarine would have been found more easily if a locator buoy with a telephone were available, thus saving precious time. Then, if all else failed, a rescue chamber could have been lowered onto the torpedo room to deliver Fitch and his five companions to freedom.

All of this was theoretically possible within a few years after the *S-4* disaster, and none of these inventions would have come to fruition if the collision had not occurred. By the time the *S-4* was finally struck from the navy list in 1936, the craft had served a useful purpose in improving submarine safety. The boat was sunk in an unmarked grave in the Pacific.

It is an old saw to say that improvements only come when there is a demonstrated need. But such was and is the case. Yet all these improvements were merely hypothetical. A real submarine disaster was needed to prove that the men of the *S-4* did not die in vain.

---

*These markers were only used during peacetime since the navy found that a depth charge from an enemy vessel could release the marker on a submarine attempting to hide.

29

Twelve Years Later . . .

ON MAY 23, 1939, THE submarine *Squalus* left the Portsmouth Navy Yard in the late morning to head to the Isle of Shoals. Like the *S-4* almost twelve years earlier, the *Squalus* was to undergo testing. The vessel was a new *Sargo*-class submarine that was at the cutting edge of submarine design. There were five officers, fifty-one enlisted men, and three civilian inspectors aboard.

Generally, the tests were to determine the boat's sea readiness. This meant diving. It had already undergone testing in April with no troubles except for some minor issues that were easily remedied at the Navy Yard. In fact, the submarine's commander, Lieutenant Oliver Naquin, was quite happy with the performance of the *Squalus* in April. The commandant of the Portsmouth Navy Yard had even sent him a congratulatory note.

In the decade after the *S-4* disaster, the navy had refined submarine construction and incorporated some of the best safety features, including some of those designed by Swede Momsen. The *Squalus* was 310 feet long, 27 feet wide—almost 100 feet longer than the *S-4*—and faster, too, with a top surface speed of 16 knots. Unlike the *S-4*, the *Squalus* had an aft torpedo room, and its battery was divided into two compartments, one immediately forward of the control room and one to the rear of it, adding an additional degree of redundancy and mechanical reliability. The aft torpedo room also contained an

escape hatch for use with the Momsen Lungs and a hatch to attach a
McCann Rescue Chamber in an emergency.

The Isle of Shoals is a collection of islands along the Maine–New
Hampshire border. Mainly devoid of boating traffic, it offered deep
stretches of water that the *Squalus* could use in its diving tests. Naquin
eased his boat along, until he came to an area where the average depth
was about 240 feet. On tap for testing that day was an emergency crash
dive while making 16 knots to a depth of fifty feet.

At 8:00 AM, Naquin gave the order for all hands to prepare for diving. Submariners raced to their stations. At 8:13, Naquin radioed his
position to Portsmouth. At 8:35, the *Squalus* reached the correct position. Naquin descended from the conning tower to the control room
and gave the order to prepare to submerge.

The alarm sounded, and the main ballast tanks' Kingston valves,
which closed off the bottom of the tanks, were opened, followed by
the main ballast tanks' vents, which allowed the trapped air in the
tanks to exit and seawater to flood in through the bottom. Indicator lights showed that all openings in the inner pressure hull were
closed—indicated by a green light. If any openings weren't closed,
then the lights would be red. It was a simple indicator that all was well.
The planesmen, following directions from the diving officer, rotated
the large control wheels on the port side of the control room, setting
both the bow and stern planes to dive.

Down went the *Squalus*.

It took one minute and two seconds for the *Squalus* to reach the
prescribed fifty feet. Naquin's executive officer, Lieutenant Walter T.
Doyle Jr., gave the order to level off at sixty-three feet. As the *Squalus*
evened out, Naquin walked to his post at the periscope.

Then the engine room called in through a telephone to the communications yeoman. The young man's eyes flew open as he said to
the captain, "Sir! The engine rooms—they're flooding!"

All hands looked to the indicator lights. All was green. *What was
going on?*

"Blow all main ballast tanks," cried Naquin.

"Blow safety and bow buoyancy," said Doyle.

Air was blown into the tanks, and the men operating the diving planes turned them to a hard rise.

But the *Squalus* continued to sink. The communications yeoman heard screaming through the telephone coming from the rearward compartments. "Take her up! Take her up!"

At eighty feet the submarine stabilized somewhat as the air blown into the tanks shifted the boat upward to 30 degrees. Men grasped levers, pipes, wheels, handles—whatever they could find—or they were tossed off their feet. The crisis mounted as there was no stopping the sea from flooding the rear compartments. Down, down went the *Squalus*.

Seemingly hundreds of small crises erupted all at once. Water flooded from the aft engine room into the aft battery through burst pipes and ventilation valves. As the sea poured in, men left their posts and scrambled to safety. Five crew members managed to claw their way out of the rear battery room, barely making it alive to the control room. The *Squalus* slammed on the bottom, the bow up at an 11-degree angle.

The lights began to flicker out. The control panels still showed all green. But somehow the main air induction valve leading to the engines had failed to close, or at least it had reopened. Officially, the accident was blamed on mechanical failure, though some people believed that somebody had accidentally opened the valve manually after the dive.

No matter the reason, the *Squalus* lay at the bottom at 243 feet. The twenty-six men in the two engine rooms and aft torpedo room had drowned—all of the men in the rear part of the vessel—but there were thirty-three men still alive in the forward part of the vessel.

There was a cold, still moment before Naquin took charge. Then he went about securing his submarine, doling out flashlights. Through the telephone system that connected to the various compartments, he found that the forward torpedo and battery rooms were safe. But there was no response from the rear of the *Squalus* either by telephone or hammering. As men began to mutter about the fate of the twenty-six drowned men, Naquin quickly squashed any more mention of it.

By telephone, Naquin ordered the torpedo room officer to release one of the innovations that was developed in the wake of the *S-4* disaster. They shot a red smoke rocket to get help to the scene. Throughout the day six of the rockets would be fired. Naquin also ordered the torpedo room release its marker buoy.

This buoy was bright yellow, about three feet wide. On the buoy was engraved, Submarine Sunk Here. Telephone Inside. It floated on the surface in the hope that somebody would notice and give a call.

Next, Naquin evacuated any men in the battery room, fearing that if salt water leaked into it that chlorine gas would form. Then, because more men were in the control room than in the torpedo room, Naquin divided the men up evenly to best conserve the breathable air. Men were ordered not to move unless commanded to do so— oxygen needed to be conserved. All the *Squalus*'s crew could do was to wrap themselves up in blankets, wait, and finger their Momsen Lungs, hoping that it would not come to that.

Naquin himself hoped not to use the rebreathers. The water off the Isle of Shoals was cold and deep. He rightfully feared that he would lose men if they tried to escape that way. Rather, Naquin hedged his bets, opting to wait for the navy to see if a rescue could be effected from outside the submarine. But first the navy would need to realize the *Squalus* was missing, and second, send a rescue squadron to them.

• • •

At the Portsmouth Navy Yard, the commandant, Rear Admiral Cyrus Cole, grew concerned when the *Squalus* failed to report in. He then gave the order to the commander of the *Sculpin*, the sister vessel of the *Squalus*, to look for the missing submarine. In the meantime, Cole contacted the New London submarine base where the venerable *Falcon* sat at berth with a McCann Rescue Chamber on its deck.

The *Sculpin* hunted for the *Squalus*. But for some unknown reason the *Sculpin* was given incorrect coordinates from the *Squalus*'s last check-in. The *Sculpin* might never have found the lost submarine were it not for a young officer who saw the sixth smoke rocket fired from the *Squalus*. The *Sculpin* hurried to the scene, where they found the marker buoy. It was gingerly brought up on deck.

"Hello, *Squalus*, this is *Sculpin*. What's your trouble?"

There was elation on the *Squalus*—for a moment—then the sea rose and tore the marker buoy, along with the connection, away.

But now the navy knew the *Squalus* was in trouble, and they knew approximately where it was. By this point, word had spread—even Edward Ellsberg had been called into action and was being flown to the site. Henry Hartley (now a commander) was on the scene as a technical advisor to Admiral Cole. After Swede Momsen was told the news, he headed immediately to the scene by seaplane. So too did Allan McCann. But, just like the *S-4*, the navy needed to buy time until the *Falcon* could arrive. The rescue ship could not hope to reach the *Squalus* until the next morning.

During these hours, Naquin doled out food to his men. Movement was still kept to a strict minimum. But the gradual increase in carbon dioxide could not be ignored. At length, Naquin opened a can of the carbon dioxide absorbent soda lime and sprinkled about a quarter of it on the deck. This was another safety precaution added since the *S-4*, which had no absorbent soda lime aboard. Naquin had flasks of compressed oxygen, which he hoarded for utmost need. In fact, Naquin purposefully kept the crew somewhat overexposed to the carbon dioxide to make them sleepy so they did not move much and use up the all-important supply of breathable air.

That night, it was dark and freezing. The men of the *Squalus* huddled in the cold. The only sounds were occasional hammer strikes in Morse, sent to the surface to communicate with the gathering rescue fleet.

The *Squalus* was luckier than the *S-4*; weather was on Naquin's side. While not optimal conditions—overcast with choppy seas—the weather was by far more moderate than the multi-day storm that plagued the *S-4* rescue efforts. By 11:30 PM, the tugboat *Penacock* managed to successfully grapple the submarine.

In the morning, the *Falcon*, now commanded not by Henry Hartley but by Lieutenant George Sharp, arrived through a fog. Sharp maneuvered the *Falcon* to a good mooring, which ate up about four hours of time. Meanwhile, the good luck continued as the weather moderated even further, and the sun came out.

There was debate on what to do. The rescue force could attempt to raise the submarine entirely, or they could work to rescue the trapped men. At length they decided that since they did not know exactly what went wrong with the *Squalus*, it would be better to attempt to rescue the men.

Momsen took direct charge of the rescue effort. He and the divers toured the *Sculpin*, using it as a model for what needed to be done. Then he selected the first diver—a man he knew well, Martin Sibitsky. At 10:14 AM, Sibitsky went down using a new helium-oxygen mixture that allowed divers to work at greater depths for longer periods of time and with shorter decompression times. Since using the helium mixture had a tendency to chill the body, Sibitsky also had the benefit of new electrically heated underwear.

Sibitsky landed forward on the *Squalus* and was greeted by joyous banging from the interior of the *Squalus*. He secured a descending line, and began hooking up guidelines for the McCann Rescue Chamber. At 10:39, he was hauled up for decompression. The work went as well as could be hoped. Next the rescue chamber, with both Momsen and McCann watching, was lowered into the water at 11:30 AM with divers John Mihalowski and Walter Harmon aboard.

There was some debate among Momsen, McCann, and Cole as to how many trips the rescue chamber needed to make. The device was only five feet in diameter and seven feet high. They feared that the risk of malfunction or accident would increase exponentially with each descent, since the depth was so great and the rescue chamber had been untested in a real disaster. At length, they decided to make four trips, retrieving seven survivors on the first, eight on the second, and nine each on the last two.

The chamber was slowly lowered down its guideline by reels. After forty-five minutes, it landed with a thud on the *Squalus*. The sound was heard through the telephone by Momsen, who later said, "I experienced a thrill I cannot possibly describe and I wonder whether any man ever could."

The chamber then sealed itself to the torpedo room hatch through the use of compressed air and the ambient sea pressure to form a seal. They then bolted down the chamber and opened the hatch. When the hatch was opened, and all could see that the chamber worked, Mihalowski said, "Well, we're here. I'm passing down soup, coffee, and sandwiches." One submariner quipped, "What, no napkins?" Another asked, "Say, where the hell have you guys been?"

Seven men were loaded into the chamber, each donning their Momsen Lungs just in case. Momsen on the surface ordered, "Unbolt. Flood lower compartment. Blow main ballast tank."

The chamber then made its long journey to the surface, following the guideline, being hauled up mechanically by the *Falcon*. At 1:42 PM, it broke the surface. The hatch opened, the men came out, and they boarded the *Falcon*. A great cheer erupted. It was a great vindication for all the effort that had been put into submarine safety and rescue since the *S-4*. When asked how he felt, Momsen replied, "Numb." He had a cup of coffee.

At that moment, a plane roared overhead. It was an Eastern Airlines plane, specially chartered to bring Edward Ellsberg to the scene. The plane made wide circles, as Ellsberg peered down to the water and saw the rescue force manipulating lines from the *Falcon* to the little rescue chamber. Ellsberg later wrote of this moment, "[I]t was evident that the task of rescue was far advanced, that Momsen had that job thoroughly under control, that from no source at all was help then needed—except such as was wholly beyond human power, to insure the continuance of the remarkably fine weather conditions favoring the rescue fleet."

Meanwhile, on the *Squalus*, Naquin evacuated the remaining men from the control room to the torpedo room. They donned their Momsen Lungs as ad hoc gas masks as they passed through the forward battery, which was poisoned with chlorine gas.

The second and third trips of the chamber went without a problem, although on the second trip there was concern because when the chamber surfaced it rose low in the water, indicating that rescuing any more than eight survivors at a time might be too many. Momsen thought a fifth trip might be necessary, but it was found

Men from the *Squalus* being taken aboard the *Falcon*.
Naval History and Heritage Command, Photo Archives, NH-97292

out that instead of the expected eight survivors aboard, a ninth had
stowed away.

By the time of the fourth trip, dark had settled, and eight men
remained inside the *Squalus*. These men then entered, with Naquin
being the last. At 7:51 PM, the *Squalus* was empty of any living man.

Slowly, the chamber made its way to the surface. But as it reached
160 feet, the hauling wire jammed. Efforts to clear the wire were useless; neither men from inside the chamber nor divers outside could
fix it. Finally, the *Falcon* sent down a diver to cut the cable from the
Squalus. The rescue chamber swung free of its reels, and it could be
hauled to the surface. But even as the chamber was slowly drawn up,
the men of the *Falcon*, to their horror, saw the steel strands of the
cable unraveling.

Momsen ordered the men in the chamber to flood their ballast
tank to maintain neutral buoyancy. In the meantime, a diver was sent
down to attach a cable to the chamber.

Naquin and the men inside the rescue chamber worked to maintain optimism. One man, a metalsmith named James McDonald, even led the men in the chamber in a rendition of "Old MacDonald Had a Farm."

Meanwhile, the diver who was sent down to hook up the new cable fouled his lines with the wiring. He managed to clear himself, but he became incoherent and could no longer work. He was brought up. A second diver was sent too, but his lamp fouled in the cable. Refusing to give up, he fought on for thirty-three minutes until he too was used up.

Momsen discussed the matter with McCann, and he advised Admiral Cole to have the men in the bell carefully blow ballast so that the chamber remained slightly below neutral buoyancy. Then, using the one remaining strand of cable left, the *Falcon* would forgo its mechanical winch and haul up the chamber by hand.

It was a delicate operation. Ten men hauled on the line, including Momsen and McCann, as they gingerly, foot by foot, drew up the chamber as the men inside carefully regulated the chamber's buoyancy. At 12:23 AM, thirty-nine hours after the *Squalus* first went down, the rescue chamber broke through the surface. All of the survivors were rescued.

EPILOGUE

AT A CHURCH IN PROVINCETOWN on Commercial Street between Dagget Lane and Anthony Street, a crowd numbering in the hundreds milled about, seeking entry to its already busy vestibule. It was overcast and chilly. The streets were wet. But today, December 17, 1937, the pastor of St. Mary of the Harbor Episcopal Church had planned something special that would bring people from far and near no matter the weather.

There were all sorts present: navy men and officers who had arrived on the destroyer *Tillman*, a color guard composed of Coast Guard personnel, a contingent from the American Legion and from the Veterans of Foreign Wars, and relatives of the *S-4*'s victims, such as Mrs. Maude Stevens, in her second visit to Provincetown. Then there were the many local people of Provincetown—the selectmen, fishermen, artists, and shopkeepers. Some who were touched by the tragedy could not make it, such as Boatswain Emmanuel Gracie, who had been afflicted with sinus troubles. But the rest had come to see Robert Wood Nicholson, the church's vicar, and two other clergy members, navy chaplain Thomas P. Thompson from the Boston Navy Yard and Howard T. Bartow, the archdeacon of New Bedford, perform a ceremony that was long overdue.

At 4:00 PM, the church's choir left the warmth of St. Mary's and entered the churchyard. Nicholson, Thompson, and Bartow solemnly followed. A hush fell as onlookers saw the procession move toward a rough-hewn wooden cross that stood in the middle of the yard. The choir began to sing:

> *O God, our help in ages past,*
> *Our hope for years to come,*

Our shelter from the stormy blast,
And our eternal home.

Under the shadow of thy throne,
Still may we dwell secure;
Sufficient is thine arm alone,
And our defense is sure.

Before the hills in order stood,
Or earth received her frame,
From everlasting, thou art God,
To endless years the same.

A thousand ages, in thy sight,
Are like an evening gone;
Short as the watch that ends the night,
Before the rising sun.

Time, like an ever-rolling stream,
Bears all who breathe away;
They fly forgotten, as a dream
Dies at the opening day.

O God, Our help in ages past,
Our hope for years to come;
Be thou our guide while life shall last,
And our eternal home.

Choir and clergy circled the cross, which had been designed by Walter Cashman from the driftwood along the local shores, reputed to come from shipwrecks. Affixed to the cross was a bronze plaque that read, "In memory of the officers and crew of the Submarine *S-4*, sunk off Wood End December 17, 1927." At the cross's base was the metal rim of a sealing ring from the submarine *S-4* that a fisherman had dredged up.

The procession entered through the church's vestibule, and the service began. Speeches were made, including one by Chief Pharmacist's Mate John Walter Maxwell, who was one of the men responsible for removing the last of the dead when the *S-4* arrived at Boston. He thanked the church.

Then the names of the forty men who were lost were read, starting with the officers:

Roy Kehlor Jones, Lieutenant Commander, Commanding Officer

William Franklin Callaway, Lieutenant Commander, Inspector from the Board of Survey and Inspection

Joseph Alfred McGinley, Lieutenant, Executive Officer

Graham Newell Fitch, Lieutenant, Junior Grade, Torpedo Room Officer

Donald Parsons Weller, Lieutenant, Junior Grade, Engineering Officer

Clarence Ferdinand Bethke, Engineman, First Class

Walter Bishop, Radioman, First Class

Earl Welsh Boone, Chief Electrician's Mate

Henry Handy Brown, Fireman, Third Class

Charles Frederick Burrell, Seaman, Second Class

Charles Beresford Calcott, Machinist's Mate, Third Class

Elmer Lyfford Cash, Chief Radioman

Russell Archibald Crabb, Torpedoman, First Class

William Dempsey, Machinist's Mate, Second Class

Robert William Diefenbach, Signalman, First Class

John Joseph Fennell, Motor Machinist's Mate, Second Class

Daniel Michael Galvin, Fireman, Third Class

Donald Fred Goering, Electrician's Mate, First Class

Peder Haaland, Machinist's Mate, First Class

Dewey Victor Haney, Commissaryman, Second Class

Buster Harris, Seaman, Second Class

Aron Albert Hodges, Chief Machinist's Mate

Arthur Frederick Hodges, Machinist's Mate, First Class

Paul Richard Kempfer, Electrician's Mate, Second Class

Jack H. Long, Fireman, Third Class

Fred Henry O'Shields, Engineman, Second Class

George Pelnar, Seaman, Second Class

John Joseph Powers, Coxswain
Rudolph James Rose, Electrician's Mate, Third Class
Alfred Eugene Seaton, Quartermaster, Third Class
Roger Leslie Short, Torpedoman, First Class
Frank Snizek, Torpedoman, Second Class
Joseph William Sternman, Engineman, Second Class
Joseph Leighton Stevens, Seaman, First Class
Carl Bernice Strange, Seaman, First Class
Mariano Tedar, Mess Attendant, Second Class
Carl Harold Thompson, Engineman, Second Class
Walter Ross Tolson, Seaman, First Class
James Johnson White, Fireman, First Class

Charles A. Ford, Civilian Draftsman from the Board of Survey
    and Inspection

Martha Atwood, who was singing along to "America" toward the close of the service, recalled afterward, "I didn't think I could go through it. One of the chaps from the *Tillman* was sitting next to me during the ceremony, and as the names of the men on the *S-4* were being read, he lost control of himself and broke into sobs. As I was singing I kept my hand on his shoulder; to comfort him. It was heartbreaking."

The service inside the church ended simply with the playing of "Taps." Then the same procession exited the church. Again, they formed a circle around the cross. Reverend Nicholson led a prayer. Then Mae Burress, national chaplain of the Fleet Reserve Auxiliary, laid a wreath at the base of the cross. A three-round volley was shot by the Coast Guard contingent, formally ending the service.

Every year, the Church of St. Mary holds its annual memorial service for the men of the *S-4*. In the early years, hundreds came from across the nation in an annual pilgrimage to remember the tragedy off Wood End. In 1940, a plaque was added to the cross, listing the names of the dead.

Typically, the subsequent ceremonies were similar to the first, with people who were involved in the disaster making speeches followed by the laying of a wreath before the cross. In those first years, those directly involved in the events of the *S-4* incident, such as Chief Boat-swain Emmanuel Gracie (who made it for the 1938 ceremony), would attend, as well as the immediate relatives of those who perished. Even fifty-five years later, in 1982, the daughter of Lieutenant Commander Roy K. Jones was present at the ceremonies.

With time, the original cross came to rot, and in 1967 it was replaced by a new cross, designed by Frederick L. Maichle Jr., and built of redwood. The new memorial, nine feet tall, still stands in the church's courtyard as of this writing.

As the decades passed, and the *S-4* gradually receded from the American memory, fewer people made the annual pilgrimage to Provincetown. In recent years, the ceremony has been moved to November to increase attendance. People still come to try to understand what happened.

• • •

Saturday, November 15, 2014, proved to be a sunny day in Provincetown. The village's many shops along Commercial Street sported signs saying, SEE YOU NEXT SUMMER. As life in the town slowed, its native beauty emerged. The Wood End and Long Point Lights still held sentinel over the town's little harbor, and the strand at Wood End from which Gracie saw the *Paulding*'s terrible course change was still lonely and beautiful.

The Church of St. Mary's of the Harbor, led by Reverend Terry Pannell, became a focus point for roughly twenty people coming from all across the nation. A contingent of submarine veterans wore their jackets and hats indicating their service. Maritime historian David Zeni made a presentation of lost newsreel footage of the *S-4* disaster. Also attending were the relations of Aron Hodges, the chief machinist's mate who was one of the first three victims recovered from the *S-4*. Robin Hodges Schwartz, researching the genealogy of her family from her home in Texas, found relatives she hadn't met that lived in Utah, Jana Ross and her daughter Ashlee. They were the great-granddaughter and great-great-granddaughter of Aron Hodges. Together these women made the pilgrimage to the *S-4* memorial, forming new bonds. Then there was the Coast Guard color guard of two young men.

Submarine veterans came forward and read excerpts from
Psalm 107:

Some went down to the sea in ships
and plied their trade in deep waters;

They beheld the works of the Lord
And his wonders in the deep.

Then he spoke, and a stormy wind arose,
which tossed high the waves of the sea.

They mounted up to the heavens and fell back to the depths;
their hearts melted because of their peril.

They reeled and staggered like drunkards
and were at their wits' end.

Then they cried to the Lord in their trouble,
and he delivered them from their distress.

He stilled the storm to a whisper
and quieted the waves of the sea.

Then were they glad because of the calm,
and he brought them to the harbor they were bound for.

In his homily, Reverend Pannell told the story of the *S-4* and the
last plea from Lieutenant Fitch: *Is there any hope?*

"There is always hope," said Reverend Pannell. "Whether submariners, Galilean fishermen, or those of us confined to terra firma, no
one knows when, where, or how tragedy will strike. For three days
extraordinary acts of courage took place in multiple attempts by deep
sea divers to rescue the survivors of the *S-4*. Their courage and the
courage of their comrades elevate all of humanity and continues to
serve as an inspiration."

Technology has improved since the *S-4* crashed into the *Paulding*
in 1927. Divers and submariners go to depths beyond what the men of
the *Falcon* may have imagined while they struggled to raise the boat in
the days after the disaster. Submarine accidents still happened, even

into the next century, precipitated by the advances in technology. The ability to dive deeper, new submarine designs, and the capacity to go to different places resulted in new tragedies. From the *Thresher* in 1963 to the Russian *Kursk* in 2000 it is shown that submarine accidents still occur. But as with the *S-4*, disaster leads to new advances. For the *Thresher*, which sank to 8,400 feet, investigations of the disaster led to the development of modern deep sea diving submersibles.

The *S-4* was a turning point. Since that disaster, American submarines have become safer. According to submarine history expert and submariner David Johnston, "When given the amount of operating hours at sea under extremely dangerous circumstances, the record of safety in the US Navy is quite amazing. Our crews were superbly trained, highly motivated, and they operated the best equipment possible. Our boats were (and still are) very safe, especially since 1940. Yes, there have been incidents and losses, but when you consider the big picture our navy has an enviable record of safety, especially when compared to the Soviets/Russians."

Complementing this comment, fellow submarine history expert and submariner Ric Hedman writes that being a submariner "is still a dangerous occupation. That is why we go through 'Qualifications.' The boat has to be well known by the crew. You never know where or when you might be the only person in a situation to save the boat. That is why we learn *every* system aboard and know the location and operation of every piece of equipment. Once you become qualified, it is a sign that you have become a competent member of the crew, and they can rely on you to have their backs just as you will have theirs in any situation. That is why sub crews are so tight—confidence in fellow crew members' abilities."

The popular image of the submarine as a steel coffin or widow maker is derived from the intense public attention given to submarine disasters when they do happen, and is undeserved.

Yet the story of the *S-4* is more than a tale of a submarine and the divers who struggled to raise it. The submarine *S-4* offers a glimpse into the American historic subconscious. The *S-4* was a blight on the penultimate year of the Roaring Twenties. Perhaps that is why, like many other American historic tragedies, it became a forgotten story—since it is so dark. It also presages the modern news cycle, and its rush for biting blame—just ask Admiral Brumby. But it is also a story of victory and endurance. The deeds of men such as Edward Ellsberg, Henry Hartley, Fred Michels, and Tom Eadie show how, even when events are balanced, as Ernest King said, "on the knee of the gods," there is ingenuity to be learned and wisdom to be had.

• • •

John S. Baylis continued to rise in the Coast Guard's ranks, was involved in several dramatic rescues, and eventually became captain of the Port of New York during the early part of World War II. As captain of the port, he was involved with the seizure of the liner *Normandie* from the French Vichy government. Despite his efforts, he could not stop the fire that destroyed the liner while it was being converted to a troop carrier. In 1942, he left New York and became district officer for the Coast Guard in Puerto Rico. He retired in 1946 with the rank of commodore. He died in 1971.

Frank Brumby remained in the navy and was promoted to vice admiral in 1933. He then took command of the navy's Scouting Force and was promoted to admiral in 1935. He then served as commandant of the Fifth Naval District and commander of the Naval Operating Base in Norfolk until his retirement in 1938. He died in 1950.

Thomas Eadie published a popular account of his exploits titled *I Like Diving* in 1931. He retired from the navy in 1939, but returned to service during World War II, when he was appointed as a chief gunner. He served at the US Naval Torpedo Station at Newport, Rhode Island. Eadie, aside from winning the Medal of Honor and two Navy Crosses, also earned the Good Conduct Medal, Victory Medal, American Campaign Medal, and World War II Victory Medal. The navy commissioned him as an officer (lieutenant), and he retired again in 1946, returning to private life and fading from the historical record. He died in Brockton, Massachusetts, in 1974.

Edward Ellsberg continued to write exciting fiction and nonfiction books throughout his life. His work *Pigboats* was the basis for a

Hollywood movie. After the United States entered World War II, Ellsberg rejoined the navy and oversaw salvage operations throughout the conflict. He retired from the navy in 1945 with the rank of rear admiral and worked as a consulting engineer until 1965. Even though he retired with flag rank, he was always popularly remembered as "Commander Ellsberg." He died in 1983.

Henry Hartley continued to rise in his "mustang" career. During World War II, he achieved the rank of captain and took part in the invasions of North Africa and Sicily. He was then promoted to rear admiral and was put in charge of the heavy cruiser *Chester*. He retired in 1947 and, in order to keep busy, took a job the next year as an inspector for the Washington DC Suburban Sanitary Commission. He died in 1953.

Ernest J. King returned to naval aviation after the *S-4* salvage, eventually becoming chief of the Bureau of Aeronautics. He was promoted to rear admiral in 1933. In 1939, he was put on the General Board instead of being given chief of naval operations, the position he long coveted. However, he was brought back into influence after America's entry into World War II. It was erroneously reported that King said, "When they get in trouble they send for the sons of bitches." When King was asked if he had indeed said this, he said that he did not, but wished he had. King did, however, say, "Any good naval officer is a son of a bitch." During the war, he became simultaneously chief of naval operations and commander-in-chief, United States Fleet. In 1944, he was promoted to the new rank of fleet admiral, the highest rank obtainable for a navy officer. He retired in 1945 and died in 1956.

Charles B. "Swede" Momsen received a letter of commendation from President Franklin Roosevelt for his work on the *Squalus* rescue. During World War II, Momsen served as commander of submarine squadrons and earned decorations including the Navy Cross and the Legion of Merit. At the end of the war, he commanded the battleship *South Dakota*. After the war, he served on the navy General Board and then as assistant chief of naval operations for Undersea Warfare and commander of Submarine Forces in the Pacific. He retired as a vice admiral in 1955 and died in 1967.

Harold E. "Savvy" Saunders served as the cartographer for the Admiral Richard Byrd expeditions to Antarctica (1928–30, 1933–35). Afterward, he did extensive work on organizing test centers for new ship designs. He was best known for his work *Hydrodynamics in Ship Design*, which became a standard text. He retired from the navy as a captain and died in 1961. The American Society of Naval Engineers presents an annual award for outstanding lifetime achievement in naval engineering in his name.

ACKNOWLEDGMENTS

I MUST FIRST THANK MY wife, Michelle, whom I tortured for months by forcing her to learn about the most esoteric facets of traditional deep sea diving and submarines. To give you an idea, at one point she threatened to wear a Mark V diving dress to bed. Her editorial eye was critical in producing a compelling narrative.

A special thanks to the dedicated submariners who run www .pigboats.org: DCC(SS/SW) David L. Johnston, USNR, and Ric Hedman TN(SS) USN. Their knowledge of submarine history and their willingness to read, answer my questions, and comment on early drafts of this book helped to create a realistic portrait of the old pigboats.

Thank you to Mr. Donald P. Brennan, whose critical eye helped me separate the wheat from the chaff in early drafts of this work.

A special acknowledgment to Captain Jack Ringelberg, PE, president of JMS Naval Architects, CEO of the Ocean Technology Foundation, and salvage expert, who provided useful comments on early versions of this manuscript.

Thank you to Mr. Gregory Murphy, who provided useful comments on the early chapters of this book.

Thank you to Ted Pollard for allowing me access to the incredible collection of materials collected by his grandfather, Edward Ellsberg.

And a special thanks to maritime historian David Zeni, a fellow traveler in my quest to understand the *S-4*.

I must also give thanks and acknowledgment to the following organizations: the librarians of the Stephen B. Luce Library, SUNY Maritime College, for providing ready assistance and maintaining the collection of manuscripts that sparked the creation of this book; the archivists of the Library of Congress Manuscript Division for providing helpful assistance in my research there; and members of the Historical Diving Society for answering queries.

NOTES

Abbreviations

BG   *Boston Globe*
BE   *Brooklyn Eagle*
EJK   Papers of Ernest Joseph King. Manuscript Division, Library of Congress, Washington, DC.
JSB   Papers of John S. Baylis, Stephen B. Luce Library, SUNY Maritime College, Bronx, NY.
NCOIT   Naval Court of Inquiry Transcripts, Papers of John S. Baylis, Stephen B. Luce Library, SUNY Maritime College, Bronx, NY.
NYP   *New York Evening Post*
NYT   *New York Times*
PA   *Provincetown Advocate*

1. The Rum-Chaser

This chapter was composed using the testimony of witnesses at the Naval Court of Inquiry. Direct quotes were taken from testimony. For information concerning the movements of the *Paulding* and the actions of the officers therein see NCOIT, testimony of John S. Baylis, Charles E. Reed, George M. Phannemiller, Walter C. Rheingans, James C. Milazzo, LeRoy Reinburg, and E. F. Gracie. For biographical information on John Baylis see JSB and US Coast Guard, "Biographical Sketch: Commodore John S. Baylis." For information concerning the *Paulding* as a rum-chaser, see Allen, *Black Ships*. This includes the *Marge* episode.

2. The Pigboat

This chapter was composed using forensic evidence and following procedures as outlined by witnesses at the Naval Court of Inquiry. While the events as depicted in this chapter cannot be absolutely verified, since there were no survivors from the *S-4*, the chapter represents the best representation based on the available evidence. For information concerning standardization trials leading up to the crash, see NCOIT, testimony of Frank L. Worden, Edmund W. Strother, L. A. Bostwick, and H. Saunders. For biographical information concerning Roy K. Jones see "Jones Served in War," NYT, December 18, 1927. For general information about submarine casualties, see US Naval Submarine School, *Submarine Casualties Booklet*. For the movements of *S-4* men and officers on the *Wandank* see NCOIT, testimony of Thomas Fertner. For a description of the interior of the *S-4* see Hedman, "The S-Boats." For the history of the development of the S-Class see Johnston, "A Visual Guide"; and Weir, *Building American Submarines*. For McGinley staying aboard the *S-4* see "All Hope of Saving Imprisoned Crew Gone," *Buffalo-Courier Express*, December 21, 1927. For Goering's letter see "Letter by *S-4* Seaman," NYT, December 22, 1927.

3. The Fate of the *Paulding*

This chapter was composed using the testimony of witnesses at the Naval Court of Inquiry. See NCOIT, testimony of Baylis, Reed, Phannemiller, Rheingans, Milazzo, and Reinburg. Direct quotations were taken directly from testimony.

4. Trapped

Events inside the *S-4* were composed using NCOIT, testimony of Saunders, E. Ellsberg, G. B. Magrath, G. H. Mankin, G.B. Dowling, and E. J. King. Testimony was also used from the second Naval Court of Inquiry, JSB; see testimony of Saunders. See also Eadie, *I Like Diving*; Ellsberg, *Men Under the Sea*; and Lockwood, *Hell at 50 Fathoms*.

5. The Boatswain

This chapter was composed using the testimony from NCOIT: Gracie and Frank E. Simmonds. Direct quotes are taken from testimony. See also *Coast Guard Log of E.F. Gracie*, JSB. It should be noted that several later secondary sources, particularly Vorse, *Time and the Town*, inflate the Gracie story or include details that are at variance with the testimony. In this chapter, I went strictly on Gracie's own testimony and his logs.

6. "Who Wants to Know?"

The primary source for this chapter is Mason, "S-4 by Semaphore," which provides the direct quotations. See also McIntire, *MacIntyre Clan*; and Spaulding, "Early Salvage Work."

7. The *Falcon*

For the account of the *Falcon* at dock and quotes therein, see EJK, handwritten and typed accounts of the *S-4* rescue and salvage operations by Henry Hartley. This includes biographical information concerning Hartley and information regarding the *Falcon*. See also NCOIT, testimony of Henry Hartley and Frank Brumby. For more information regarding the *Falcon*, see Mooney, ed., *Dictionary of American*

Naval Fighting Ships. For information regarding Saunders and Strother on the *Bushnell* and their investigation into the disaster, see NCOIT, testimony of Saunders, Strother, and Gracie.

8. The Ace of Divers

This chapter was composed using NCOIT, testimony of Thomas Eadie; and Eadie, *I Like Diving*. See also Brady, "Gambling with Death." The best of these sources for biographical information on Eadie is *I Like Diving*.

9. Hide and Seek

This chapter was composed using NCOIT, testimony of Gracie, Saunders, and Hartley; and EJK, manuscripts of Henry Hartley.

10. Where's Ellsberg?

This chapter was composed using Ellsberg, *On the Bottom*; Ellsberg, *Men Under the Sea*; Ellsberg, "Interview with Rear Admiral Edward Ellsberg"; and Alden, *Salvage Man*. "The *S-4* is in 102 feet of water . . .": NYT, December 19, 1927.

11. "An Olympian Zeus"

This chapter was composed using Buell, "Prewar Career of Ernest King" and *Master of Sea Power*; King and Whitehill, *Fleet Admiral King*; and NCOIT, testimony of King.

12. One Man Down

The narrative of this chapter was composed using Eadie, *I Like Diving*; EJK, manuscripts of Hartley; NCOIT, testimony of Eadie, Hartley, and King; and US Navy, *Diving Manual* (1916). "If the grapnel catch proves to be the *S-4* . . .": EJK, manuscripts of Hartley. "OK on Eadie": Eadie, *I Like Diving*, 29. "On the submarine . . .": NCOIT, testimony of Eadie and Hartley; EJK, manuscripts of Hartley; and Eadie, *I Like Diving*, 148–154.

13. Six Taps

Hartley's feelings about discovering men alive on the *S-4*: EJK, manuscripts of Hartley. King's arrival: NCOIT, testimony of King. Quotes from Eadie found in Eadie, *I Like Diving*, 148–152; and EJK, manuscripts of Hartley.

14. Blowing the Ballast Tanks

Weather conditions: NCOIT, testimony of King. Officers present: NCOIT. Decision to blow the ballast tanks: NCOIT, testimony of King, Brumby, Ellsberg, Saunders, and Hartley. Technical information about compartment salvage air valve can be found in NCOIT, testimony of Ellsberg and King. For the *S-5* incident see Hill, *Under Pressure*. Continued problems with reporters: EJK, manuscripts of Hartley; see also "Divers for *S-4* See Winter's Job Ahead," BG, December 26, 1927. Carr's dive: NCOIT, testimony of W. Carr, Hartley, King, and Saunders; see also Eadie, *I Like Diving*. "You can't work as fast as on the surface . . .": Eadie, *I Like Diving*, 178. Maneuvering the *Falcon*: NCOIT, testimony of Hartley, Ellsberg, and King; see also EJK, manuscripts of Hartley.

15. "How Long Will You Be?"

Information about Fessenden may be found in Fessenden, *Fessenden, Builder of Tomorrows*. For the *S-8* using its oscillator prior to the first dive, see "Men Who Are Trapped in *S-4* Believed Alive," NYP, December 19, 1927. For the list of messages from the *S-4* and times, see "*S-4*'s Tragic Taps Revealed by Navy," NYT, January 6, 1928; and "Navy Makes Public Messages from *S-4*," BG, January 6, 1928. Failure to blow the ballast tanks: NCOIT, testimony of King, Brumby, Saunders, Hartley, and Ellsberg. See also EJK, manuscripts of Hartley.

16. "Tonight or Never"

For weather conditions see NCOIT, testimony of King and Hartley. King maintained a log of the weather that was read into testimony that was particularly valuable. The narrative of this chapter was composed using NCOIT, testimony of King, Hartley, and F. Michels. See also EJK, manuscripts of Hartley; Ellsberg, *Men Under the Sea*; and Brady, "Gambling with Death." In some accounts, particularly those of Hartley, there are slight variations in the details, which I attempted to reconcile by comparing the testimony of those also present at the time of Michels's descent. "I have just been in consultation with the admiral . . ." and further quotations: NCOIT, testimony of Hartley; and EJK, manuscripts of Hartley.

17. Two Men Down

The most direct source material of Eadie's rescue of Michels comes from Eadie's somewhat dramatized memoir, *I Like Diving*, and his testimony at the NCOIT. When Eadie's testimony conflicted with his later writing I chose to follow the testimony, since it was given only a month after the disaster. The other most accurate account comes from Hartley's testimony and his own recollections found in EJK. Direct quotations used in the narrative were given as quotations in these documents, with the exception of the following. "I have never known . . .": EJK, recommendation of Frank Brumby for Tom Eadie to receive a medal of honor. "The annals of the navy . . .": Edward Ellsberg, "Ellsberg Relates Heroic Divers' Work," BG, December 25, 1927.

18. Inside the Iron Doctor

For Ellsberg's journey to the *Falcon* see Ellsberg, *Men Under the Sea*; and NCOIT, testimony of Ellsberg. Much of Ellsberg's account, while dramatized, is corroborated in other sources, such as EJK. See also Ellsberg, "Interview with Rear Admiral Edward Ellsberg."

19. The Six

"There was no fluttering . . .": Eadie, *I Like Diving*, 199. For the list of messages from the S-4 and times, see "S-4's Tragic Taps," NYT; and "Navy Makes Public Messages," BG. Biographical information concerning the six men trapped in the torpedo room can be found in JSB, service records of the crew of the S-4, as well as clippings. "We could get to Boston and back . . .": EJK, manuscripts of Hartley. "Blowing compartment salvage air line . . .": JSB, telegrams sent out from the rescue force. Tom Eadie notifying Michels's wife: Eadie, *I Like Diving*. "I am feeling perfectly fine . . .": "Diver Is Recovering Rapidly in Hospital," BG, December 21, 1927.

20. "It's Terrible, It's Terrible"

"The townsfolk . . ." and accommodations made by residents of Provincetown: "Wreck Activities Stir Provincetown," NYT, December 19, 1927; and Joseph S. Ward Jr., "Desolation Marks Place of Disaster," BG, December 19, 1927. "The news ran like fire . . .": Vorse, *Time and the Town*, 226. "McGuiggan told King . . . ": King and Whitehill, *Fleet Admiral King*, 198; Ernest King states in a footnote that the reporters did not come aboard until after "the gale broke." However, the telegram quoted was from December 19 at 5:05 AM, well before the storm ended. While King was probably correct in identifying McGuiggan and the Associated Press, he was incorrect on when they actually went aboard the *Falcon*. "We read those newspaper articles . . .": Eadie, *I Like Diving*, 169. "Respectfully protest method . . .": JSB, telegrams. "There were broadcasts . . ." and media coverage: "WEEI Stays on Extra Hour to Give Globe's News on Wreck," BG, December 19, 1927. "A photographer who went out in one of the smaller craft . . .": "Wreck Activities Stir Provincetown," NYT. The photograph of the press boats may be found in EJK. "The newspapermen, who were paying . . .": Joseph S. Ward Jr, "Did Navy Do Its Best?" BG, January 1, 1928. For telegrams sent to next of kin of S-4's crew see JSB. "It is hard to hope . . .": "Desolation Marks Place of Disaster," BG, December 20, 1927. For information about Snizek see untitled article, NYT, December 20, 1927; and "Desolation Marks Place of Disaster," BG. For information about Galvin see "Catapulting of Prisoners from S-4 in Torpedo Tube Seen as Means of Escape," BE, December 20, 1927; and "Men Who Are Trapped in S-4," NYP. "I don't think there is a chance . . .": "Men Who Are Trapped in S-4," NYP. "Judging from past experience . . .": "The Latest Submarine Disaster," BE, December 19, 1927. "Once he was with the submarine S-7 . . .": *Chicago Daily Tribune*, December 19, 1927. "It is customary when a submarine . . .":

"Some Hope Is Held That Air Will Last," BG, December 20, 1927. "After the *S-51* debacle . . .": JSB. "With the *S-4* on the bottom . . .": "Men Who Are Trapped in *S-4*," NYP. "It all depends on how many men . . .": "Chance of Saving Crew Very Slim, Declares Expert," BE, December 19, 1927.

21. "Is There Any Hope?"

A timeline of the *Falcon*'s movements was given by Hartley and King at their testimony to NCOIT. "If a fleet of ships anchored stem . . ." and other suggestions given to the rescue force: JSB, telegrams. Information concerning the SC tubes may be found in Friedman, *U.S. Submarines Through 1945*. How the rescue force decided to use the SC tubes may be found in NCOIT, testimony of King, Ellsberg, and Saunders. See also Eadie, *I Like Diving*; and Saunders, *Salvage Report*, 31. For movements of the *Falcon* see JSB, telegrams. For the list of messages from the *S-4* and times, see "S-4's Tragic Taps," NYT; and "Navy Makes Public Messages," BG. For preparation of materials to be put through torpedo tubes, see Saunders, *Salvage Report*, 31–32. "Advisory northwest storm warnings . . .": JSB, telegrams.

22. "Y-E-S"

For the list of messages from the *S-4* and times, see "S-4's Tragic Taps," NYT; and "Navy Makes Public Messages," BG. "The heating and regular lighting systems . . .": "Torture Chamber of Submarine Is Few Feet from Supply of Air," BG, December 20, 1927. "We went to Boston to save a man's life . . .": Joseph S. Ward Jr., "Hope for *S-4* Survivors Dies After Brave 'All's Well,'" BG, December 21, 1927. "What makes you think that?": Ibid. "Get out of here . . .": Ward, "Did Navy Do Its Best?" "We have normal quarters . . ." EJK, manuscripts of Hartley. Regarding Wickwire and Kelley see "Police of Brooklyn Find Two Divers for Ellsberg," BG, December 20, 1927. "Are you going to try to send . . .": "Signals from *S-4* Growing Weaker," NYP, December 20, 1927. "How long it will take us . . .": Ward, "Hope for *S-4* Survivors Dies." "I am strong . . .": "Mrs Weller Offers Plan to Aid Rescue," BG, December 21, 1927. For unorthodox suggestions see JSB, telegrams. For the magnet and flowering plants ideas see "Suggestions to Aid *S-4* Include Magnet and Flowering Plants," BG, December 23, 1927. Regarding the *Falcon*'s actions after the storm broke see NCOIT, testimony of Hartley, King, Ellsberg, Saunders, and Brumby; see also EJK, manuscripts of Hartley. "It was like a fog . . .": Joseph S. Ward Jr., "Divers Get Air into Torpedo Room of *S-4*," NYT, December 22, 1927. "Gave out his orders . . .": Nat A. Burrows, "All Cool on Falcon as Divers Go Below," BG, December 22, 1927. "Please move so our boat . . .": EJK, manuscripts of Hartley. For Mark McIntyre's involvement see Mason, "S-4 by Semaphore." Regarding Volton's boat see Ward, "Divers Get Air into Torpedo Room." Brumby's anger: "Air Is Pumped into S-4 but Divers Rap in Vain," BG, December 22, 1927. Hawes's strike: EJK. Daniel Burd's dive is described in "Air Is Pumped into S-4," BG. For the last-moment rescue attempts see NCOIT, testimony of Ellsberg, Hartley, King, and Saunders; see also EJK.

23. Carr's Cross

For McGinley and Crabb's actions in Provincetown see "Father of McGinley Sees *Paulding* Chief," BG, December 23, 1927. Ellsberg's dive is described thoroughly in Ellsberg, *Men Under the Sea*. See also Ellsberg, "Interview with Rear Admiral Edward Ellsberg"; Eadie, *I Like Diving*; "New Gale Stops Work of Divers," NYT, December 24, 1927; and untitled article, BG, December 24, 1927.

24. Christmas Eve

For Mrs. Stevens's story see "S-4 Man's Mother Goes with Wilbur," NYT, December 25, 1927; and "McClintic Demands S-4 Be Raised Now," BG, December 25, 1927. See also JSB, service records of *S-4* crew. "The navy is plainly not doing what it could . . .": Untitled article, BG, December 22, 1927. "Down in that dark hull . . .": "McClintic Demands S-4 Be Raised," BG. For Loring Black see "Wilbur Goes to S-4 Wreck as Criticism Increases; House Inquiry Indicated," NYT, December 24, 1927. "It appears to me . . .": "Naval Court to Sit Here After Holiday," BG, December 21, 1927. "It may be necessary . . .": "Wilbur Goes to S-4 Wreck," NYT. "Its members are civilians . . .": "Suggests Disaster Probe by Naval Academy Board," BG, December 25, 1927. For Fitch and Jones telegrams see "Wilbur Goes to S-4 Wreck," NYT; and "Andrews Forgives Uninformed Critics," BG, December 25, 1927. "The submarine tragedy . . .": "Why Remain Helpless?," *Hyannis Patriot*, publishing an article originally appearing in the *Boston Post*, December 22, 1927. Inventors denouncing rescue efforts: "Noted Inventors Denounce Navy for *S-4* Disaster," BE, December 25, 1927. For Fessenden see "Fessenden Assails Sinking of the *S-4*," NYT, December 23, 1927. "Not, we hazard . . .": Rowland, "The 'Why' of the 'S-4' Disaster." "There is nothing that either of them . . .": "Wilbur Trip Seen as Move to Quiet *S-4* Criticisms," BE, December 25, 1927. For the continued interchange between Hughes and Stevens see "Wilbur Orders Navy to Raise the S-4 Now If Weather Permits," NYT, December 25, 1927. Wilbur's press conference was pieced together using questions and answers found in the December 25, 1927, editions of NYT, BG, BE, *Chicago Tribune*, and *Washington Post*. "If the submarine was inside . . .": "Wilbur Orders Navy to Raise the S-4," NYT. Damage control by the Navy is described in Ward, "Did Navy Do Its Best?" "Further recognition of the deed . . .": Eadie, *I Like Diving*, 180. "Exceptionally kind, sympathetic . . .": EJK, manuscripts of Hartley. For Hartley's dog see untitled article, BG, December 26, 1927. "I have been in a mining town . . .": Vorse, *Time and the Town*, 228. For the ceremony at Skarloff's Wharf see Joseph S. Ward Jr., "Provincetown Pays Honor to *S-4* Dead," BG, December 25, 1927.

25. Bringing Up the Bodies

A description of the Salvage Force may be found in Saunders, *Salvage Report*, 41–51. "Provided readily . . .": King and Whitehill, *Fleet Admiral King*, 200. Transfer of Brumby: "Brumby Transferred to Manoeuvre Duty," NYT, January 26, 1928. For a detailed description of salvage operations see Saunders, *Salvage Report*, 59–99;

see also NCOIT, various testimony covering salvage operations until mid-January. Eadie's rescue of Mattox is covered in Eadie, *I Like Diving*. Ellsberg's departure and Michels's return: "Navy Says Only Six Survived *S-4* Crash," BG, January 2, 1928; and "Have New Theory on Condition of *S-4*," NYT, January 2, 1928. See also Ellsberg, *Men Under the Sea*; and Eadie, *I Like Diving*. "We could not buck the elements . . .": "Michaels [*sic*] Defends Navy Work on *S-4*," NYT, December 26, 1927. For information concerning "Jake" the dummy diver and freezing in the divers' hoses see EJK, manuscripts of Hartley; and Saunders, *Salvage Report*, 76–83. "There is more misinformation loose . . .": "LaGuardia Defends *S-4* Rescue Work," Hartford *Courant*, January 5, 1928. King's credit to La Guardia: King and White-hill, *Fleet Admiral King*, 199. For information concerning the retrieval of bodies see Saunders, *Salvage Report*, 93; and Eadie, *I Like Diving*, 195–201. "The bodies were almost the specific gravity . . .": Eadie, *I Like Diving*, 195. "I had found two of them . . .": Ibid. For another description of the bodies see NCOIT, testimony of Saunders and Magrath. Concerning problems entering the torpedo room see Eadie, *I Like Diving*, 203–204; and Saunders, *Salvage Report*, 94–99. "Please demand that my husband's body . . .": "Demands Husband's Body," NYT, January 15, 1928. "You couldn't pull yourself up . . .": Eadie, *I Like Diving*, 204. For technical troubles of salvage operations see Saunders, *Salvage Report*, 102; EJK, manuscripts of Hartley and Harold Saunders. Information concerning after the new air conditioning system was installed may be found in EJK, manuscripts of Hartley; Saunders, *Salvage Report*, 79–83; and Eadie, *I Like Diving*. "The air had a peculiar smell . . .": Eadie, *I Like Diving*, 205. "The adverse effect of the partly dehydrated . . .": EJK, manuscripts of Hartley. "As happy as a kid": Eadie, *I Like Diving*, 211. Washing tunnels: Saunders, *Salvage Report*, 143–144. For the nor'easter, see EJK, manuscripts of Hartley.

26. "The Knee of the Gods"

"All ships take stations . . .": EJK, manuscripts of Hartley. "I think we can make it almost . . .": "Navy Raises the *S-4*," NYT, March 18, 1928. For the timeline of when compartments were blown see Saunders, *Salvage Report*, 168–178. "There she is": "Navy Raises the *S-4*," NYT. For the perilous trip to Boston see Saunders, *Salvage Report*, 179–183; and King and Whitehill, *Fleet Admiral King*, 200–203. "To please not give up . . .": Buell, *Master of Sea Power*, 78. Griffin's poem: Griffin, "Speech in the House of Representatives."

27. "My Body to Pelnar"

For coverage of the *S-4* at dry dock see untitled article, *Hartford Courant*, March 20, 1928; "Opening of the *S-4* Shows Calm Death After Life Battle," NYT, March 20, 1928; "Board to Comb Interior of *S-4* in New Inquiry," BG, March 20, 1928; and "*S-4* Yields Bodies; Struggle for Life in Hull Disclosed," *Washington Post*, March 20, 1928. For the assessment of the interior of the *S-4* see Saunders, *Salvage Report*, 191–207; and JSB, revised hearings of the Naval Court of Inquiry, testimony of Harold Saunders. For the effects of the victims of the *S-4* see "Soggy Marriage Certificate, Photographs, Letters Bare Private Lives of S-4 Victims," BE, March 28,

1928; and untitled article, BG, March 23, 1928. "They died like rats . . .": "Absence of Escort for Victim of S-4 Stirs Jersey Town," *Brooklyn Standard Union*, March 23, 1928. "We cannot understand why . . .": NYP, March 23, 1928. Medals and awards: EJK. For Eadie's winning the Medal of Honor see Eadie, *I Like Diving*. "This is not going to be any whitewashing . . .": "*S-4* Inquiry by Navy Opens at Yard Here," BG, January 5, 1928. For findings of the Court of Inquiry and reactions to it see JSB. For the Coast Guard Board of Inquiry findings see JSB. For Wilbur's exoneration of Jones and Brumby see "Admiral Brumby Exonerated," NYT, April 16, 1928.

28. Of Lungs and Bells

For legislation regarding submariners see "An Act Granting Double Pension." Pay raises are discussed in "Submarine Pay Advanced," NYT, April 14, 1928. For an excellent biography on Momsen see Maas, *The Rescuer*. Most of the biography of Momsen was composed using the Maas source, which includes the direct quotations. See also Moss, "How They Sank and Saved the *S-4*," for the *S-4*'s use as an experimental vessel. The scrapping of the *S-4* is found in "Government Sends *S-4* to Sea Grave," PA, September 1, 1936; and Mooney, ed., *Dictionary of American Naval Fighting Ships*.

29. Twelve Years Later . . .

Peter Maas's books *The Rescuer* and *The Terrible Hours* contain the best accounts of the rescue of the *Squalus*. Maas had direct access to Momsen in the research of his books. For Ellsberg's account see Ellsberg, *Men Under the Sea*. Also, the original documents digitized by the Naval History and Heritage command at www.history .navy.mil/research/histories/ship-histories/danfs/s/squalus-ss-192/squalus-ss -192-sinking-rescure-of-survivors-and-salvage.html were particularly useful.

Epilogue

For the first memorial service held at St. Mary's Episcopal Church and information regarding the cross, see "Simple Cross Says 'We Understand," PA, December 9, 1937; "Church Dedicates Disaster Memorial," PA, December 16, 1937; "Cross Is Dedicated to Memory of Victims of *S-4* Disaster," PA, December 23, 1937; "*S-4* Disaster Recalled Today," BG, December 17, 1937; and "Provincetown Pays Honor to *S-4* Crew," BG, December 18, 1937. For other early ceremonies see "Service in Memory of *S-4* Disaster," PA, December 8, 1938; "Tribute Is Paid to *S-4* Victims," PA, December 21, 1938; and "Services Mark Sub *S-4* Tragedy," PA, December 19, 1940. Almost yearly coverage was given by the *Provincetown Advocate* to the service. The names of the victims of the *S-4* were compiled from the official service records found at JSB. The 1967 cross is described in an untitled article in PA, September 14, 1967; "Memorial Service Sunday for *S-4*," PA, September 14, 1967; and "Talents of Artists Went into Church," PA, December 21, 1967. Information regarding the 2014 ceremony was gathered directly by the author, who attended and recorded the service. Johnston and Hedman's quotes were taken from e-mail correspondence, November 8, 2014.

BIBLIOGRAPHY

The majority of text in this book was derived from archival sources, contemporary newspaper accounts, and memoirs. Supporting secondary sources provided insight into other submarine disasters, diving practices, and biographical details of some of the key characters. Of particular value to any serious researcher of the *S-4* disaster are the archival papers of John S. Baylis, Edward Ellsberg, and Ernest J. King.

Archival Collections

Papers of Edward Ellsberg. Maintained by Ted Pollard.
This private collection, maintained by a descendant of Edward Ellsberg, contains clippings, correspondence, articles, and photographs.

Papers of Ernest Joseph King. Boxes 24 and 25. Manuscript Division, Library of Congress, Washington, DC.
King's papers focus more on the salvage operations and include salvage reports. However, there are a good number of photographs in the collection and accounts of the disaster by other persons. In particular, there are two accounts of the rescue operations written by Henry Hartley—one handwritten, the other typed—prepared for King to use in his autobiography. There are also documents by Harold Saunders concerning the salvage and diving in general.

Papers of John S. Baylis. Boxes 7, 8, and 9. Stephen B. Luce Library Archives, SUNY Maritime College, Bronx.
This collection contains a wide range of materials, including a full transcription of the navy's Court of Inquiry and its findings, correspondence, Coast Guard logs, Coast Guard reports, navy telegrams during the disaster, photographs, and service records of the men aboard the *S-4*. Of primary importance to the composition of this book were the Court of Inquiry transcripts and a reconvened Court of Inquiry transcript that occurred after the *S-4* had been raised in March 1928.

Newspapers

Atlanta Constitution
Baltimore Sun
Boston Globe

Boston Herald
Brooklyn Eagle
Brooklyn Standard Union
Buffalo Courier Express
Cape Cod Times
Chatham (MA) Monitor
Chicago Tribune
Christian Science Monitor
Hartford (CT) Courant
Harvard Crimson
Hyannis (MA) Patriot
Los Angeles Times
New York Evening Post
New York Herald-Tribune
New York Sun
New York Times
Philadelphia Enquirer
Provincetown (MA) Advocate
Washington Post

Books, Articles, Government Documents

"An Act Granting Double Pension in All Cases to Widows and Dependents When an Officer or Enlisted Man of the Navy Dies from an Injury in Line of Duty as the Result of a Submarine Accident," Pub. L. No. 70-323, 70th Cong., 1st sess. (1928).

Alden, John D. *Salvage Man: Edward Ellsberg and the US Navy.* Annapolis, MD: Naval Institute Press, 1998.

Allen, Everett S. *The Black Ships: Rumrunners of Prohibition.* Boston: Little, Brown, 1979.

Barnes, Robert Hatfield. *United States Submarines.* New Haven, CT: H. F. Morse Associates, 1946.

Bartholomew, Charles A., and William I. Milwee Jr. *Mud, Muscle and Miracles: Marine Salvage in the United States Navy.* 2nd ed. Washington, DC: Naval History & Heritage Command, 2009.

Brady, John T. "Gambling with Death." *Popular Mechanics,* May 1928.

Braisted, William R. "Charles Frederick Hughes." In *The Chiefs of Naval Operations,* edited by Robert William Love Jr. Annapolis, MD: Naval Institute Press, 1980.

Buell, Thomas B. "The Prewar Career of Ernest J. King." In *Changing Interpretations and New Sources in Naval History: Papers from the Third United States Naval Academy History Symposium,* edited by Robert William Love Jr. New York: Garland Publishing, 1980.

———. *Master of Sea Power: A Biography of Fleet Admiral Ernest J. King.* Annapolis, MD: Naval Institute Press, 1980.

Delgado, James P. *Silent Killers: Submarines and Underwater Warfare.* New York: Osprey Publishing, 2011.

Eadie, Tom. *I Like Diving: A Professional's Story.* New York: Houghton Mifflin, 1929.

Ellsberg, Edward. "Interview with Rear Admiral Edward Ellsberg." Transcript of an interview conducted by Captain Bruce McCloskey, 1972. Edward Ellsberg official website. www.edwardellsberg.com/audio/EllsbergTranscript11181972.pdf.

———. *Men Under the Sea.* New York: Dodd, Mead & Co., 1939.

———. *On the Bottom.* New York: Dodd, Mead & Co., 1929.

Fessenden, Helen May Trott. *Fessenden, Builder of Tomorrows.* New York: Coward-McCann, 1940.

Friedman, Norman. *U.S. Submarines Through 1945: An Illustrated Design History.* Annapolis, MD: US Naval Institute Press, 1995.

Frost, Frank T. "Scyllias: Diving in Antiquity." *Greece & Rome.* 2nd series, vol. 15, no. 2 (October 1968): 180–185.

Gray, Edwyn. *Disasters of the Deep: A Comprehensive Survey of Submarine Accidents and Disasters.* Annapolis, MD: Naval Institute Press, 2003.

Griffin, Anthony J. "Speech of the Hon. Anthony J. Griffin of New York in the House of Representatives." Washington, DC: Government Printing Office, March 30, 1928.

Harrington, John Walker. "Making Submarines Safe." *Popular Science,* March 1928.

Hartley, Henry. "Some Historical Facts on Diving." *U.S. Naval Institute Proceedings,* March 1931, 341–349.

Hedman, Ric. "The S-Boats." PigBoats.com, accessed March 17, 2015. http://pigboats.com/subs/s-boats.html.

Hill, A. J. *Under Pressure: The Final Voyage of Submarine S-Five.* New York: Free Press, 2002.

Hill, Sir Leonard. *Caisson Sickness and the Physiology of Work in Compressed Air.* New York: Longmans, Green & Co., 1912.

Homer. *The Iliad.* Translated by Samuel Butler. Chicago: Encyclopaedia Britannica, 1955.

Johnston, David L. "A Visual Guide to the S-Class Submarines." PigBoats.com, 2007. www.pigboats.com/dave6.html.

King, Ernest J., and Walter Muir Whitehill. *Fleet Admiral King: A Naval Record.* New York: W. W. Norton, 1952.

Lockwood, Charles A., and Hans Christian Adamson. *Hell at 50 Fathoms.* Philadelphia: Chilton Co., 1962.

Maas, Peter. *The Rescuer.* New York: Harper & Row, 1967.

———. *The Terrible Hours: The Man Behind the Greatest Submarine Rescue in History.* New York: Harper Collins, 1999.

Martin, Robert C. *The Deep-Sea Diver: Yesterday, Today, and Tomorrow.* Cambridge, MD: Cornell Maritime Press, 1978.

Martin, Robert E. "Beating Death at the Sea's Bottom." *Popular Science,* April 1928.

Mason, John. "The S-4 by Semaphore." *Yankee,* December 1964.

McIntire, Robert Harry. *The MacIntyre, McIntyre and McIntire Clan of Scotland, Ireland, Canada, and New England.* N.p.: self-published, 1949. Available at the Internet Archive, www.archive.org/details/macintyremcintyr00mcin.

Mooney, James L., ed. *Dictionary of American Naval Fighting Ships.* Washington, DC: Naval History Division, Department of the Navy, 1981.

Moss, William W. "How They Sank and Saved the *S-4.*" *Popular Science,* March 1929.

Rowland, John T. "The 'Why' of the 'S-4' Disaster." *Scientific American* 138, no. 3 (March 1928).

Saunders, Harold E. *Salvage Report of U.S.S. S-4.* Washington, DC: Government Printing Office, 1929.

Spaulding, Mark McIntyre. "Early Salvage Work on the U.S.S. *S-51.*" *U.S. Naval Institute Proceedings*, March 1936, 329–336.

Submarine Board. *Report and Recommendations on Submarine Safety and Salvage by the Submarine Board Appointed by the Secretary of the Navy, June 29, 1928.* Washington, DC: Government Printing Office, 1929.

US Coast Guard. "Biographical Sketch: Commodore John S. Baylis." Washington, DC: Public Information Division, US Coast Guard Headquarters, November 1971. Available at US Coast Guard official website. www.uscg.mil/history /people/Flags/BaylisJBio.pdf.

———. "Harry G. Hamlet." US Coast Guard official website, November 17, 2014. www.uscg.mil/history/people/HGHamletBio.asp.

US Naval Submarine School. *Submarine Casualties Booklet.* New London, CT: US Naval Submarine School, 1966.

US Navy. *Diving Manual.* Washington, DC: Government Printing Office, 1916.

———. *US Navy Diving Manual.* Revision 6. Washington, DC: Government Printing Office, 2008.

US Senate. "Investigation of the Sinking of the Submarine 'S-4.'" Hearings Before the Subcommittee of the Committee on Naval Affairs, US Senate, 70th Cong., 1st sess., April 27–May 26, 1928. Washington, DC: Government Printing Office, 1928.

Vorse, Mary Heaton. *Time and the Town: A Provincetown Chronicle.* New York: Dial Press, 1942.

Weir, Gary E. *Building American Submarines, 1914–1940.* Washington, DC: Naval Historic Center, Department of the Navy, 1991.

INDEX